POLITICAL MUSLIMS

Contemporary Issues in the Middle East
Mehran Kamrava, *Series Editor*

Select Titles in Contemporary Issues in the Middle East

Colonial Jerusalem: The Spatial Construction of Identity and Difference in a City of Myth, 1948–2012
    Thomas Philip Abowd

Democracy and the Nature of American Influence in Iran, 1941–1979
    David R. Collier

In the Wake of the Poetic: Palestinian Artists after Darwish
    Najat Rahman

Iraqi Migrants in Syria: The Crisis before the Storm
    Sophia Hoffmann

Islam, Arabs, and the Intelligent World of the Jinn
    Amira El-Zein

Law of Desire: Temporary Marriage in Shiʻi Iran, Revised Edition
    Shahla Haeri

The Mizrahi Era of Rebellion: Israel's Forgotten Civil Rights Struggle, 1948–1966
    Bryan K. Roby

Shahaama: Five Egyptian Men Tell Their Stories
    Nayra Atiya

POLITICAL MUSLIMS

Understanding Youth Resistance in a Global Context

EDITED BY
TAHIR ABBAS
AND SADEK HAMID

SYRACUSE UNIVERSITY PRESS

For a listing of books published and distributed by Syracuse University Press, visit www.SyracuseUniversityPress.syr.edu.

ISBN: 978-0-8156-3565-9 (hardcover)
    978-0-8156-3583-3 (paperback)
    978-0-8156-5430-8 (e-book)

Library of Congress Cataloging-in-Publication Data

Names: Abbas, Tahir, 1970– editor. | Hamid, Sadek, editor.

Title: Political Muslims : understanding youth resistance in a global context / edited by Tahir Abbas and Sadek Hamid.

Description: Syracuse, New York : Syracuse University Press, 2019. | Series: Contemporary issues in the Middle East | Includes bibliographical references and index.

Identifiers: LCCN 2018049036 (print) | LCCN 2018051092 (ebook) | ISBN 9780815654308 (E-book) | ISBN 9780815635659 (hardcover : alk. paper) | ISBN 9780815635833 (pbk. : alk. paper)

Subjects: LCSH: Muslim youth—Political activity. | Muslims—Political activity. | Social change.

Classification: LCC BP188.18.Y68 (ebook) | LCC BP188.18.Y68 P65 2019 (print) | DDC 322.4088/297—dc23

LC record available at https://lccn.loc.gov/2018049036

Manufactured in the United States of America

Contents

Acknowledgments

Given the profound importance of young Muslims globally, we undertook the task of assembling a volume that highlights their roles in combatting extremism by finding new ways of integrating Islam and Islamic thinking into their solutions for problems in various social settings. This book does not reproduce the cultural versus structural conundrum on the question of Muslim political activism or the issues behind radicalization and extremism. It instead attempts to provide an in-depth perspective on how a stigmatized group of young people remain socially engaged despite difficult conditions. The contributions use a social sciences approach to emphasize nuanced instances of participation and engagement in society.

This collection would not have seen the light of day without the tremendous efforts made by all of the contributors, who enthusiastically and patiently remained dedicated to the project. We are thoroughly grateful to them and to Suzanne Guiod at Syracuse University Press for her initial interest in the project and for her encouragement in seeing it through to completion. We are especially indebted to Alison Maura Shay and Kelly L. Balenske at the press for their dedicated support in the book's preparation.

Tahir Abbas
Sadek Hamid

POLITICAL MUSLIMS

Introduction

Global Political Muslim Youth

TAHIR ABBAS and SADEK HAMID

An intense popular and academic interest in Islam and Muslims has emerged since the attacks in the United States on September 11, 2001 (9/11), and the instances of terrorism on European soil in the new millennium. Driven by the need to understand what causes these tragic events, the study of Muslims and their faith has grown at an unprecedented rate. A flood of scholarly work explores the religion in its different regions, politics, cultures, and economic conditions in an effort to comprehend the motivations behind these acts of violence. We arguably know more about Muslim values and practices than ever, but many people in Western societies remain concerned about the Muslim presence among them as a small number of Muslims perpetuate these anxieties in carrying out terrorist plots against fellow citizens. Islamophobic interest groups have also exploited this apprehension in an attempt to advance their own political agendas (Kumar 2012; Lean 2012; Kundnani 2013).

Young Muslims in particular have become the focus of this unease in both Western and Muslim-majority nations, feared for their disruptive potential and vulnerability to radicalization. A regular flow of media headlines reinforce the fear of disaffected Muslim young people being radicalized on the Internet as thousands have migrated to theaters of conflict, posing a security threat upon return to their countries of origin (Cottee 2015). These stories appear to vindicate negative conclusions gleaned from certain polls that suggest that young Muslims are less integrated, have less in common with their non-Muslim peers, possess ambivalent

1

loyalties, and indicate a preference for Islamic schools and sharia law (Mirza, Senthilkumaran, and Ja'far 2007). However, less attention has been paid to how young Muslims participate in reshaping their societies in a positive way (Herrera and Bayat 2010; Ahmad and Seddon 2012; Masquelier and Soares 2016b). Yet there are indeed numerous interpretations of the faith that allow young Muslims to adhere to religious principles but also encourage their critical engagement and effective participation in the societies in which they live.

This volume challenges the dominant one-dimensional representations of Muslim youth by disrupting reductive stereotypes and illustrating the nature of their critical roles in the world today. It therefore offers a panoramic snapshot of Muslim youth activism within a range of key sites across the globe. It explores how they engage in transformative politics, social activism, and religious revival. We explore these spaces by de-exceptionalizing and normalizing the experiences of being young and Muslim in ten countries—the United States, Canada, Great Britain, the Netherlands, Switzerland, Turkey, Afghanistan, Pakistan, Kashmir, and Indonesia. Most of the chapters are case studies of urban youth phenomena in various socioeconomic strata, highlighting how young Muslims practice and negotiate resistance and change.

The contributions to this collection address a wide variety of themes, including the development of hybrid identities, student activism, securitization and deradicalization, the strategic use of music and social media, nonviolent social mobilization, new political movements, and historical assessments of youth activism. They offer a polyphonic (re)presentation of Muslim youth activism written from a variety of disciplinary positions and perspectives. This introduction delineates the wider sociopolitical contexts of this vibrancy and deconstructs the narratives of and relationships between Muslim youthfulness, Islamism, radicalization, and Islamophobia. It concludes with an overview of the chapters in the collection.

The Power of Muslim Youthfulness

The term *youth* refers to a broad chronological scale of young people in the age range thirteen to twenty-five, though in some societies this range may stretch to age thirty, indicating "the extent to which the cultural age category of 'youth' has expanded to include some who are legally recognized elsewhere in society as children, and some who are legally recognized elsewhere as adults" (Nilan and Feixa 2006, 1). The terms *youth* and *young people* are social categories that describe a particular state of consciousness relating to being young and youthful. As social constructs, they suggest certain behavioral characteristics that describe a period of transition and are treated here "as a social and mutable category that continues to have different meanings in different times and places" (Nayak 2003, 3). The sociologist Asef Bayat defines youthfulness as "a series of dispositions, ways of being, feeling, and carrying oneself" (2010a, 118). It also signifies a "particular habitus, behavioural and cognitive dispositions that are associated with the fact of being 'young'—that is[,] a distinct social location between childhood and adulthood" (Bayat 2010b, 28).

Like members of other religious traditions, young Muslims are heterogeneous, including those who retain a form of emotional attachment to their faith but are not necessarily observant in their everyday lives. Some alternate between phases of commitment and indifference; a significant number are deeply observant; many have strong secular outlooks that foreground ethnic diaspora identities or national identifications over a religious one; and others strategically deploy different identities depending on context. This strategic deployment may manifest in sympathy with transnational causes as well as with the idea of an *ummah*, or global Muslim community, integrating different elements creatively in order to adopt a variety of hyphenated, bicultural self-definitions. Writing about the specificities of Muslim youthfulness, Adeline Masquelier and Benjamin Soares point out that "much of what makes them Muslim youth is a whole politics about Islam: the landscape of geopolitical conflicts and loyalties, new media, global markets, consumption patterns, and cultural forms, all of which influence their ways of being in the world in the post–9/11 era" (2016a, 3). Any discussion of "Muslim youth" must therefore avoid the risk of essentialization because young people often subscribe to conflicting identities shaped by multiple dynamics in a continuous state of reconfiguration based on culture, ethnicity, tribe, nationality, religiosity, sexuality, class, education, and politics—all of which constantly influence their identities, experiences, and politics. The political impulse is of particular interest to us in this volume because there is a great deal of anxiety and expectation about Muslim young people's politically transformative capacity in their societies given the emergence of new national and global social movements that address issues such as human rights, economic justice, racial equality, and sexual freedom.

In light of the fact that young people in Muslim-majority nations often become politicized through their involvement in Islamist movements, their power to disrupt is often negatively interpreted, even if their disruption is of a peaceful nature in silent protests or active participation in faith-based revivalist organizations. Young people make up the core recruits of most of the different religious-reform trends across the world and cause alarm for their participation in extremist violent groups. Because of this alarm, securitized discourses frame many studies of Muslim youth.

These debates often do not reflect the diversity of lived experiences or the nature of youth activism, both of which are manifested in surprisingly counterintuitive ways. In the Islamic Republic of Iran, for instance, young women challenge the state's religious authority and its policing of public morality with what can be called "sartorial resistance" by donning headscarf styles that border on the illegal and by developing subcultures that "reimagine their Islam in order to accommodate youthful desires for individuality, change fun and 'sin' within the existing moral order" (Khalaf and Khalaf 2011, 11).

The world's Muslim population is expected to increase to 2.2 billion by 2030, with approximately 28 percent of them being between the ages of fifteen and twenty-nine. Globally over the next fifteen years, the Muslim demographic will grow at about twice the rate of the non-Muslim demographic. If current trends continue, by 2030 Muslims may make up around 26 percent of the world's total projected population of 8.3 billion (Grim and Karim 2011, 13). According to the Pew Research Center, between 2010 and 2050 higher fertility rates combined with improved health and economic conditions in Muslim-majority states will cause their populations to grow more than twice as fast as the overall world population. By the second half of this century, Muslims might surpass Christians as the world's largest religious group (Lipka and Hackett 2015). Approximately 60 percent of Muslims live in the Asia-Pacific region, and about 20 percent live in the Middle East and North Africa (MENA) states, where youth constitute 40 to 50 percent of their societies.

The populations of Muslim minorities in Europe and America are also set to rise owing to immigration and natural growth. By 2030, the number of Muslims in Europe could increase to around 58 million and in the United States to more than 6 million (Miller 2017). This changing demographic profile could profoundly alter the makeup of Western societies, with their ageing populations and relatively lower reproductive rates. The sheer numbers of Muslim young people in majority and minority contexts will become highly significant as they become social actors, participate in politics, and generate social movements. Clearly, Muslim youth have a global physical presence, with many of them also inhabiting globalized virtual spaces that are at the cutting edge of societal change.

Since the 1960s and in other periods of recent history, young people have been at the forefront of revolutionary political mobilizations and countercultural movements in the West. In some instances, this position has led to their being framed as a "social problem" and as the cause of a "moral panic" owing to their apparent rebellion against traditional social norms and antagonistic youth subcultures. Part of large-scale changes in societal morality, family life, and patterns of education, employment, and consumption, young people were at the forefront of demonstrations in the Islamic Revolution in the late 1970s and of social mobilizations organized by various Islamist movements in Muslim-majority societies in the 1980s and 1990s. Some of these young people were inspired by religion, whereas others were motivated by social justice concerns. In the MENA region, their activism became increasingly visible during the 1990s and 2000s, presaging their participation in political movements, civic organizations, and online networks that we witness at today.

The most recent turning point occurred during the upheavals in the Arab world that began in early 2011. Hundreds of thousands of young Arab Muslims in half-a-dozen MENA countries coordinated peaceful protests against their ruling elites. The early stages of these protests were described as an "Arab spring" because they expressed the energy, hopes, and aspirations of millions of Muslim youth that there would be a dramatic reconfiguration of politics in a region where "young people straddle a fault line between hope and despair" (John 2017, 4). The waves of violence, repression, and instability that followed in the years have highlighted an all too obvious divide between the lives of youth in Syria, Iraq, Yemen, and the lives of youth in prosperous Persian Gulf states. The two most common grievances among young people in these nations were about not being able to enjoy all the rights and opportunities they are entitled to and about feeling constrained by different forces in their society, including family, society as a whole, and government (Issam Fares Institute 2011). The situation was then and still is generally graver for young women as they experience gendered inequalities in education, employment, civic and political participation, and access to health and legal services because of the persistence of traditional patriarchal structures and attitudes that limit their decision-making powers.

A striking feature of this street-level resistance and mobilization against authoritarian social control was the use of online media. Even though digital access is unevenly spread in the region, young female and male activists skillfully rearranged the political discourse, shaped the public sphere, and challenged power structures in unprecedented ways. Young people on the ground disseminated information about the protests in real time by texting, tweeting, and using Facebook groups and YouTube uploads. Middle Eastern youth are increasingly engaged in "civic activism" through "a mix of public education and consciousness raising, political lobbying, street activism, [and] volunteerism and community service . . . around a single common cause" (Khouri and Shehata 2011, 17).

The explosion of social media has produced one of the most important transitions in recent decades. Young people are able to have huge social impact by blending digital media with traditional political activism and social entrepreneurship in ways that bypass state control. This is important to note because although some young Muslims are attracted to Islamist politicized movements, the overwhelming majority of them gravitate toward secular forms of social activism, as illustrated in many of the contributions to this collection.

Understanding Islamism and Radicalization

The term *Islamism* has become synonymous with *radicalization* and *religious extremism*. However, most Islamists are not jihadists or members of al-Qaeda or of the Islamic State of Iraq and al-Sham (ISIS), which are a violent minority within a spectrum of Muslims who follow different political and ideological strategies (Fuller 2004; Martin and Barzeger 2009). Many different shades of Islamism exist, from political and cultural movements to ideological and religious trends. The different shades have also emerged in different historical and social milieu. All of the mainstream Islamist movements across the globe have gained some influence by their largest manifestations—the Muslim Brotherhood (Ikhwan al-Muslimoon) in the Middle East and the Islamic Assembly (Jamaati-Islami) in South Asia. Known for their pragmatic gradualism and willingness to work within existing state structures, both groups are also currently undergoing processes of evolution (Hamid and Mccants 2016).

More than two decades ago, Olivier Roy (1996) and Gilles Kepel ([2000] 2009) in different ways predicted the failure of political Islam. Their arguments appear vindicated in light of Islamist movements' inability to acquire mass followings and their failure to capture the majority of seats in elections. When Islamists have gained political power, most recently in the case of Egypt, one of the most frequent criticisms leveled against them is their inability to provide socioeconomic policies that offer anything distinctly new from the previous regime. Though these Islamist organizations may fail to convince most people, they remain potent in tapping into religious sentiment deeply embedded in Muslim cultures, even while facing competition from a new generation of religious reformists. People disillusioned with Islamism but committed to their faith have transformed their energies into what Bayat has dubbed "post-Islamism": "a political and social condition in which after a phase of experimentation, the appeal, energy, and sources of legitimacy of Islamism get exhausted even among its once-ardent supporters" (2010a, 243). This new generation of religiously inspired social activists is spearheaded by pious Muslims who attempt to "fuse religiosity and rights, faith and freedom, Islam and liberty. It wants to turn the underlying principles of Islamism on their heads by emphasizing rights instead of duties, plurality in place of a singular authoritative voice, historicity rather than fixed scripture, and the future instead of the past" (Bayat 2010a, 243). This post-Islamist trend continues to evolve as more traditional forms of Islam go through their own internal transformations. As recent observers have noted, even though politicized forms of Islam continue to make advances in regions such as the Middle East, Islamism as a broad ideological alternative is splintering, with intense intragroup competition for membership, resources, and survival taking place between movements in the political sphere owing to a combination of specific localized conditions. As Avi Max Spiegel observes in the Moroccan context, rival organizations try to attract new recruits "not through organizational rigidity—firm lines of hierarchy and control—but rather by promising and preaching personal choice, autonomy and freedom, by offering the ability to carve out what young people want: their own individual identities" (2015, 8).

Although there are many highly nuanced studies of Islamically inspired politics, research into the relationship between Muslims and militancy is often reliant on functionalist social-psychological approaches (Wiktorowicz 2004). Moreover, ideology, deprivation, and alienation cannot entirely explain what draws young people to violent Islamism. Religious belief interacts with other aspects of people's contextual experiences at various individual, group, institutional, and state levels. A fluid mix of variables can align to influence why young Muslims choose to join extremist groups: racism; Islamophobia; anger at Western foreign policy; a search for identity, status, adventure, justice, or revenge; perspectives that resonate with their perceptions of the world. Nevertheless, a dominant analytical standpoint focuses on the role of ideology as the primary causal dynamic behind violent radicalization. Here, sociological conditions at the level of the individual, the family, the neighborhood, the city, the nation-state, and the world are clearly important. At a structural level, the specific quandaries of ethnic and racial inequality affect Muslim communities in disproportionate ways, especially in western European economies (Heath and Martin 2013).

Muslims in Europe are now third-generation minorities, and the issues of educational underachievement, limited skills and training, underemployment, unemployment, and discrimination continue to affect their social mobility and opportunities for integration. These predicaments can thus lead to alienation, frustration, disenfranchisement, and ultimately stress and anxiety (Abbas 2011). This combination of effects attracts some to criminality and violence, which emerge because of the state's symbolic violence and biopolitics (Foucault 2003). At the family level, intergenerational disconnect can play a role in this process. Grandfathers and fathers who were invited to or migrated to western European countries with large Muslim populations, such as France, Britain, and Germany, brought with them patriarchal values found in parts of South Asia, North Africa, and Anatolian Turkey.

A form of cultural hierarchy maintains the male head of household as the final arbitrator in domestic decisions, including regulating the role of women in the family. However, although fathers maintain a certain level of influence over their sons in the home, wider society determines their sons' social mobility, which catches young Muslim men in a double bind. At one level, they are subject to the authority of the male head of household, but at the same time, on other level, they are demonized or rendered invisible in the public sphere. This can create a sense of psychological dislocation among European-born young men and women who wish to attain a certain degree of individuality and cultural affinity with a host society that does not fully accept them.

Perpetuating Islamophobia

A set of dominant hegemonic discourses referred to as the "Muslim question" has come to define social debates about the visibility of the followers of Islam (Norton 2013). These discourses shape public perceptions about immigration, crime, violence, terrorism, and gender inequality and allege that Islam perpetuates them, but they do so without questioning the West's commitment to its own ideals. Meanwhile, wider social and economic inequalities continue to deepen as various counterterrorism interventions shrink hard-won freedoms in the name of protecting liberty (Abbas and Awan 2015). Society champions individuality and competitiveness, while the frontiers of the welfare state are ever in retreat, and those at the bottom of society are increasingly required to fend for themselves at times of economic hardship, ironically by seeking help from the very state that presents them as the undeserving. Distracting public opinion is a tried and tested political strategy: every time a terrorist incident implicates an individual who claims his or her actions were taken in the name of Islam, somehow all Muslims are made accountable.

In the United Kingdom, policy think tanks such as the Centre for Social Cohesion, the Henry Jackson Society, and the Quilliam Foundation frequently accuse Muslim communities of not doing enough to challenge extremism and blame Islamism for providing the "mood music for terrorism." These institutions conceptually subscribe to a primordialist view of religion that ignores the reality of how actors in struggles and conflicts that are in fact secular in nature instrumentalize Islam. Such organizations also have dubious links with Far Right groups in the United States and across Europe and have influence among senior government ministers and counterterrorism policy circles that invariably support the status quo.

In spite of the growth of "Islamophobia studies," problems of classification, categorization, and generalization afflict the term *Islamophobia*. Some regard Islamophobia as a *process*, whereas others sees it as a *product*. The former relates to patterns of prejudice and marginalization measured as distinct forms of racial, cultural, and religious discrimination. The latter manifests itself in history as well as in contemporary politics. There remains an analytical gap between conception, perception, and ultimately realization (Allen 2010). For others, the ambiguity of the concept is its strength in that Islamophobia takes many different shapes and forms depending on context and opportunity. These forms have local and global manifestations in specific intellectual, political, cultural, and social ontologies (Sayyid and Vakil 2011). Other scholars have come to interpret Islamophobia's relationship to existing patterns of xenophobia, Orientalism, and imperialism that affect liberal democracies and the constructions of multiculturalism found within them (Esposito and Kalin 2011). Racism is not the preserve of Far Right groups or institutionalized only in the workings of state apparatus—"Islamophobia, like other forms of racism, can be colour-coded, i.e., it can be biological (normally associated with skin colour) and can be cultural (not necessarily associated with skin colour), or it can be a mixture of both" (Cole 2009, 251–52).

In America, neo-Orientalist scholarship has worked to justify US foreign policy in the Middle East, pathologizing Muslims for not being ready for democracy and thus in need of Western patronage. This cultural-deficit framework reemerged vigorously after the events of 9/11, and it remains an ongoing phenomenon in the United States. It further perpetuates Islamophobia (Kumar 2010) and the objectification of American Muslims (Bayoumi 2015). An accompanying development has been another industry—one that focuses on radicalization and deradicalization. A large number of institutions and self-styled experts have come forward to endorse government approaches to tackling Islamic political radicalism (Kundnani 2009). They help to sustain the view that the problem of violent extremism originates within ideology rather than within sociology and conflict. This view takes attention away from concerns relating to structural disadvantage, discrimination, and policies that are arguably the more significant drivers in declining urban areas (Alexander 2004). Some government departments also support this view in their own research (Travis 2008). The increasing gap between the rich and poor has contributed to the current period of global economic insecurity. Even in Western nations such as the United Kingdom, higher education does not necessarily lead to employment. In light of the austerity measures introduced in the wake of the global financial crises of 2008, labor markets have shrunk, limiting the aspirations of young graduates. In Britain, countering terrorism has led to the perverse situation in which a liberal democracy is developing illiberal policies (Williamson and Khiabany 2011).

Many Muslims living in the Middle East and other Muslim-majority contexts suffer the turmoil of despotism and cronyism in addition to problems posed by climate change, economic underdevelopment, and social unrest. They also experience acute levels of underdevelopment in economic and educational infrastructures as well as of militarization. One of the most pressing challenges facing young people in Muslim-majority societies is the increasing gap between education or skills and employment. Approximately 100 million youth are in dire need of employment in the MENA region alone (World Economic Forum 2012). The often talked about demographic "youth bulge" is also occurring at time of increasing risk and uncertainty in many of these Muslim-majority societies, where young people struggle with disaffection, marginalization, and contradictions within their cultures. As observers note, young people in Arab societies have to deal with a variety of issues as well as with "disparate and conflicting messages: religious authority, state, national or secular ideologies, family and kinship groups, peer subculture, popular and cyber culture and as of late the seductive global allures of commodified consumerism, virtual images and lifestyles" (Khalaf and Khalaf 2012, 9). With the myriad challenges facing Muslims across the world, scholars and practitioners are in a position to point to various ways forward. Populations in uneven power relationships cannot challenge in isolation the dominant social structures and institutions, hence the need to reconceptualize Muslim agency in the sphere of social and political conflict.

Content of the Volume

Second- and third-generation young people in North America and western Europe are at the forefront of adapting to and reinterpreting Islam in ways that seek to reconcile their faith with secular Western cultures. These efforts are resulting in critical new thinking and cultural bricolage. Most of these youth have little interest in perpetuating their parents' ethnic and linguistic traditions and are more concerned with achieving their full rights as equal citizens. The situation in the United States is important to consider given that it is the most powerful nation on earth, has many geostrategic interests in Muslim-majority countries, and possesses a significant domestic Muslim population.

Young people growing up in the post-9/11 era have had to cope with being defined as a "problem," being objects of suspicion, having their loyalty questioned, undergoing surveillance, and suffering increasing levels of racism and Islamophobia (Bayoumi 2009). As a result, some have become politically active, whereas others have tried to evade public scrutiny by de-emphasizing their Muslimness or even by leaving the faith (Sirin and Fine 2008).

American Muslims include African Americans as well as immigrant and minority groups from all over the globe. American Muslim youth consist of many subgroups that live in diverse contexts shaped by their race, ethnicity, socioeconomic status, and ancestral heritage. As contributors Sameera Ahmed and Hadiyah Muhammad note in chapter 1, "despite having their identity and roots stripped from them, many African Muslims resisted their slave master's domination by orally transmitting Islamic knowledge and beliefs, maintaining Islamic dietary restrictions, growing beards, and sometimes wearing turbans." Malcolm X and Muhammad Ali "are recognized . . . as cultural icons who embodied the resistance to a White hegemonic paradigm." Given the significance of African American political and cultural history, "Black Muslim youth have been able to create pathways that simultaneously resist institutionalized oppression and embrace their racial, religious, and national identities."

In chapter 2, Jasmin Zine and Asma Bala explain how university campuses in Canada are important sites where young Muslims articulate what it means to be both Muslim and Western. University student societies are often active spaces in which young people find solace and comfort among likeminded people as well as the opportunity to engage in the most pressing concerns in wider society. Government counterterrorism narratives that single out Muslim young people as potential risks on campuses are counterproductive, undermining the traditional opportunities for dialogue and debate between students groups. For Zine and Bala, these student organizations are "more than just clubs. Rather, they form a subaltern Muslim counterpublic and are constituted as campus-based social movements. They assist students in aligning their faith and activism in ways that create Islamic subcultures on campus and guide students in pious living."

This invasive securitization is also creeping into the policies of many western European states: "Casual, everyday European Islamophobia has led to a series of moral panics over women wearing headscarves and burqas and Muslim youths more generally" (Masquelier and Soares 2016a, 8). In chapter 3, Martijn de Koning observes how in the Netherlands the ultraconservative form of Islam known as Salafism is marked as a specific concern for policy makers, who regard it as a driver in the path toward violent extremism. Salafi Muslim youth, targeted as a source of extremism in many Western countries, receive the brunt of attention even though few of them espouse violence, as de Koning states: "there is no evidence that the Salafi networks in the Netherlands are seeking to implement sharia or prepare for an Islamic revolution to create an Islamic state in the Netherlands." But rather than be trapped by a seemingly closed-ended scenario, these young radicals have opportunities for "reversal/inversion and escape." De Koning argues that participation in the arts, politics, and society can enable young Dutch Muslim men to channel into positive forms of empowerment and resistance the frustration and anger they feel because of their alienation. In chapter 4, Aminul Hoque discusses the tensions involved in the processes of integration for second- and third-generation British Bangladeshi Muslims. He notes how "many young Bangladeshis contest, reject, and reconstruct national (British) and ethnic (Bangladeshi) identity categories to make them meaningful" and concludes by arguing that confident and progressive British Islamic identities have emerged. These young Muslims are expecting recognition and demand to play a role in national politics.

Switzerland is a unique nation. It has close ties with France, Germany, and Italy at its borders, all shaping the internal Swiss national social composition and political outlook. Andreas Tunger-Zanetti and Jürgen Endres contend that protest is not the only way to deal with the challenges of discrimination and racism facing Muslims in Switzerland. They describe in chapter 5 how being "scouts in rough terrain" appeals to Muslims between the ages of fourteen and nineteen. Young Muslims work with civil society, volunteer, and engage with mainstream society through various charitable and community-oriented action. The youth groups offer protected spaces where Islam can be discussed and difficult questions can be asked and debated. In these groups, young people "are exploring ways to live in an environment characterized by rough terrain (structural obstacles) and often inhospitable weather (media 'storms' and individual discrimination)." In these spaces, they can move beyond ritualism and dogmatic thinking embedded in certain community settings. In the context of the limited scope of the state's investment in youth work and community education (especially for Muslim youth), the presence of these Muslim groups provides dividends to Muslims and society as a whole.

South of Europe, Turkey is a nation undergoing a period of substantive change as it has grown into a regional power over the past decade. In chapter 6, Yusuf Sarfati details the transformative impact of the Islamist Justice and Development Party government on Turkish political culture. He discusses how the party's increasingly authoritarian policies have alienated significant sections of the population that voted for it. These tensions have escalated after repeated accusations of state corruption and suppression of dissent, and they reached a critical juncture after the Gezi Park protests in 2013, which accelerated the creation of a number of new youth-led social movements—the new "Islamic Left," according to Sarfati. The Anticapitalist Muslims and Labor and Justice Platform represent a new, alternate Islamic formation that emphasizes an egalitarian and socially conscious Islamic politics. This formation is indicative of the intergenerational shifts taking place within the post-Islamist discourse.

Farther east, a rich diversity of South Asian Islam and distinct Muslim nations share a common heritage but are also experiencing historical ruptures and political differences that have exacerbated existing divisions between them, preventing them from meaningful cooperation. The combined Muslim populations of Pakistan, Kashmir, India, Bangladesh, and Afghanistan total more than half a billion, but ongoing divisions and conflict mean that these societies could not be farther apart. Following the events of 9/11 and the subsequent "war on terror," Afghanistan and Pakistan in particular have suffered, while Kashmir remains a thorny subject for both Pakistan and India, with their ever-vociferous competing claims over it. As the squabbling continues and the animosity between two nations torn apart from one goes on, the people of Kashmir feel persecuted by the Indian occupation, a view seldom reported in India or even in the West. Pakistan has struggled immeasurably in the post-9/11 era, where much of the political violence has been carried out by Muslims against each other through the rise of sectarianism against Shias as well as increased intolerance of Christian groups. Muslim young people are the most frequent casualities of these conflicts, which are sustained by

Western governments' economic sanctions, drone attacks, and support for authoritarian regimes.

In Afghanistan, ethnic rivalries have been aggravated by foreign intervention, decades of war, manipulation by religious factions, and constant instability that has fractured much of what remains of Afghan civil society. In this milieu, the Internet is one of the few spaces allowing young women to express their voices and challenge the dominant paradigms that marginalize them. In this regard, blogging is an important tool for empowerment, representation, and engagement. Shehnaz Haqqani argues in chapter 7 that "Pashtun women bloggers from Afghanistan and Pakistan challenge . . . common Western perceptions of their identities, cultures, and native countries." Rather than be cast as victims of their own social order, however, these young Pashtun women achieve empowerment and demonstrate they are both "performers in and creators of a third culture of which they are not only valuable members but also primary mediators." Empowerment through music has also arisen among young Muslims in Pakistan who share similar fears. In chapter 8, Chloe Gill-Khan discusses how music has long been an important part of the cultural history of Pakistan, particularly folk music variants rooted in Sufism. Politicized pop music continues to grow in popularity, helped by a technologically savvy youth population connected to the Internet. With lyrics whose topics range from "corporate feudalism" to "conspiracy theories," "internal discord," and high-level politics, the songs discussed envision multiple horizons for ideological, political and structural change.

At the same time, significant spaces have emerged for public engagement. In chapter 9, Munazza Yaqoob examines how youth organizations and networks in Pakistan have engaged in educational and peace-building strategies as a bulwark against issues of radicalization in society. Yaqoob describes the work of several civil society projects but focuses specifically on the contributions of the Critical Thinking Forum. How the forum engages young women in education and research activities to enhance achievement, social inclusion, and participation in political and sociocultural debates, especially on campuses, suggests that universities remain critical sites for engagement. In the troubled state of Kashmir, a youthful demographic has seen little else but conflict. In chapter 10, Idrisa Pandit describes how young activists have used text as a tool of resistance in the public square. Pandit highlights the critical role of young women who utilize their writing, poetry, and other art forms to document human rights violations, sometimes at the risk of being harassed, attacked, and labeled as troublemakers. Pandit writes, "Women's voices have been ever present in the Kashmiri struggle. From the very beginning, women—mothers, wives, and daughters—have paid a heavy price in the current uprising as victims of brutalization and oppression." This bravery and sacrifice continues to give hope.

In Southeast Asia, Indonesia is home to 220 million Muslims. It is the largest single Muslim-majority nation in the world and the farthest away from the geographical heart of Islam. In Indonesia, young people have engaged in various forms of political resistance, which range from street demonstrations and electoral politics to religiously inspired popular culture. After the Suharto era ended in the 1990s, Indonesia became a political, economic, and cultural powerhouse in the region. Although political institutions protect the rights and freedoms of all religious communities in the nation, with the national motto "Unity within Diversity" being upheld with confidence, the question of youth radicalism has surfaced in recent periods, especially after the Bali terror attacks in 2002. Despite a growing economy, widening divisions between rich and poor have also become acute. There have been intermittent episodes of social unrest. In chapter 11, Carool Kersten documents the activism of young Muslim Indonesians historically and observes that

> Indonesia has also developed a distinctly Indonesian Islamic discursive tradition. Shaped by this tradition's dynamics of patronage and mentoring, custodial care and critique, Muslim youth activists have played and continue to play an important role in its articulation and dissemination. It has resulted in vibrant intra-Muslim debates. In recent years, however, it has also led to a polarization of positions not just between Muslims and non-Muslims but also and perhaps even more sharply among Indonesian Muslims themselves.

This discursive tradition represents aspects of the difficult terrain that Muslim youth activists must navigate in their various national contexts.

The conflicts taking place in Muslim-majority states are occurring for many different reasons. First, geopolitical factors affect an overriding dynamic that shapes individual contexts (Mandaville 2007). Second, sectarianism is an internal quagmire that traps groups in Muslim-majority nation-states (Berkey 2003). Third, a spiritual versus material conflict exists in Muslim societies wrestling with how to deal with a godly world without God, as they see it (Asad 2003). All of these factors lead to inequality, social conflict as the norm, and competition for resources. For some, the need for the spiritual is paramount, hence ongoing internal uncertainty. Important questions remain regarding how outside forces can influence the situation in these countries, considering the lack of internal change and development to meet the people's expectations.

Much of the angst expressed over Muslims in Western societies is a projection of nations trying to define their role in a global era. In a postcolonial, multipolar world, western Europe is experiencing an identity crisis—struggling to reconcile the failures of the European Union against the historical construction of a continental identity. Ironically, the idea of Europe was in part a response to the encroaching power of the Ottoman Empire and the denial of a civilizational debt to Islam. Much of "Old Europe" presently resists a responsibility to accept and incorporate its Muslim minorities (Marquand 2012). The presence of Muslims in Europe is indisputably redefining Europe, reconfiguring notions of European-ness and thereby of other national identities across western Europe (Allievi 2012). One encouraging sign that the conflicts between Muslims and non-Muslims can be resolved is that many Muslims and members of other faith groups in Europe and elsewhere are working together to constructively challenge the counterproductive policies of state institutions (Back et al. 2009). Young Muslims in particular are increasingly at the forefront of these initiatives, demonstrating their capacity to affect positive social change. This volume offers numerous glimpses of these developments.

This international collaboration draws upon a rich set of empirically and theoretically informed frameworks. Scholars from a variety of backgrounds, such as anthropology, sociology, political science, religious studies, and international relations, address the conceptualization of global

Muslim young people and resistance. All use innovative methodologies grounded in the micro understanding of the everyday social, economic, and political realities of young people.

The result of these scholars' work is an interdisciplinary analysis of emerging patterns of social change among young Muslims from around the world. This analysis makes this collection one of the few works to examine social transformation generated by every society's most dynamic element—young people. This volume is groundbreaking in the rich diversity of global perspectives it offers and in its decentering of the one-dimensional representations of Muslim young people today. It reflects both specific and broader challenges facing young people in both Muslim-minority and Muslim-majority contexts, religious and secular, and it points to the importance of listening to and understanding young people, who are ultimately the future of Islam in general and of societies with Muslim populations in particular.

References

Abbas, Tahir. 2011. *Islamic Radicalism and Multicultural Politics: The British Experience.* London: Routledge.

Abbas, Tahir, and Imran Awan. 2015. "Limits of UK Counterterrorism Policy and Its Implications for Islamophobia and Far Right Extremism." *International Journal for Crime, Justice, and Social Democracy* 4, no. 3: 16–29.

Ahmad, Fauzia, and Mohammed S. Seddon, eds. 2012. *Muslim Youth: Challenges, Opportunities, and Expectations.* London: Continuum.

Alexander, Claire. 2004. "Imagining the Asian Gang: Ethnicity, Masculinity, and Youth after 'the Riots.'" *Critical Social Policy* 24, no. 4: 526–49.

Allen, Chris. 2010. *Islamophobia.* Farnham, UK: Ashgate.

Allievi, Stefano. 2012. "Reactive Identities and Islamophobia: Muslim Minorities and the Challenge of Religious Pluralism in Europe." *Philosophy and Social Criticism* 38, nos. 4–5: 379–87.

Asad, Talal. 2003. *Formations of the Secular: Christianity, Islam, Modernity.* Stanford, CA: Stanford Univ. Press.

Back, Les, Michael Keith, Azra Khan, Kabir Shukra, and Johon Solomos. 2009. "Islam and the New Political Landscape: Faith Communities, Political Participation, and Social Change." *Theory Culture Society* 26, no. 4: 1–23.

Bayat, Asef. 2010a. *Life as Politics: How Ordinary People Change the Middle East.* Amsterdam: Amsterdam Univ. Press.

———. 2010b. "Muslim Youth and the Claim of Youthfulness." In *Being Young and Muslim: New Cultural Politics in the Global South and North*, edited by Linda Herrera and Asef Bayat, 27–48. Oxford: Oxford Univ. Press.

Bayoumi, Moustafa. 2009. *How Does It Feel to Be a Problem? Being Young and Arab in America.* New York: Penguin.

———. 2015. *This Muslim American Life: Dispatches from the War on Terror.* New York: New York Univ. Press.

Berkey, Jonathon P. 2003. *The Formation of Islam: Religion and Society in the Near East, 600–1800.* Cambridge: Cambridge Univ. Press.

Cole, Mike. 2009. "Critical Race Theory Comes to the UK: A Marxist Response." *Ethnicities* 9, no. 2: 246–84.

Cottee, Simon. 2015. "Pilgrims to the Islamic State: What Westerners Migrating to ISIS Have in Common with Westerners Who Sympathized with Communism." *Atlantic*, July 24. At https://www.theatlantic.com/international /archive/2015/07/isis-foreign-fighters-political-pilgrims/399209/.

Esposito John, and Ibrahim Kalin, eds. 2011. *Islamophobia: The Challenge of Pluralism in the 21st Century.* New York: Oxford Univ. Press.

Foucault, Michel. 2003. *Society Must Be Defended: Lectures at the Collège de France, 1975–1976.* Edited by Mauro Bertani and Alessandro Fontana. Translated by David Macey. London: Picador.

Fuller, Graham E. 2004. *The Future of Political Islam.* Basingstoke, UK: Palgrave Macmillan.

Grim, Brian J., and Mehtab S. Karim. 2011. *The Future Global Muslim Population Projections for 2010–2030.* Washington, DC: Pew Research Center Forum on Religion and Public Life.

Hamid, Shadi, and Will Mccants. 2016. *Rethinking Political Islam.* Washington, DC: Brookings Institution Press. At http://www.brookings.edu/research /reports2/2015/08/rethinking-political-islam.

Heath, Anthony, and Jean Martin. 2013. "Can Religious Affiliation Explain 'Ethnic' Inequalities in the Labour Market?" *Ethnic and Racial Studies* 36, no. 6: 1005–27.

Herrera, Linda, and Asef Bayat, eds. 2010. *Being Young and Muslim: New Cultural Politics in the Global South and North.* Oxford: Oxford Univ. Press.

Issam Fares Institute for Public Policy and International Affairs, American University of Beirut. 2011. *A Generation on the Move: Insights into the Conditions,*

Aspirations, and Activism of Arab Youth. Beirut: Issam Fares Institute for Public Policy and International Affairs, American Univ. of Beirut.

John, Sunil. 2017. *The Arab Youth Survey 2017*. Dubai, United Arab Emirates: ASDA'A Burson-Marsteller.

Kepel, Giles. [2000] 2009. *Jihad: The Trail of Political Islam*. London: I. B. Tauris.

Khalaf, Samir, and Roseanne Saeed Khalaf. 2011. Introduction to *Arab Youth: Social Mobilisation in Times of Risk*, edited by Samir Khalaf and Roseanne Saeed Khalaf, 7–32. London: Saqi Books.

Khouri, Rami G., and Dina Shehata. 2011. "Youth Civic and Political Participation: Apathy amidst New Forms of Activism." In *A Generation on the Move: Insights into the Conditions, Aspirations, and Activism of Arab Youth*, edited by the Issam Fares Institute for Public Policy and International Affairs, American University of Beirut, 16–19. Beirut: Issam Fares Institute for Public Policy and International Affairs, American Univ. of Beirut.

Kumar, Deepa. 2010. "Framing Islam: The Resurgence of Orientalism during the Bush II Era." *Journal of Communication Inquiry* 34, no. 3: 254–77.

———. 2012. *Islamophobia*. New York: Haymarket.

Kundnani, Arun. 2009. "Radicalisation: The Journey of a Concept." *Race & Class* 54, no. 2: 3–25.

———. 2013. *The Muslims Are Coming! Islamophobia, Extremism, and the Domestic War on Terror*. London: Verso.

Lean, Nathan. 2012. *The Islamophobia Industry: How the Right Manufactures Fear of Muslims*. London: Pluto Press.

Lipka, Michael, and Conrad Hackett. 2015. *Why Muslims Are the World's Fastest-Growing Religious Group*. Washington, DC: Pew Research Center, Apr. 25. At http://www.pewresearch.org/fact-tank/2017/04/06/why-muslims-are-the-worlds-fastest-growing-religious-group.

Mandaville, Peter. 2007. "Globalization and the Politics of Religious Knowledge: Pluralizing Authority in the Muslim World." *Theory, Culture & Society* 24, no. 2: 101–15.

Marquand, David. 2012. *The End of the West: The Once and Future Europe*. Princeton, NJ: Princeton Univ. Press.

Martin, Richard C., and Abbas Barzeger, eds. 2009. *Islamism: Contested Perspectives on Political Islam*. Stanford, CA: Stanford Univ. Press.

Masquelier, Adeline, and Benjamin F. Soares. 2016a. "Introduction: Muslim Youth and the 9/11 Generation." In *Muslim Youth and the 9/11 Generation*, edited by Adeline Masquelier and Benjamin F. Soares, 1–30. Albuquerque: Univ. of New Mexico Press.

———, eds. 2016b. *Muslim Youth and the 9/11 Generation*. Albuquerque: Univ. of New Mexico Press.

Miller, Emily McFarlan. 2017. "Europe's Muslim Population Growing—but Won't Be a Majority Anytime Soon." Religion News Service, Nov. 29. At http://religionnews.com/2017/11/29/europes-muslim-population-growing-but-wont-be-a-majority-anytime-soon/.

Mirza, Munira, Abi Senthilkumaran, and Zein Ja'far. 2007. *Living Apart Together: British Muslims and the Paradox of Multiculturalism*. London: Policy Exchange.

Nayak, Anoop. 2003. *Race, Place, and Globalization: Youth Cultures in a Changing World*. Oxford: Berg.

Nilan, Pam, and Carles Feixa. 2006. "Introduction: Youth Hybridity and Plural Worlds." In *Global Youth? Hybrid Identities, Plural Worlds*, edited by Pam Nilan and Carles Feixa, 1–13. London: Routledge.

Norton. Anne. 2013. *On the Muslim Question*. Princeton, NJ: Princeton Univ. Press.

Roy, Olivier. 1996. *The Failure of Political Islam*. Cambridge, MA: Harvard Univ. Press.

Sayyid, Salman, and Abdoolkarim Vakil, eds. 2011. *Thinking through Islamophobia: Global Perspectives*. New York: Columbia Univ. Press.

Sirin, Slecuk R., and Michelle Fine. 2008. *American Muslim Youth: Understanding Hyphenated Identities through Multiple Methods*. New York: New York Univ. Press.

Spiegel, Max A. 2015. *Young Islam: The New Politics of Religion in Morocco and the Arab World*. Princeton, NJ: Princeton Univ. Press.

Travis, Alain. 2008. "MI5 Report Challenges Views on Terrorism in Britain." *Guardian*, Aug. 20. At https://www.theguardian.com/uk/2008/aug/20/uk security.terrorism1.

Wiktorowicz, Quintan, ed. 2004. *Islamic Activism: A Social Movement Theory Approach*. Bloomington: Indiana Univ. Press.

Williamson, Milly, and Gholam Khiabany. 2011. "State, Culture, and Anti-Muslim Racism." *Global Media and Communication* 7, no. 3: 175–79.

World Economic Forum. 2012. *Addressing the 100 Million Youth Challenge Perspectives on Youth Employment in the Arab World in 2012*. Washington, DC: World Economic Forum.

1

Black American Muslim Youth

Navigating Environments, Engaging New Pathways

SAMEERA AHMED
and HADIYAH MUHAMMAD

> I can't really separate my Black and my Muslim identity. Like I said,
> I walk around every day, Black, you know. So how the world inter-
> acts with me on a day to day basis first, actually, is Black—unless
> they see my name first, then it's Muslim, or no most of the time then
> it's still Black, just with a funny name.
>
> —quoted in Sameera Ahmed, Sultan
Sharrief, and Cynthia Arfken, "Juggling
Cultural Identities" (2009)

Despite composing the largest percentage of native-born Muslims (40 percent) in the United States (Pew Research Center for the People and the
Press 2011), Black Muslims are a severely under-researched group. African American or Black Muslim youth are a unique group that experiences
life at the intersections of anti-Black attitudes, institutionalized racism,
and increasing Islamophobia. Black Muslim youth's experiences differ
from those of their immigrant Muslim peers because of their erasure and
invisibility as Muslims, which are primarily owing to a societal attempt
to define Islam as a religion of recent "immigrants" and to marginalize it
as "other" rather than see it as part of American history largely through
the Black American experience. Black Muslim youth are challenging
White supremacy and anti-Blackness while deriving strength and connection from their religious and cultural heritage. They also, however, play
a critical role in the indigenization of Islam in America because they are

privileged with a cultural capital that allows them to be seen as American and Black rather than as foreign and "Other." This chapter aims to increase understanding of Black Muslim youth by highlighting their unique developmental context and to explore the varying pathways they are choosing. This chapter draws on data collected from fieldwork interviews with Black American Muslim young people on this subject matter.[1]

Contextualizing Black American Muslims Developmental Needs

Human development is bidirectional and must account for the impact of the environment on the individual and the individual's impact on his or her environment (Lerner and Kauffman 1985). Furthermore, development must consider the bidirectional interaction of the individual's characteristics, the varying environments the person is embedded within, and the fluidity of development to account for the variety in developmental paths observed (Abo-Zena and Ahmed 2014). How these factors interact and affect Black Muslim youth are discussed later. The individual characteristics of Black Muslim youth, such as physical, cognitive, and personality traits, contribute to varying developmental outcomes. In one interview, a Black Muslim male college student noted a stark example of how physical traits have a significant impact on the lives of Black Muslim youth's daily interactions with society: "My roommate is Arab, but I'm Black. When we are late for Fajr [dawn] prayers at the mosque, he doesn't get it! I can't just leave [the apartment] without my [driver's] license. I keep tellin' him, 'Bro, I'm Black. We just can't drive a car without a license and proof [of ownership] in the car. You're bound to get stopped by the police!'"

Other examples of person-centered factors such as health, personality, and physical attractiveness. How society perceives these traits influence how a young person interacts and experiences his or her environment. Similarly, what a Black Muslim youth searches for in a religious experience (e.g., fellowship, mentorship, guidance, structure) shapes the experiences

---

1. Unless otherwise noted, quotations from Black youth in this chapter come from interviews we conducted in 2009.

that individual seeks out in his or her environment. Racial and religious identities may fluctuate with age, context, and societal events. For example, cognitive development and the task of identity formation may lead some individuals to question their belief system. In addition, Black Muslim youth's racial identity may be influenced by the presence or absence of racial socialization opportunities in their environment. In focus-group discussions, young Black Muslim emerging adults described their racial and religious identities as interacting and evolving over time (Ahmed, Sharrief, and Arfken 2009). Some young people described having a "vacation" from Islam, where they consciously chose not to practice or identify with Muslims and instead to blend in with their Black peers. Black Muslim youth converts often describe this developmental stage associated with introspection that leads to re-evaluating their life, eventual conversion. An individual's identification may fluctuate based on his or her immediate context. One young Black emerging adult discussed her racial and religious identities:

> I feel like I'm both [Black and Muslim] simultaneously. I can flick and put a spotlight on one and kinda shade out the other for certain settings and stuff. Because I'm very passionate about both. I like to be very involved with things that are like Black based . . . discussions on, you know, where we are in, in the Black community . . . because that is so much a part of my life. And so much a part of my identity. . . . And a lot of times like when I'm out and about . . . you're gonna see . . . I'm Black. But at the same time, I umm like, I like to let people kinda find out that I'm Muslim. That's kinda how, how I do it. (quoted in Ahmed, Sharrief, and Arfken 2009)

Despite the importance of individual characteristics, Black Muslim youth are also developing within various milieus. These contexts—including but not limited to historical, societal, socioeconomic, neighborhood, educational, family, peer, and congregational cultural contexts—overlap and sometimes conflict with each other in terms of cultural values, norms, and expectations. The individual's ability to navigate through these multiple contexts results in varying developmental trajectories. Black Muslim youth are not insulated from the racial realities of the Black community or from the Islamophobia that exists in America. Although Islam's roots in America predate the coming of Christopher Columbus, the first wave of Muslims arrived as a result of the forcible enslavement of millions of West Africans during the transatlantic slave trade (Diouf 1998). Despite having their identity and roots stripped from them, many African Muslims resisted their slave masters' domination by orally transmitting Islamic knowledge and beliefs (McAdams-Mahmoud 2005), maintaining Islamic dietary restrictions, growing beards, and sometimes wearing turbans (Diouf 1998). Resistance would take different forms from one generation to the next, but these efforts by enslaved African Muslims are still important aspects of Black Muslim youth identity. For example, when asked about factors that contribute to their identity, a young Black Muslim replied, "I think about . . . you know . . . the whole struggle thing. The coming up from slavery, cause we're Black. We're slave descendants, so there is a certain struggle [that we carry on]" (quoted in Ahmed, Sharrief, and Arfken 2009). The struggle may represent the initial and collective trauma that continues to manifest itself in anti-Black attitudes, discrimination, and disparities in the lives of Black youth.

During the early twentieth century, the Black community was introduced to Islam through proto-Islamic movements that used cultural symbols (e.g., the crescent and stars), Arabic words, and Arabic dress (e.g., the turban). Groups such as the Moorish Science Temple and the Nation of Islam (NOI), combined Black nationalism with aspects of Islamic teachings to uplift the Black community (McAdams-Mahmoud 2005.) In particular, the NOI had a significant role in normalizing Islam within the Black community. It presented an alternative of moral confidence, self-discipline, and financial independence from systems that oppressed the Black community. Black converts to the NOI founded the proto-Islamic movement to serve as both a spiritual and an ideological protest to an oppressive White hegemonic culture. The public transformation of Malcolm Little, who changed his name to Malcolm X and became NOI's most prominent member, and the posthumous publication of *The Autobiography of Malcolm X* as told to Alex Haley (1965) have been instrumental in educating generations of people about Islam and continue to serve as a source of inspiration. Similarly, the example set by Muhammad Ali and his willingness to sacrifice his boxing title and career for his religious beliefs resulted in worldwide admiration among many within the Black community. Black Muslim youth recognize both men as cultural icons who embodied the resistance to a White hegemonic paradigm. Many other individuals who began with the NOI would replicate Malcolm X and Muhammad Ali's journey to orthodox Islam. After his father's death, Imam Warith Deen (W. D.) Muhammad became the national leader of the NOI and led many of its members to orthodox or Sunni Islam by renouncing his father's prophecy and the deification of Wallace Fard Muhammad.

Not all individuals converting to Islam within the Black community came through the NOI. Prior to Imam W. D. Muhammad's leading of many NOI members to Sunni Islam, Dar ul-Islam was the largest indigenous group of Black Muslims. Founded in the 1960s, this group focused on introducing Blacks to orthodox Islam (Ahmed 1991). They emphasized the Qur'an and sunna (Prophetic example) and provided community services and prison outreach. This group eventually disbanded in 1980 after internal disagreement regarding the movement's direction (Ahmed 1991). Many mosques previously affiliated with Dar ul-Islam then joined the community of Imam Jamil Al-Amin, a highly revered Black Muslim leader who has been imprisoned under false pretenses since 2000 and was formerly known as H. Rap Brown, a leader of the Student Nonviolent Coordinating Committee in the 1960s. The impact of different mosque pathways to Islam (NOI, Dar ul-Islam, the W. D. Muhammad community, etc.) influence the current norms, cultures, and experiences of Black Muslim youth. The acceptance and practice of Islam by the parents and grandparents of Black Muslim youth during the Civil Rights Movement (1955–68) may be viewed in part as resistance to structural oppression and racism. The sociopolitical climate of the Civil Rights Movement was instrumental in motivating these individuals to explore and accept Islam, resulting in the formation of a new identity. The cultural capital gained from Black Muslims' efforts during the 1960s and 1970s resulted in greater familiarity with and acceptance of Islam within the Black community.

The impact of racism on the development and well-being of Black Muslim youth cannot be overstated. Negative racial stereotypes and attitudes have served to institutionalize racism, affecting their socio-economic mobility, living conditions, and unequal access to essential resources (Williams and Williams-Morris 2000). An integral component of minority youth development is the awareness that they belong to a stigmatized group within the dominant society (McKown and Weinstein 2003). In addition to the typical microaggressions their immigrant Muslim peers experience, Black Muslim youth experience incidents of racial profiling and harassment. They are also disproportionately incarcerated, profiled, policed, and arrested (Kerby 2012). They have higher rates of juvenile incarceration and are more likely to be sentenced to adult prison. In fact, although Blacks make up only 13 percent of the US population (US Census Bureau 2013), Black men make up 40 percent of the US prison population (Sentencing Project 2018)—statistics that highlight the school-to-prison pipeline reality for young Black males. In addition, Black Muslim youth must also contend with the negative images of what it means to be a Black person promoted by the media and entertainment industry. The social pressure to engage in a negative lifestyle that is inconsistent with their religious beliefs is often challenging. The onslaught of negative messages regarding purported cultural norms affects Black Muslim youth's perception of themselves in particular and of their racial group as a whole. As one young man explained,

> You know the media . . . they make us challenge ourselves so much as far as they jam pack this rap music and they jam pack all this negativity into our lifestyles. . . . They jam-pack selling crack. Everybody is selling drugs, ain't making money, bla bla bla. Or they jam-pack selling, everybody wanna sleep with your girl or everybody, you know what I'm sayin'? They don't wanna have no family structure.

Not only are Black Muslim youth part of a racially stigmatized group, but if they choose to identify with Islam, they are also a part of a religiously stigmatized group. American Muslims report that 60 to 75 percent of them have experienced discrimination (Pew Research Center 2017), and anti-Muslim attitudes and incidents appear to have increased after the 2016 presidential elections (Southern Poverty Law Center 2016). For

Black Muslim youth living in predominantly Black communities, the anti-Muslim attitudes generally found outside these communities may not be so prevalent because of the historical contribution by and respect afforded to Muslims in the non-Muslim Black community. Black Muslims are often viewed positively in these spaces, so Black Muslim youth's identification with Islam and Muslims may be empowering and a source of pride there. However, in communities with negative perceptions of Islam and Muslims, Black Muslim youth may encounter repeated discrimination and microaggression and so in certain instances may choose to disassociate with Islam and the Muslim community altogether. The societal messages absorbed by Black Muslim youth affect how these individuals see themselves and how they believe society (the dominant community, the Black community, and the Muslim community) view their group and them as individuals.

Institutionalized racism directly affects the socioeconomic conditions and opportunities afforded to Black Muslim youth (Elliot 2016). One of the major determinants of socioeconomic status is employment status. The unemployment rate among US Blacks is generally double the rate of Whites (e.g., in 2011 Blacks had an unemployment rate of 16 percent and Whites a rate of 8 percent [US Census Bureau 2013]). In the past decade, racial inequalities in hiring practices have not changed, with White applicants continuing to get 36 percent more callbacks from employers than equally qualified Black applicants (Quillian et al. 2017). As a result, Black children are more likely than White children to live in poverty (34 percent versus 10 percent) (*National Assessment of Education Progress* 2011) and to stay in that same income bracket when they become adults (42 percent among Blacks versus 17 percent among Whites) (Hertz 2005). Poverty among children has been associated with poor health conditions, lower educational achievement, and increased rates of risk-taking behaviors. In 2012, the median annual income for Black families was $39,988 in comparison to $67,892 for White families (US Census Bureau 2012). At present, no known studies have compared median incomes of American Muslims by racial/ethnic subgroups. However, in a study of American Muslims conducted by Pew, 26 percent of foreign-born American Muslims reported incomes greater than $75,000 compared to 17 percent of native-born

American Muslims, 40 percent of whom identified as Black (Pew Research Center for the People and the Press 2011). It is unclear what the current socioeconomic conditions are for Black Muslims as a subgroup. Field evidence indicates that conditions for them are more likely similar to those of the general Black population than to those of the immigrant Muslim community. The difference in the socioeconomic conditions of Black and immigrant Muslim communities often results in differing opportunities for young people. In addition, American Muslim immigrants operating businesses in predominantly Black neighborhoods do so through cultural exclusion and economic exploitation of the Black community. The tension, mistrust, and resentment that exists between residents and business owners are produced by the idea that the upward mobility of immigrant business owners is achieved at the expense of Blacks in the latter's own neighborhoods.

Black Muslim youth reside in diverse settings, which can have varying impacts on their development (Mock 2015). Black families have historically been redlined, a practice by federal agencies, banks, and businesses in which services, such as mortgages, are denied based on race (Madrigal 2014). Current-day redlining practices include companies' refusal to provide services to or their provision of only limited access to essential resources in Black neighborhoods (Mock 2015). Neighborhood settings with concentrated poverty can result in negative community cohesion and greater mistrust (Massey and Denton 1993), increased youth violence and delinquency, increased risk of a continued downward trajectory on the socioeconomic ladder, and negative impacts on community resources needed to support young people and their families (Pinderhughes et al. 2001; Wickrama and Bryant 2003). Higher levels of residential stability and community support are more likely to promote youth development (Hurd, Stoddard, and Zimmerman 2012). Some Blacks are migrating to suburbs (Sullivan 2011) or sending their children to live with relatives in suburbs with better schools and neighborhoods in the hope that they will be provided with a more positive peer influence and better job prospects. However, Black youth residing in suburban neighborhoods may struggle with integration issues owing to racism, differences in cultural normative behaviors, and speech (e.g., their use of Black vernacular English). In addition, these Black youth may experience loss of culturally affirming activities and programs, a loss that may negatively affect their racial identity development, so that they may seek to return "home" to urban environments, rich with Black cultural experiences. Neighborhood settings and Black Muslim youth's experiences within these settings vary and have profound long-term impacts on each individual's choices, opportunities, and resources.

The educational environment serves as an important socializing agent that may serve to influence young Black Muslims' development (Reardon 2016). Educational environment and opportunities can affect the young person's social mobility, connectedness to society and community, as well as sense of self and confidence to navigate the real world. Unfortunately, US schools are more segregated today than they were in the 1950s, continuing a legacy of unequal education that ultimately affects access to college and jobs (Orfield and Chungmei 2007). Educational disparities may be related to socioeconomic status, with Black youth being more likely to attend high-poverty schools (US Department of Education 2007), which are of poor quality both physically and educationally and have lower numbers of certified teachers compared to White-majority schools (Presidential Task Force on Educational Disparities 2012). Half of Black male students and one-third of Black female students have been suspended or expelled from school, compared to one-fifth of White male students and one-tenth of White female students (*National Assessment of Education Progress* 2011). The differing rates of suspension and expulsion are likely related to factors such as racial bias, cultural mismatch, and stereotypes of academic behavior of minority youth (Gregory, Skiba, and Noguera 2010). The differences in cultural expectations and norms between teacher and student may result in behaviors that are considered normative by students but interpreted as hostile, threatening, and defiant by teachers owing to the teachers' racial bias. Challenges in navigating the path to academic success may explain why 34 percent of Black children do not graduate high school on time (National Kids Count 2013) and only 32.1 percent of eighteen- to twenty-four-year-old Blacks are enrolled in college or university, compared with 44.2 percent of Whites (*National Assessment of Education Progress* 2011). One result of this often unhealthy academic environment is an increase in the number of Black families that turn to homeschooling as an option to provide their children with a positive educational experience. Currently, Black youth make up 10 percent of homeschool student populations and 16 percent of public-school student populations (US Department of Education 2014; Huseman 2015). Parents who choose to homeschool are often motivated by the need for "racial protectionism" because of school-related racism, a culture of lowered expectations, and lack of positive, affirming Black role models (Mazama and Lundy 2012, 724).

There are currently no known studies looking at the education patterns and outcomes of US Muslims by subgroup. Most Black Muslim youth attend public schools, but a growing number are going to charter schools. Parents who seek a religious environment for their children choose to send their children to Islamic school or consider homeschooling. Islamic school experience may vary depending on the school makeup and administration. For example, Black Muslim children who attend Sister Clara Muhammad schools are more likely to be exposed to a culturally affirming programming, whereas those who attend immigrant-run Islamic schools may be exposed to other Muslim cultures but at the same time to anti-Black racism within the Muslim community. It is thus important to understand the nuanced nature of Black Muslim youth's educational context to understand the impact it has had on their development.

Historical, societal, and socioeconomic factors have a direct influence on Black Muslim families, which serve as the primary source of socialization and development for Black Muslim youth. Among Black children, 33 percent live in a two-parent family, and 67 percent live in a single-parent family or reside with relatives or other individuals. Factors contributing to the difference in family structure can be traced to increased family stress owing to institutionalized racism. Currently, there are no known statistics on the family structure and composition of Muslim subgroups. However, Black Muslim families are more likely to vary in their family structure compared to immigrant Muslim families. Black Muslim family structure may range from traditional two-parent families to blended, polygamous, or single-parent families or families with multiple generations living together or families made up of fictive kin.

For Black Muslim youth raised in Muslim families, their lived experiences may be shaped by parents' practice of Islam and religious socialization of their children. A young female described her experience:

> There was definitely a conscious effort from my parents to kinda separate us from like the masses and getting too far into, you know, blending in with the, you know, the outside. Like as far as . . . going to parties and staying out late, and you know, just being able to do anything that I wanted. A lot of my other friends were able to do a lot of things like that but I couldn't. . . . A lot of times you don't really understand why, but as you get older, you know, you understand.

Parenting styles and religious socialization practices also vary and may affect gender roles, parent-child relationships, and the acceptance of religious practices such as polygamy (McAdams-Mahmood 2005). However, differences are less apparent for some Black Muslim youth. A young male reported, "Did we act as, as Muslims? No, you couldn't tell, when we was out there in the streets, no. When we was in the house, even if we prayed, we prayed kinda as if a Catholic repents. But it, it was strictly just knowledge. I didn't see it change us from the next door neighbors." Black Muslim youth are more likely to live in pluralistic religious settings compared to most immigrant Muslim youth. Black Muslim youth may be the only Muslim in their families in the case of converts or one of few in the case of second- or third-generation Muslims (i.e., their parents or grandparents converted to Islam). The Black community is traditionally more religious than other communities in American society, with 79 percent of those surveyed reporting religion to be important in their lives (compared to 56 percent of US adults) and 53 percent reporting weekly religious attendance (Sahgal and Smith 2009). Non-Muslim Black extended family members' reaction to young Black Muslims' practice of their faith may range from outward rejection or indifference to respect and admiration. Most Black Muslim youth have non-Muslim relatives with whom they may interact on a regular basis and who thus shape their interaction and connection with both the Black community and society in general.

These experiences often give Black Muslim youth the social capital needed to normalize Islam and thus be at the forefront of the indigenization of Islam in America.

Understanding the varying factors that affect Black Muslim families—such as family dynamics and structure, parental religious socialization, socioeconomic status, and extended family influence—should also be considered when exploring Black Muslim youth development. Peer influence can also be positive or negative in its impact on a young person's development (Jaccard, Blanton, and Dodge 2005; Barry and Wentzel 2006). Black Muslim youth must traverse varying aspects of adolescent and emerging adult cultures, some of which may conflict with their religious beliefs. As one young person stated, "Everything as far as going out clubbing, drinking up, and partying, that's really the definition of fun . . . of what fun is for our generation right now. And so I'm not going to sit here and try to say that I've never done any of that stuff." Young people often struggle with the desire to fit in with their peer group, especially if they feel their group is stigmatized and they want to avoid further stigmatization. This struggle can increase pressure on Muslim youth to engage in risky behaviors despite religious prohibitions. For example, although the rates of substance use (e.g., alcohol, drugs, and tobacco) is lower among Black youth than among White youth (Blum et al. 2000), Black youth who do use such substances are more likely to experience problems because of their use (Zapolski et al. 2014). Teenage pregnancy continues to be greater among Black youth than among Whites (5 percent versus 2.5 percent) (Centers for Disease Control and Prevention 2012), and 35 percent of gang members identify as Black (National Gang Center 2013). Specific to Black youth, peer influence may also deter academic achievement by peer policing of students who are perceived to be "acting White" by gaining academic success (Ogbu 2008).

Black Muslim youth are embedded within such peer contexts and report struggling to navigate peer norms while attempting also to maintain their religious principles. How Black Muslim youth navigate these conflicting spaces may be related to their previous developmental experiences, their sources of support, and the availability of culturally and religiously appropriate alternatives. Prior studies have found that peer presence can increase the likelihood that young people will make risk-taking decisions (Kretsch and Harden 2013). In a pilot study on Black Muslim youth, 71 percent reported they had consumed alcohol, and 48 percent reported using marijuana (Ahmed, Sharrief, and Arfken 2009). In addition, 85 percent of the sample reported that they had dated, and 55 percent reported having had nonmarital sexual intercourse (Ahmed, Sharrief, and Arfken 2009). Despite engaging in behaviors prohibited by their faith, most participants in the study identified themselves as very to moderately religious, which potentially highlights cognitive dissonance between beliefs and behaviors. Although the study did not directly measure peer influence, it did identify that Black Muslim youth opted to participate in these risky behaviors while in the presence of both Muslim and non-Muslim peers. Black Muslim youth may identify more with their Black non-Muslim peers than with their non-Black Muslim peers because of similar lived experiences (Khan and Ahmed 2010). As one participant described, "I can relate [to immigrant Muslim peers] but I don't feel like we can still relate on a on a certain level. I don't still feel like . . . I mean . . . I feel okay they're my brother and sisters in Islam, but at the same time, like, they don't know the struggles that I face as an African American" (Khan and Ahmed 2010).

The lack of shared experience owing to racial difference (i.e., historical, socioeconomic, family, and son) and the impact this lack has on one's lived experience (i.e., institutional injustice) may contribute to a lack of understanding and support between Black Muslim and immigrant Muslim youth. This lack of understanding often results in the inability to develop a positive support network that expands beyond race and ethnicity. Religious communities within the Black community have historically been critical in the development and socialization of Black youth. Black Muslim religious communities are multifaceted and include variations in cultural focus, historical pathways to Islam, religious and ideological interpretation, and congregational cultures.

The cultural focus of Black Muslim communities can be conceptualized along three main categories: cultural nationalists, Sunnis with African American centered leadership, Sunnis with immigrant-centered leadership (McAdams-Mahmood 2005). Cultural nationalist communities are often found in urban settings, have a religious leadership that is Black, stress the importance of Black nationalism and Islam, and preach separation and independence from the dominant society. These communities often focus on Black history and heritage, encourage financial independence through small businesses, and emphasize the importance of group goals as well as uniformity. Religious communities that are Sunni with African-centered leadership are also found mostly in urban settings and have Black religious leadership. These Black Sunni communities may stress self-determination and racial pride and adhere to the tenets of Islam but may not place a high emphasis on behaviors such as uniformity, collective identity, or independence from the dominant society. Black Muslim youth associated with both of these communities are more likely to be exposed to programs promoting positive racial identity but have minimal to no interaction with the immigrant Muslim community. The Black religious leadership of these communities may be more understanding of the unique challenges facing Black Muslim youth because of the shared cultural history, racial identity, and daily experiences of institutionalized racism.

Black Muslim youth may also be embedded in Sunni religious communities with immigrant-centered leadership. These communities may be located in either suburban or urban settings and have religious leaders who are immigrants. The congregational focus is often on the universality of religion, with little to no recognition of Black culture and issues that affect Blacks' lives (e.g., racial profiling, police brutality, etc.). Black Muslim youth raised in immigrant-dominant religious communities are exposed to different ethnic groups but often report experiences of racism and feel Black culture is not accepted as an equally valid racial/ethnic identity and culture within the Muslim community (Khan and Ahmed 2010). As a result, some of them may choose to shed aspects of their racial culture in order to be accepted by their coreligionists; others may choose to attend Black-dominant religious congregations instead; and yet others may choose to disconnect altogether from the religious community.

In addition to variations in cultural orientation, ideological variations within religious communities should be considered. Some of the more common ideological approaches include espousing a literalist interpretation of religious texts (Salafi) and focusing on proselytizing Islam (Tablighi

Jama'at). Communities with such ideological interpretations often encourage the learning of Arabic, memorization of the Qur'an, and application of specific Prophetic practices. They may also have rigid gender roles and gender-segregated programs and activities, adopt certain ethnic cultural practices (e.g., Arab or South Asian), and encourage limited interaction with non-Muslim society. Other communities have adopted a spiritual or mystical interpretation of Islam (Sufism). Individuals ascribing to such an approach may be visible in their adoption of ethnic clothing (Arab or West African) and *dhikr* beads or staff and may encourage obedience to a spiritual guide. Some Black communities may have no specific ideological orientation that dominates the congregational culture. Ideological interpretations may empower some Black Muslim youth's involvement but in other cases may result in their rejection of these interpretations of their faith or in religious self-doubt. Finally, each religious community may have its own congregational culture that affects a young person's development and connection to that community. Congregational cultures may be affected by geographic location, congregational historical background, or congregants' personal backgrounds. As one young Black male described his religious community's culture, "It was more gangster [laughs]. I don't wanna go into depth, but more of gangsters in the *masjid* [mosque]. And I grew up in a certain lifestyle. . . . So it was a lot of different mentalities. So that played a real major part on why I don't have a community that I'm close to now because of my upbringings. Like they ran us away from the *masjid*!"

The presence or lack of a youth-affirming religious community; relevant, religious, and cultural discourse and programming; and rigid, harsh, or hypocritical behaviors of religious role models can have an impact on Black Muslim youth's development. Such experiences can have long-term positive or negative effects on the individual's religious practice, connection to his or her religious community, and his or her development. The practice of religion is one critical way that people respond to their lived experience. How Islam is experienced and practiced in one context may vary from how it is experienced and practiced in another context. With differing levels of identification and practice, Black Muslim youth's practice of Islam varies.

Given the historical and societal factors discussed previously, it is not surprising that Black youth convert to Islam. For some Black youth, the process of exploring one's roots (i.e., West Africa and enslavement) may result in their rejection of Christianity because of its historical role in the subjugation of the Black community and eventually lead to their conversion to Islam. Black youth may also be introduced to Islam while incarcerated. Among inmates, the rationales for conversion vary and include social support and privilege among Muslim inmates, protection from gangs, and forgiveness of one's criminal behavior. Some Black youth engage in their faith through developing religious and cultural agency. These individuals seek to acquire competence in the Sunni tradition by learning Arabic and Islamic sciences and by applying Islamic principles to their unique perspective in order to create a sustainable practice of Islam in America (Jackson 2005). In the process of becoming agents in their Islamic identity (integrating their Black, American, and Muslim social identities), these individuals have also become authorities within the larger American Muslim community. For other Black Muslim youth, their engagement with Islam does not extend beyond their cultural-historical recognition of being Muslim. A young Black Muslim said, "The role that Islam plays in my life now . . . is, is more so like just history to me and knowledge."

Among these youth, their practice of Islam is tenuous at best. Numerous factors may contribute to their limited religious engagement, such as the lack of positive religious socialization by family and religious congregation, anti-Black racism within the Muslim community, the desire to fit in with their peers, and difficulty practicing a religion that is stigmatized by society. Finally, some Black Muslim youth also respond to their lived experience by choosing to leave Islam. Little is known about the prevalence of and reasons for apostasy among this group. Reasons for apostasy may include acceptance of the norms and values of the dominant culture, lack of knowledge of or conviction in Islam, and the belief that Islam is not relevant to their reality as Black Americans. Some converts leave Islam because of a lack of support from the Muslim community, lack of Islam's perceived relevancy to their lived experience, or pressure from family to return to their former religion. Black Muslim youth who leave Islam may choose to adopt another faith or to have no faith at all.

Pathways to Muslim Youth Engagement

Owing to their lived experiences, many Black Muslim youth are keenly aware of the inequities and disparities that exist in their environment. These youth actively engage non-Muslim society via their career or volunteer choices and attempt to address the disparities observed in their communities while maintaining their multiple social identities (e.g., Black, Muslim, American, professional, activist). This section highlights the varying areas and methods of societal engagement by Black Muslim youth and millennials.

Like their parents and grandparents before them, some Black Muslim youth are also active in social justice campaigns within the Black community. Increased police brutality and the unwarranted deaths of unarmed Black youth, such as Trayvon Martin, Michael Brown, Tamir Rice, and countless others, have led to numerous community-based responses. Black Muslim youth have been involved in supporting movements, such as Black Lives Matter (BLM), a decentralized movement of activists who organize demonstrations and protests to maintain sustained national and media attention on the unjust killings of unarmed Black men and women. Black Muslim youth contribute to BLM in numerous ways, including but not limited to participating in and organizing rallies, raising awareness of social injustice, and highlighting the intersection of their Black and Muslim identities. They have also been involved in other efforts such as the 300 Men March Movement in Baltimore (2015), which used Street Engagement Units to decrease shootings and homicides in targeted neighborhoods by talking to angered residents before they chose to participate in violent protests.

Black Muslim youth have used social media to call attention to gender, racial, religious, cultural, educational, and political inequities. Their efforts have sparked conversation, shifted community-based policy, challenged the American Muslim narrative, and confronted the American Muslim establishment. When the misappropriation of the BLM hashtag (#BlackLivesMatter) to #AllLivesMatter or #MuslimLivesMatter occurred, Black Muslim youth were at the forefront of calling attention to the fact that the use of such hashtags served as a distraction and derailment of BLM's specific goals. Their efforts helped to reduce the usage of these misappropriations within the American Muslim community. Similarly, when eight Black churches burned in the wake of the Emanuel African Methodist Episcopal church killings in 2015, Faatimah Knight, a young Black Muslim used crowdsource funding through social media to help the Black Christian community rebuild. Black Muslim youth are harnessing the energy of social media to engage their social networks and environment and to reach a greater audience beyond their immediate social circles.

Black Muslim youth have been instrumental in helping to raise awareness of social injustice within the American Muslim community. Black Muslim emerging adults have been involved in the formation of organizations such as the Muslim Anti-Racism Collaborative. The collaborative gives the Muslim community an entry point to support, organize, and participate in policy reform around such issues related as police brutality and anti-Black and intracommunity racism, providing a tool kit with general tips for organizing dialogues. Programs such as the Deeply Rooted Emerging Leaders Fellowship, organized by Muslim Wellness, have created safe spaces for young Black Muslim activists to be emotionally nurtured, supported, and mentored while engaging in spiritually grounded social justice efforts. Activism through online fora have given voice to Black Muslim youth, who are otherwise rendered silent and invisible. Successful campaigns such as #BlackInMSA (Muslim Anti-Racism Collaborative) and #BlackMuslimFamily (Muslim Wellness Foundation) created space for Black Muslim youth to share the pain they have experienced from intracommunity racism and encouraged the broader Muslim community to engage in discussions about macro- and microaggressions experienced by Black Muslim youth. Black Muslim youth are also choosing to educate and mentor other Black youth as teachers in varying school settings (e.g., public, charter, Islamic, and home schools), in after-school programs (e.g. Global Youth Empowerment), and in religious and community-based youth groups. As one Black Muslim youth explained, "There is an absence of positive male role models in our community, which gets lots of kids into trouble. I lost too many of my friends to death or jail. I need to do something to change our community. Or else what's gonna happen to my son? I can't just sit by and let things happen the way they have been."

Black Muslim youth choosing academic routes as a means to effect change also have an increasing number of young professional Black Muslim role models. For example, Intisar Rabb's development of SHA-RIAHSource, a scholarly website on Islamic legal issues, revolutionizes accessibility to reliable information on Islamic legal issues. Other role models include Muhammad Khalifa, who highlights the need for more culturally responsive school environments, and Irshad Altheimer, who conducts research on gun violence, correctional facilities, and criminal justice policy to effect change at the macrolevel. Others have chosen to document their own history, issues, and experiences rather than continue being the subject of outsiders' research: for instance, Precious Muhammad and Rebecca Hankins are documenting the history of Islam in America; Jamillah Karim is documenting the experiences of American Muslim women; Donna Auston is exploring race, gender, and religious practice; and Su'ad Abdul-Khabeer is investigating the intersection of religion, race, music, and space as well as centering the Black and Muslim experience in the United States via the online forum Sapelo Square, which she founded and serves as senior editor. Others, such as Kameelah Mu'min Rashad, have chosen to address issues affecting both micro and macro levels by focusing on mental health efforts in the Black Muslim community through the Muslim Wellness Foundation and the Black Muslim Psychology Conference.

Using numerous forms of artistic expression such as literature, poetry, comedy, film, music, and fashion to illuminate their lived experience, engage their environment, and express their unique identity, Black Muslim youth are actively participating in narrating their lived experience as Muslims in America. Individuals such as Umm Juwayriyah (pen name for Maryam Sullivan) have sought to introduce the Black urban Muslim experience into children's literature. In addition, a number of young Black women have been involved in the creation and development of magazines, such as *Azizah*. Black youth have used blogs as a means of expressing themselves and their experiences. For example, Ihsaan Tahir uses her blog *Muslimnlove* to explore the journey to find a husband (Tahir 2013). Although their experiences may have occurred in the past, current social media tools allow for greater audience reach to share the experience and feel less isolated. Similarly, poetry has been used to give voice to Black Muslim youth's lived experience, to raise consciousness, and to spur people toward social change. Black Muslim youth may use poetry to express everything from their sadness and happiness while navigating the complexities of their lives to their feelings of disenfranchisement owing to institutional inequities and their efforts to resist the dominant culture. The prominent Black Muslim spoken-word poet and hip-hop artist Amir Sulaiman explains in his poem "Dead Man Walking,"

> I wish I could sing for justice
> But I know no such song
> I know about Shahadah
> Salat and Quran
> Jihad, martyrdom, and homemade bombs
> I know you think I'm wrong
> For talking about homemade bombs
> But the leader of the free world
> Can drop A-bombs and napalm
> And got the nerve to ask
> "Why do they hate us?"
>
> (Sulaiman n.d.)

Some Black Muslim youth are engaging with their environment through comedy. Sharing the complexities of their lives through humor, comedians are able to break down barriers and educate non-Muslim audiences about the lived experiences of Islam and Muslims. Comedians such as Preacher Moss and Omar Regan not only serve as role models for younger Muslim (both Black and non-Black alike) but are also able to use their skills to help normalize the Muslim experience for non-Muslim audiences and to highlight similarities in lived human experiences. Non-Muslim audiences may perceive the use of comedy as a unique, disarming response. Other comedians, such as Dave Chappelle, may choose not to address their faith in their comedy but may make that faith clear through other means. Young Black Muslims are also securing opportunities to depict their experiences in film, simultaneously entertaining and educating their audiences. Although it is challenging to navigate the movie-making industry, Black Muslim film producer-directors, such as Sultan Sharrief (*Bilal's Stand* [2010]) and Qasim Basir (*Mooz-lum* [2011]) are emerging and serving as role models for other Black Muslim youth wanting to enter the industry. Their semiautobiographical movies about Black Muslim boys growing up in America highlight the intersection of race, religion, and identity within the American landscape. For many, film may be the only medium in which they can comfortably observe the lived experiences of others. Whereas *Mooz-lum* addresses the struggle to define one's identity and the impact of the attacks on September 11, 2001 (9/11), on a young Muslim man, *Bilal's Stand* draws attention to the overlapping and conflicting developmental contexts that challenge urban youth who are trying to attain academic success. Remarkably, these movies are among the first to portray Black Muslim families as part of the fabric of America rather than in opposition to it (as in, e.g., Spike Lee's film *Malcolm X* [1992]). The success of these independent films opens doors for future Black Muslim youth to explore similar topics on-screen.

Music also captures the zeitgeist of the day, making the creation, procurement, and consumption of music a response to one's environment. How Black Muslim youth relate to music may depend on their own or their parents' beliefs regarding the permissibility of music in Islam, ranging from categorical prohibition to the acceptance of music with or without string or wind instruments. For those who believe in the acceptability of music that doesn't use string or percussion instruments, groups such as Native Deen, an Islamic hip-hop group composed of three Black Muslim men—Joshua Salaam, Naeem Muhammad, and Abdul-Malik Ahmad— are popular and serve as an alternative. Such groups focus on Islamic themes and American Muslim experiences and are often more popular within the larger immigrant Muslim community (Oppenheimer 2011). Hip-hop is particularly popular among Black Muslim youth. It originated in the 1970s as an underground urban musical expression that gave urban Black youth an opportunity to respond to an inequitable environment following the civil rights movement. As hip-hop artist Yasiin Bey (formerly known as Mos Def) raps,

Hip-Hop past all your tall social hurdles
Like the nationwide projects-prison-industry complex.

(Yasiin Bey 2018)

The emergence of hip-hop in the 1970s was highly influenced by the NOI and other proto-Islamic movements such as the Five Percent Nation (Abdul-Khabeer 2007). Both Muslim and non-Muslim artists commonly used Islamic themes, ideologies, and terminologies in their music, thus further inculcating Islam in the larger Black community. Islamic themes and terminologies used in hip-hop music can normalize Islam as a minority religion, rendering its practice something familiar rather than "Other," as illustrated by Lupe Fiasco's song "Muhammad Walks": "The Most Forgiving will forgive it if you stay repentant. . . . You gotta stay on your salats, your zakats, your Quran" (Fiasco 2018).

The reciprocal relationship between Blackness and Islam with hip-hop as a medium of exchange is what defines the concept of "Muslim Cool." More than just an influence on lyrics, "for Muslim Cool Blackness is a point of opposition to White supremacy that creates solidarities among differently racialized and marginalized groups in order to dismantle overarching racial hierarchies" (Abdul-Khabeer 2016, 5). The success of Black Muslim hip-hop artists who embody the idea of Muslim Cool, such as Yasiin Bey, Freeway, and Lupe Fiasco, serves as a model for Black Muslim youth to recognize Islam as a faith that culturally belongs to them and to indigenize Islam in America through their practice of that faith. Creative forms of cultural expression among Black Muslim youth are also manifested in other creative sectors, such as the fashion industry. Young Black Muslim women are articulating their own ideas about Muslim women's fashion by creating affordable modest clothing. New York City high-fashion designer Nzinga Knight sells her collection Nzinga Knight New York internationally and became the first American Muslim woman wearing *hijab* to be featured as a contestant on the design competition show *Project Runway*. Not long after that, fashion designer Ayana Ife had her debut on *Project Runway* and became the first Muslim woman finalist to showcase her collection at New York Fashion Week (Wheeler 2017). Through their collections, Knight and Ife are carving out space in the

Muslim fashion industry to communicate designs reflective of their identities, experiences, and customers.

Finally, Black Muslim youth professional athletes often look to boxing and basketball legends Muhammad Ali and Kareem Abdul-Jabbar for inspiration in their balancing of high-profile careers and religious practices. Husain Abdullah left the National Football League (NFL) to make the pilgrimage (the hajj) to Mecca and garnered national attention because his decision to fulfill his religious obligations was thought to jeopardize his career. After returning to the NFL and scoring a touchdown, Abdullah prostrated on the field to show his gratitude to God. The NFL considered his behavior to be excessive celebration and penalized him, drawing the ire of fans and Muslim organizations, who argued that Christian players are not penalized for similar acts of worship. The NFL later admitted Abdullah should not have been penalized. Abdullah's public identification and practice of his faith made him a role model for many Muslim youth. Similarly, young Muslim females have an increasing number of female athlete role models. American fencer Ibtihaj Muhammad won a Bronze medal in sabre fencing at the Summer Olympics in Rio de Janeiro in 2016 and was the first American Muslim woman to compete in *hijab*. Bilqis Abdul Qaadir played college basketball at the University of Memphis and Indiana State University and was the first college athlete to play in a basketball game wearing *hijab*. Abdul Qaadir sought to play professional basketball overseas, but the International Basketball Federation prevents headgear more than five centimeters in width, which hindered her ability to wear *hijab* while play. Qaadir is developing her own nonprofit organization, Muslim Girls Hoop Too, to raise awareness and fight the federation's ban on *hijab* (Muslim Girls Hoop Too 2017). By honoring their Islamic beliefs, these athletes have made it easier for those coming after them to be fully seen and respected as a Muslim playing a professional sport.

Conclusion

Black Muslim youth and emerging adults are a diverse group of individuals with shared experiences and factors that have affected their developmental trajectories. Their individual traits interact with their overlapping and sometimes conflicting developmental contexts and are influenced by factors that are fluid and constantly changing. These intersections are critical to understand and integrate into research, public policy, education, and community-based initiatives. The cultural and religious history of Black Muslims in America is defined by resilience and empowerment. Despite living in an alleged postracial, post-9/11, Islamophobic environment, Black Muslim youth have been able to create pathways that simultaneously resist institutionalized oppression and embrace their racial, religious, and national identities. Black Muslim youth's identity development is different from that of their parents in that many are actively engaging in and embracing both their religious heritage and their racial heritage, confidently fusing their multiple social identities. They are using their cultural capital as Black Americans and engaging with their religious values and communities as active agents of change. Black Muslim youth are contributing to their racial and religious communities as well as to national conversations. An increasing number of Black emerging adults are engaged in social justice efforts, in careers that have an impact, and in the development of a unique cultural narrative. Yet although diverse pathways and mediums of social engagement are emerging, the paucity of current research on this important subgroup of Muslims must be underscored. This sizeable and influential subgroup needs further exploration. Future efforts to understand American Muslim youth must include the voices and experiences of Black Muslim youth. As the late El Hajj Malik El Shabazz (Malcolm X) said, "Education is our passport to the future, for tomorrow belongs to the people who prepare for it today" (Malcolm X 1964).

References

Abdul-Khabeer, Saud. 2007. "The Rhyme and Reason of American Islamic Hip Hop." *Muslim World* 97, no. 1: 125–41.

———. 2016. *Muslim Cool: Race, Religion, and Hip Hop in the United States.* New York: New York Univ. Press.

Abo-Zena, Mona M., and Sameera Ahmed. 2014. "Religion, Spirituality, and Emerging Adults: Processing Meaning through Culture, Context, and Social Position." In *Emerging Adults' Religiousness and Spirituality: Meaning-Making in an Age of Transition*, edited by Carolyn McNamara Barry and Mona M. Abo-Zena, 220–36. New York: Oxford Univ. Press.

Ahmed, Gutbi Mahdi. 1991. "Muslim Organizations in the United States." In *The Muslims of America*, edited by Yvonne Yazbeck Haddad, 11–23. New York: Oxford Univ. Press.

Ahmed, Sameera, Sultan Sharrief, and Cynthia Arfken. 2009. "Juggling Cultural Identities: Challenges for Second Generation African American Muslim Youth." Paper presented at the 117th Annual Convention of the American Psychological Association, Toronto, Aug. 7, 2009.

Barry, Carolyn McNamara, and Kathryn R. Wentzel. 2006. "Friend Influence on Prosocial Behavior: The Role of Motivational Factors and Friendship Characteristics." *Developmental Psychology* 42, no. 1: 153–63.

Blum, Robert W., Trisha Beuhring, Marcia L. Shew, Linda H. Bearinger, Renée E. Sieving, and Michael D. Resnick. 2000. "The Effects of Race/Ethnicity, Income, and Family Structure on Adolescent Risk Behaviors." *American Journal of Public Health* 90, no. 12: 1879–84.

Centers for Disease Control and Prevention. 2012. "Teenage Childbearing, by Age and Detailed Race and Hispanic Origin of Mother: United States, Selected Years 1970–2010." National Center for Health Statistics, table 4. At http://www.cdc.gov/nchs/data/hus/2012/004.pdf.

Diouf, Sylviane A. 1998. *Servants of Allah: African Muslims Enslaved in the Americas*. New York: New York Univ. Press.

Elliot, Diana. 2016. "Two American Experiences: The Racial Divide of Poverty." *Urban Wire* (Urban Institute), July 22. At https://www.urban.org/urban-wire/two-american-experiences-racial-divide-poverty.

Fiasco, Lupe. 2018. "Muhammad Walks" (lyrics). At http://www.gotbars.com/lupe-fiasco-muhammad-walks-lyrics.8185.html.

Gregory, Anne, Russell J. Skiba, and Pedro Noguera. 2010. "The Achievement Gap and the Discipline Gap: Two Sides of the Same Coin?" *Educational Researcher* 39:59–68.

Hertz, Tom. 2005. "Rags, Riches, and Race: The Intergenerational Economic Mobility of Black and White Families in the United States." In *Unequal Chances: Family Background and Economic Success*, edited by Herbert Gintis, Samuel Bowles, and Melissa Osborne Groves, 165–91. New York: Russell Sage Foundation; Princeton, NJ: Princeton Univ. Press.

Hurd, Noelle M., Sarah A. Stoddard, and Marc A. Zimmerman. 2012. "Neighborhoods, Social Support, and African American Adolescents' Mental

Health Outcomes: A Multilevel Path Analysis." *Child Development* 84, no. 3: 858–74.

Huseman, Jessica. 2015. "The Rise of Homeschooling among Black Families." *Atlantic*, Feb. 17. At http://www.theatlantic.com/education/archive/2015/02/the-rise-of-homeschooling-among-Black-families/385543/.

Jaccard, James, Hart Blanton, and Tonya Dodge. 2005. "Peer Influences on Risk Behavior: An Analysis of the Effects of a Close Friend." *Developmental Psychology* 41, no. 1: 135–47.

Jackson, Sherman A. 2005. *Islam and the Blackamerican: Looking toward the Third Resurrection*. New York: Oxford Univ. Press.

Kerby, Sophia. 2012. "The Top 10 Most Startling Facts about People of Color and Criminal Justice in the United States." Center for American Progress, Mar. 13. At http://www.americanprogress.org/issues/race/news/2012/03/13/11351/the-top-10-most-startling-facts-about-people-of-color-and-criminal-justice-in-the-united-states/.

Khan, Farah, and Sameera Ahmed. 2010. "Peer Relations and Risky Behaviors of African American Muslim Youth." Paper presented at the 118th Annual Convention of the American Psychological Association, San Diego, Aug. 14.

Kretsch, Natalie, and Kathryn Harden. 2013. "Pubertal Development and Peer Influence on Risky Decision Making." *Journal of Early Adolescence* 34, no. 3: 339–59.

Lerner, Richard M., and Marjorie B. Kauffman. 1985. "The Concept of Development in Contextualism." *Developmental Review* 5, no. 4: 309–33.

Madrigal, Alexis C. 2014. "The Racist Housing Policy That Made Your Neighborhood." *Atlantic*, May. At https://www.theatlantic.com/business/archive/2014/05/the-racist-housing-policy-that-made-your-neighborhood/371439.

Malcolm X. 1964. Speech at the founding rally of the Organization of Afro-American Unity, June 28, New York. At http://www.Blackpast.org/1964-malcolm-x-s-speech-founding-rally-organization-afro-american-unity.

Massey, Doreen S., and Nancy A. Denton. 1993. *American Apartheid: Segregation and the Making of the Underclass*. Cambridge, MA: Harvard Univ. Press.

Mazama, Ama, and Garvey Lundy. 2012. "African American Homeschooling as Racial Protectionism." *Journal of Black Studies* 43, no. 7 (Oct.): 723–48. doi:10.1177/0021934712457042.

McAdams-Mahmoud, Vanessa. 2005. "African American Muslim Families." In *Ethnicity and Family Therapy*, edited by Monica McGoldrick, Joe Giordan, and Nydia Garcia-Preto, 138–52. New York: Guilford.

McKown, Clark, and Rhona S. Weinstein. 2003. "The Development and Consequences of Stereotype Consciousness in Middle Childhood." *Child Development* 74, no. 2: 498–515.

Mock, Bretin. 2015. "Redlining Is Alive and Well—and Evolving." CITYLAB,
Sept. 28. At https://www.citylab.com/equity/2015/09/redlining-is-alive-and
-welland-evolving/407497.

Muslim Girls Hoop Too. 2017. "How Can I Help?" At https://muslimgirlshoop
too.weebly.com/how-can-i-help.html.

National Assessment of Education Progress, 2011. 2011. At https://catalog.data
.gov/dataset/2011-national-assessment-of-educational-progress.

National Gang Center. 2013. *National Youth Gang Survey Analysis.* Tallahassee,
FL: National Gang Center. At http://www.nationalgangcenter.gov/Survey
-Analysis.

National Kids Count. 2013. "High School Students Not Graduating on Time, by
Race and Ethnicity." Data center, June. At http://datacenter.kidscount.org
/data/tables/7755-high-school-students-not-graduating-on-time-by-race
-and-ethnicity?loc=1&loct=2-detailed/1/any/false/809,712,517,516,515/141,7
25,4041,1,12,13/14945.

Ogbu, John. 2008. *Minority Status, Oppositional Culture, and Schooling.* New
York: Routledge.

Oppenheimer, Mark. 2011. "A Diplomatic Mission Bearing Islamic Hip-Hop."
New York Times, July 23. At https://www.nytimes.com/2011/07/23/us/23
beliefs.html.

Orfield, Gary, and Lee Chungmei. 2007. *Historic Reversals, Accelerating Resegre-
gation, and the Need for New Integration Strategies.* Los Angeles: Civil Rights
Project, Univ. of California at Los Angeles.

Pew Research Center. 2017. *U.S. Muslims Concerned about Their Place in Society,
but Continue to Believe in the American Dream: Findings from Pew Research
Center's 2017 Survey of U.S. Muslims.* Washington, DC: Pew Research Center, July 26. At http://www.pewforum.org/2017/07/26/findings-from-pew
-research-centers-2017-survey-of-us-muslims/.

Pew Research Center for the People and the Press. 2011. *Muslim Americans: No
Signs of Growth in Alienation or Support for Extremism.* Washington, DC:
Pew Research Center. At http://www.people-press.org/2011/08/30/section
-1-a-demographic-portrait-of-muslim-americans/.

Pinderhughes, Ellen E., Robert E. Nix, Michael Foster, and Damon Jones.
2001. "Parenting in Context: Impact of Neighborhood Poverty, Residential

Stability, Public Services, Social Networks, and Danger on Parental Behaviors." *Family Journal of Marriage and Family* 63, no. 4: 941–53.

Presidential Task Force on Educational Disparities. 2012. *Ethnic and Racial Disparities in Education: Psychology's Contributions to Understanding and Reducing Disparities.* Washington, DC: American Psychological Association. At http://www.apa.org/ed/resources/racial-disparities.aspx.

Quillian, Lincoln, Devah Pager, Ole Hexel, and Arnfinn H. Midtbøen. 2017. "Meta-analysis of Field Experiments Shows No Change in Racial Discrimination in Hiring over Time." *Proceedings of the National Academy of Sciences* 114, no. 41: 10870–75.

Reardon, Sean F. 2016. *School Segregation and Racial and Academic Gaps.* Center for Education Policy Analysis (CEPA) Working Paper no. 15-12. Stanford, CA: CEPA, Stanford Univ. At http://cepa.stanford.edu/wp15-12.

Sahgal Neha, and Greg Smith. 2009. *A Religious Portrait of African-Americans.* Washington, DC: Pew Research Center

Sentencing Project. 2018. "Racial Disparity." At https://www.sentencingproject .org/issues/racial-disparity/.

Southern Poverty Law Center. 2016. "Update: 1,094 Bias-Related Incidents in the Month Following the Election." Hate Watch, Dec. 16. At https://www .splcenter.org/hatewatch/2016/12/16/update-1094-bias-related-incidents -month-following-election.

Sulaiman, Amir. n.d. "Dead Man Walking." LyricsWorld. At https://www.elyrics world.com/dead_man_walking_lyrics_amir_sulaiman.html. Posted Aug. 25, 2017.

Sullivan, John. 2011. "Blacks Moving South—and to the Suburbs." *Race, Poverty & the Environment* 18, no. 2: 16–19.

Tahir, Ihssan. 2013. "Black + Muslim + Woman." *Muslimnlove*, Sept. At http:// muslimnlove.com/.

US Census Bureau. 2012. *The Black Population: 2010.* Washington, DC: US Department of Commerce, Sept. At http://www.census.gov/prod/cen2010 /brief/c2010br-06.pdf.

———. 2013. *U.S. Census Bureau: State and County QuickFacts.* Washington, DC: US Department of Commerce, June 27. At http://quickfacts.census.gov /qfd/states/00000.html.

US Department of Education, National Center for Education Statistics. 2007. *The Condition of Education.* Washington, DC: US Government Publishing Office.

————. 2014. "State Nonfiscal Survey of Public Elementary and Secondary Education, 2002–3 and 2012–13," and "National Elementary and Secondary Enrollment Projection Model, 1972–2024." Common Core of Data. *Digest of Education Statistics 2014*, table 203.50. At https://nces.ed.gov/programs /digest/d15/tables/dt15_203.50.asp.

Wheeler, Kayla. 2017. "It's 'Been' Cool to Cover: Why Ayana Ife Matters." Sapelosquare, Nov. 21. At https://sapelosquare.com/2017/11/21/its-been-cool-to -cover-why-ayana-ife-matters/.

Wickrama, K. A. S., and C. M. Bryant. 2003. "Community Context of Social Resources and Adolescent Mental Health." *Journal of Marriage & Family* 65:850–64.

Williams, David, and Ruth Williams-Morris. 2000. "Racism and Mental Health: The African American Experience." *Ethnicity and Health* 5, nos. 3–4: 243–68.

Yasiin Bey. 2018. "Mathematics" (lyrics). At http://rapgenius.com/Yasiin-bey -mathematics-lyrics.

Zapolski, Tamika C. B., Sarah L. Pedersen, Denis M. McCarthy, and Gregory T. Smith. 2014. "Less Drinking, yet More Problems: Understanding African American Drinking and Related Problems." *Psychological Bulletin* 140, no. 1: 188–223.

2 Faith and Activism

Canadian Muslim Student Associations
as Campus-Based Social Movements
and Counterpublics

JASMIN ZINE and ASMA BALA

In a climate of Islamophobia and racial securitization created by the "war on terror," Muslim student groups on university campuses are seen as breeding grounds of Islamist radicalism. Many of the youth connected to the bombings in London on July 7, 2005, and the "Toronto 18 case" in Canada in June 2006 were university students, so campus groups have become sites of interest for the security and intelligence community and also, accordingly, for social justice educators concerned with the politics of campus culture and the surveillance of Muslim youth in a climate of fear and distrust. Muslim identities have come under siege owing to the war on terror and related domestic policies of racialization and securitization. Islamophobia and anti-Muslim racism are by-products of the aftermath of the attacks in the United States on September 11, 2001 (9/11), and the ongoing war on terror. It is in this volatile political context that Canadian Muslim Students Associations (MSAs) operate as collaborative sites promoting Islam and Muslim identification on campuses across North America. These organizations create a space for Islamic subcultures to flourish within university campuses and provide spiritual support, affinity, and camaraderie among Muslim students. They are also sites of political negotiation, struggle, and activism.

Drawing on social movement theory and contested theories of the public, we embed this discussion within a broader analysis and critique of the politics of empire as it plays out in the lives of Muslim youth. We examine the Islamic subcultures of MSAs in Canadian universities and the way they negotiate the bordered spaces of race, religion, gender, politics, and identity and how the resulting tensions produce a sphere for social activism and resistance. Based on qualitative research, this chapter examines how these groups operate as campus-based social movements and counterpublics that promote specific religious ideologies and goals and connect Muslim youth with national and transnational struggles that politicize their identities as Canadian Muslims. Our analysis is also attentive to the way the politics of race and empire affects and shapes the lives, experiences, and subjectivities of Muslim youth in Canada (see also Maira 2009).

There is little research on Muslim youth in Canada and even less that focuses on the national network of MSAs in universities across Canada. The largest wave of Muslims to Canada occurred after the official policy on multiculturalism came into effect in 1971 (Memon 2009). A large percentage of these Muslim immigrants had entered Canada for the purposes of higher education and began to develop campus-based Islamic movements as a means to retain ties of heritage and identity, both formally and informally. By 1963, there was a critical mass of Muslims across university campuses in the United States that led to the establishment of the Muslim Students Association National. The association was officially formed by students attending an Islamic conference at the University of Illinois at Urbana-Champaign. According to the organization's official history, the founding members consisted of Muslims from around the world, each of whom sought to create a unified body to oversee the concerns of Muslim students in North America who were (a) away from familiar ties of religiosity and (b) studying in a land where Islam was still a foreign conception.[1] Although the original mandate of MSA National was to serve the needs of both Canadian and American Muslims students and subsequently the broader Muslim community, the organizational structure shifted over time. Linked together through a sense of common history, both organizations MSA and MSA National have operated independently of each other

---

1. As explained on the MSA National website at http://msanational.org/.

since the mid-1990s. At present, the organization MSA National operates as two autonomous entities: the Islamic Society of North America (ISNA) US and ISNA Canada. Most major Canadian universities have an MSA group on their campuses that is largely Sunni dominated; however, some larger universities also have Shia, Ismaili, and Ahmadiyya groups.

The findings in this chapter are part of a larger qualitative research study that examines the politics of race and empire on citizenship identity and belonging among Canadian Muslim youth.[2] We conducted more than 130 interviews with Muslim youth across Canada—in Ontario, Quebec, Vancouver, and New Brunswick—from 2009 to 2014. The data for this chapter are drawn from a subset of the larger sample and focus on undergraduate Muslim university students. The students interviewed come from South Asian, Arab, Somali, and Kurdish backgrounds and represent both Sunni and Shia groups.

Framing the Research: Social Movement Theory, Activism, and Counterpublics

Drawing on the understandings provided by social movement theory, we critically unpack how some MSAs are engaged as political actors in what Quintan Wiktorowicz describes as "'the mobilization of contention' to support Muslim causes" (2004, 2). Wiktorowicz identifies broad-based activities that constitute Islamic activism as ranging from "propagation movements, terrorist groups, collective action rooted in Islamic symbols and identities, explicitly political movements that seek to establish an Islamic state, and inward looking groups that promote Islamic spirituality through collective efforts" (2). Islamic social movements thus range from grassroots protests to organized efforts seeking political change and transformation. They hold with a wide range of ideals—some steeped in radical Islamism and others concerned with broader social justice issues such as war, human rights, and civil liberties.

2. This study was funded by the Social Sciences and Humanities Research Council of Canada.

We locate the role of MSAs within this constellation of Muslim activism and social movements with a view to understanding their role on Canadian campuses. To this end, we focus on the role of MSAs in specific campus-based politics such as Israeli Apartheid Week, Hijab Solidarity Day, as well as more religiously oriented lectures and events. The variegated nature of MSAs as campus-based social movements and the interests they purvey are critical in examining how young Muslims locate themselves within the nation and as transnational actors connected to the broader Muslim *ummah*, or global community of believers.

MSAs are purveyors of Islamic knowledge, rooted mostly in conservative orientations of Islam, which are disseminated through formal means in *halaqa*s (study circles), *khutba*s (sermons), and public lectures and forums as well as through informal means such as social interaction and the normative standards enforced for Islamic conduct and practice within the MSA subculture. These activities serve to socially regulate and discipline Muslim identities in accordance with these groups' dominant religious and ideological framework. We argue that this ideological role positions MSAs as discursive actors that form a Muslim counterpublic that operates in both religious and political ways. As powerful discursive sites, MSAs police the boundaries of Islamic identity and practice among their members and constitute epistemic and ontological formations for a campus-based Islamic public that creates the foundations for social movement activism.

Part of the discursive role of MSAs is the religious education and support they provide to Muslims on campus, making them powerful spaces for the production and dissemination of Islamic knowledge. This knowledge is too often filtered through particular ideological lenses that stem from conservative, patriarchal religious views. In a surprising development, we discovered that more ideologically oriented groups, such as Party of Liberation (Hizb ut-Tahrir), had a presence on some Canadian campuses. This group advocates a return to a central Islamic authority through the caliphate system. The fact that MSAs are sites for this type of religious movement to develop speaks to the way they operate as discursive communities that wield religious authority on campus and can be utilized for building specific kinds of social movements. Jürgen Habermas's

(1991) notion of the public sphere is defined as the arena where private persons come together to create public opinion. The distinctive features of this sphere posit that all individuals come together around issues of general interest, without concern for social status, and achieve consensus by means of critical rational discussion (Ambrozas 1998; Calhoun 1992; Fraser 1990). Habermas's theory implies that the public sphere is open and accessible to all and further assumes that logical ideas put forward by participants—not social status, gender, wealth, and so on—are legitimizing factors in the discursive arena (see Habermas 1991).

Though his theory is valuable in conceptualizing the public sphere, Habermas fails to take into consideration the realities of class-based societies and other forms of social difference and exclusion; as a number of authors have observed, his model assumes that these differences can be bracketed (Calhoun 1992). Nancy Fraser (1990) notes that for centuries the broader public sphere in Western societies has marginalized individuals based on gender, religion, class, and other forms of social difference. She argues that the exclusionary effect of these factors limits marginalized groups' access within a dominant public sphere. No less important, Habermas also assumes that discourse in the public sphere should be restricted to the common good. Again, this assumption rests on the premise that all persons have equal access to the public sphere, have bracketed their status/difference, and have defined the "common good" as that which benefits all, not just the privileged class. For Fraser, it is imperative to recognize that subordinate groups do not have the privilege of being heard in the broader public and are therefore relegated to a position as a "subaltern counter-public" (1990, 1995).

When conceptualizing the university as a public, Diana Ambrozas (1998) draws on Fraser's framework and goes further to contend that the public sphere is made up of multiple intersecting publics where issues are discursively constituted and contested and, moreover, where there are no a priori determinations of what is considered "rational." Ambrozas notes, "The university today is not, strictly speaking, a single public but a number of intersecting weak and strong publics. These publics are constituted by women's studies departments, ethnic students' associations, unions, electronic mail lists for 'academic freedom,' and so on" (1998, 12). Although the associations that Ambrozas notes do constitute multiple and overlapping publics, we would argue that in the context of Canadian public universities they operate within a dominant Eurocentric, secular, male-dominated, able-bodied, and heterosexist environment that would relegate them to the position of subaltern publics. Universities are not level playing fields for members of marginalized groups, whether faculty or students; therefore, the associations located outside of dominant structures of power and privilege occupy a subordinate status within these hierarchical sites. On university campuses, MSAs operate as "Muslim counterpublics" through which religious discourses and practices are purveyed within the organization and among fellow Muslims. These practices are aimed at perpetuating Islamic values on campus and are a means to cultivate a particular type of Islam and Muslim subject.

Charles Hirschkind's (2006) ethnographic study of religious sermon cassette tapes in Egypt revealed that the widespread circulation of these tapes served to expand the arena of Islamic argumentation and debate in Egypt through what he termed an "Islamic counter public." Given the context of his research in Egypt, Hirschkind's use of the concept of counterpublic differs from Fraser's conception of the counterpublic in the West. Gregory Starrett notes that Hirschkind draws from Michael Warner and Isaiah Berlin's notion of the public sphere as a "self-organizing space for open debate," in which popular media forms have been used either as "mechanisms allowing for open deliberation, or as disciplinary instruments meant to shape consciousness in predetermined ways" (2008, 1043). Hirschkind thus examined these emerging Islamic publics as sites free from state control where ideas of the common good based on religious virtues and piety provided the basis for ethical living and were not necessarily forms of religious indoctrination. Both Fraser's and Hirschkind's notions of the counterpublic provide important ways of understanding how MSAs are constituted as subaltern and Islamic counterpublics. We have already noted the way MSAs operate as a subaltern counterpublic in Canadian university settings in their contestation of the dominant secular, Euro-centered public sphere through social justice, advocacy, and equity-based activism. Hirschkind's conception of an Islamic counterpublic is also relevant in understanding how MSAs operate as purveyors of Islamic knowledge through their *halaqa*s, *da'wa* (preaching), public lectures, and events. The dissemination and circulation of this knowledge are targeted at the Muslim public on campus as well as at the broader multiple publics that compose the campus. The MSAs' role of providing religious guidance and instruction is aimed at strengthening the faith of Muslims on campus and at building a model for pious living.

Instead of using the term *Islamic counterpublics*, we have opted to use the terms *Muslim publics* and *Muslim counterpublics*. Whereas Hirschkind's use of the term *Islamic counterpublics* is well applied in the Egyptian context based on the dominant structures of religious authority, the term *Muslim* is more appropriate to the context of Canadian MSA diasporic subcultures and the more limited structures of knowledge and authority the MSAs employ as student groups. The term *Muslim* denotes more variability in what Muslims as social and discursive actors construct, create, and purvey as opposed to the more fixed norms that are codified within Islamic traditions. In the context of undergraduate student groups, the students' religious formation and knowledge of Islam are reflective of their developing understandings of the faith as well as of their age, social location, and the cultural norms they have grown up with as opposed to a rigorous approach to Islamic knowledge or hermeneutics. Therefore, we locate their articulations of religious knowledge as being "Muslim" rather than "Islamic."

In the narrative analysis that follows, we discuss the religious, social, ideological, and political roles of MSAs as campus-based social movements and subaltern Muslim counterpublics based on the interviews we conducted with Muslim youth at university campuses across Canada. This discussion will help to elucidate the challenges faced by the 9/11 generation of Muslim youth and how that tragedy has affected and shaped the development of MSA subcultures, their modalities of resistance, and their broader political commitments. The discussion demonstrates how faith, activism, and citizenship are intertwined through the work of these student organizations as they represent campus-based social movements and Muslim counterpublics.

Creating an Islamic Subculture and Muslim Public

MSAs on university campuses provide spaces of spiritual support, affinity, and camaraderie among students. These organizations help build a sense of community, solidarity, and affective support among religiously observant students navigating a secular and Eurocentric academy. The university campus can be an alienating environment for students who want to live according to Islamic codes of behavior and conduct and to maintain their religious obligations toward the five pillars of Islam.[3] The pillars that most affect their day-to-day activities at school are praying five times a day at appointed times and fasting in the month of Ramadan. The ability to carry out these obligations has been enabled through MSAs' lobbying for more-inclusive campus environments, where prayer rooms, facilities for preritual washing, and halal food are made available. Most Canadian universities have provisions for these accommodations, and students report that these provisions enhance their sense of belonging and their experience at university (see Asmar, Prude, and Inge 2004; Peek 2005; Canadian Federation of Students Task Force 2007). Mahvish, a student at one Ontario university, described the accommodations provided at her institution but was still skeptical of the impact that other interventions designed to promote multicultural activities may have had on the overall context of the university and the general university population's understanding of Islam and Muslims:

> We brought halal food to campus that was fabulous. . . . We have the prayer room in which we are sitting right now, conducting this interview. Certain things had to be respected when students are fasting during Ramadan, and there's exams or lectures. I've heard a lot of professors courteous enough to give a five to ten minute break to pray and eat and then resume class. When we have celebrations when we have

3. The five pillars of Islam are believing in one God and in Prophet Muhammad as his last messenger, performing obligatory prayer, paying alms to the less fortunate, performing the pilgrimage to Mecca, and fasting in the month of Ramadan. For more details, see Hussain and Ayoub 2007.

Islam Awareness Week . . . all of this has been facilitated, but I don't
know about the sincerity of it. I still question the sincerity of all that. I
have yet to see a shift in attitudes, and while the displays may go up and
the artwork is there and the speakers come in, and I don't know who's
really listening and who's not. I think that this might be formality we
do because we are an institution of higher learning, but I question the
validity of the true intentions behind it.

MSAs in the post-9/11 era, when Muslim identity and practices have
come under broader public scrutiny, provide a network that allows Muslim students to connect with their coreligionists on campus. The MSA
also provides a "safe space" where members can discuss and practice their
beliefs and strengthen their religious identities (Peek 2005, 228). Sohail,
an Ontario-based international student, described the sense of family and
community he derived from his MSA and how it has strengthened his
identity and practice as a Muslim:

On a personal note, the MSA for me, being an international student,
this is my first year with the MSA. On a religious note, I made a jump; I
guess I realized it was due time that I found a sense of belonging. I had
always felt that way about my religion, but now I feel I'm really getting
there, so the MSA is like a family. It's home away from home. I'm here
without my family. It's where I am five to six days a week, helping out my
brothers and sisters with everything possible. From prayer to how to do
MSA services, it really helps you to become an active member, and it has
given me an opportunity to reflect on my identity as a Muslim and as a
person and as an individual within society, and it has really helped me
redefine my goals. That's what the MSA has done for me.

The MSA is constituted as a public through the modalities of social and
affective support it provides along with the discourses that shape these
modalities. These social ties are also formed through the fictive kinship
identification of "brothers" and "sisters" within Islam as well as through
the notion of the MSA as family and the concept of the *ummah* as a supra-
national organizing principle.

Gender Equity

Research has indicated that there has been varying commitment to gender equity in MSAs (see, e.g., Mir 2006, 2007). Interestingly, it is often women who support the patriarchal structures of male authority that are predominant in these organizations. Zabeda, a student from British Columbia, explained that although she and her MSA would be open to female leadership, there were reasons why she preferred that role be passed on to the brothers:

> In the MSA, yeah, I would say [the distribution of power between men and women] is pretty fair. I know our president is male, and it could have easily been a female. Personally I preferred [and] most of us preferred for it to be a male just because the president has to go through a lot of things. People yell at him, call him late at night. And we didn't want a sister to have calls from random guys late at night. So we looked at those types of things. But it technically could have been anyone. It is just what we wanted. I wanted that, too.

In some instances, female leaders have successfully run MSA chapters; however, these examples have been few and were not found in the data we collected, with the exception of the recent election of Huda (whom we discuss later) as the new president in her chapter. Nonetheless, as Uthman explained, his MSA has made a commitment to having equal say for male and female executive members:

> Every single person sitting in that room has a say, and it's not that, oh, there's only three sisters, ha ha, and there's five brothers, so you lose. We don't have that going on. It's like if you're three sisters, you're as equal to the five brothers, the five of us. The same thing. If one sister has an opinion, we all go back and forth, and it's like a collective thing, and it's basically like a family, and we're just debating how we can make MSA better so that people can actually show up and how can we provide more services to Muslims, so that they'll say, "Look, MSA is actually doing something."

Although Uthman reinforced his MSA's egalitarian position, which is very positive, such a move remains more a form of "benevolent patriarchy" until there is true gender parity in representation and leadership authority. Nonetheless, Zabeda found that on occasion if the female executives were more vocal and passionate in executive meetings, they had greater pull in the decision making. Gender segregation is customary in many MSA social events—a practice that is in line with the organization's more conservative orientation of maintaining social distance between men and women. For some women, this segregation was not an exclusionary act but one they preferred based on their sense of ease and comfort within female-centered spaces, as Farheen explained: "We had separate [*halaqas*, or study circles] for girls as well, so we could talk about things that you wouldn't normally feel comfortable talking about in front of guys." Farheen's example provides evidence of how MSAs create spaces where women can discuss issues they would otherwise be uncomfortable speaking about in front of men. Yet she also sees the value that MSAs place on female modesty through gender segregation and the conservative dress codes as having a more performative element. Shabana Mir describes in her study of Muslim women in US college campuses how one female MSA executive member admitted to behaving more conservatively with her male friend—also an MSA executive—when they were in MSA settings as opposed to outside of them (2009, 248). The pressure to maintain more traditional norms and conventions oftentimes stems from the social disciplining that takes place within MSA spheres in accordance with the conservative gender relations they impose. Muslim women's acquiescence to the MSA's patriarchal structures can be seen as capitulating to a patriarchal subculture that keeps women within their own spheres of influence, yet it is actually more in line with the kind of empowered female agency that Saba Mahmood describes in her study of the Cairene women's piety movement. Mahmood argues that "women's active support for socio-religious movements that sustain principles of female subordination can be a dilemma for feminists" (2011, 5), but her fieldwork work goes on to demonstrate how women find ways to maneuver within traditional patriarchal spaces to fulfill their needs without necessarily resignifying or contesting the validity of these norms but instead creating the "capacity to realize one's own interests against the weight of custom, tradition, transcendental will or other obstacles (whether individual or collective)" (8). Moreover, the creation of female-centered spaces contributes to the strengthening of sisterhood and solidarity of women who are normally involved both behind the scenes and in frontline MSA activism despite being shut out of the top leadership positions in many chapters.

Religious Authority

As discursive actors, MSAs provide religious education to Muslims on campus through religious study circles, or *halaqas*—public talks, lectures, and events. Through these communicative forms, they disseminate Islamic beliefs and practices based on the ideological orientations determined by the executive body of the group that are based on the teachings of religious leaders deemed to be the most valid and authoritative sources for sharia-based guidance. According to Charles Hirschkind and Brian Larkin (2008), the circulatory forms through which religious publics constitute themselves and their members are often established in relation to or in opposition to competing forms of identity. Within MSA subcultures, this oppositional positioning is furthered by religious chauvinism, sectarianism, and the exclusion or alienation of those who do not share the same religious perspectives. In many cases, these epistemic boundaries are policed and regulated, and it is one's adherence to the association-approved principles of belief and practice that determines belonging to and membership in the group. The guidelines for pious behavior are circumscribed by those who wield religious authority, usually members of the group's executive. These guidelines are largely unspoken but nonetheless determine the legitimacy of group membership and the boundaries of inclusion and exclusion. For example, it is unlikely that a Muslim who identifies as gay, lesbian, or transgender would find a comfortable home within a traditional MSA group.

Some Pakistani students felt the effects of religious disciplining when trying to form a cultural group for themselves on one campus. Huda related how MSAs can become the "halal police" on campus, determining what behavior is right and righteous and imposing these standards on

Muslim students. She described how the MSA at her school tried to block the development of a Pakistani Student Association (PSA) at a neighboring university and even protested outside one of the PSA's cultural events because there was music and free intermingling between men and women, which violated the MSA's beliefs about righteous conduct for Muslims. This protest inhibited attempts to develop a PSA on her university campus because students were wary of being harassed by the MSA.

One MSA president we interviewed felt strongly that although the previous administration had a single-minded ideological framework, his new administration was committed to promoting a broader notion of Islam. Hamza explained his perspective on Islam as a diverse rather than narrow path by noting, "That is another thing that was not accounted for before [by the former MSA exec] . . . making sure that Islam is not just one stroke of color; Islam is diverse, and that's why it's beautiful because it's amazing how there are so many different ways that people can express their Islam." This particular MSA administration sought to break with the ideologically driven agenda of the past executive and create a more inclusive environment where a wide variety of Muslim opinions could be accommodated. This positive development demonstrates how inclusive forms of leadership can reshape the discursive boundaries that define belonging and the voices that can claim legitimacy within the Muslim public sphere on campus.

Bigotry and Religious Chauvinism

Unfortunately, not all MSAs can claim such enlightened leadership. Bigotry and religious chauvinism often come into play in them. Most MSAs in Canadian universities are Sunni and both marginalize and alienate Shia students and other non-Sunnis. The hegemony of Sunni Muslims and Sunni Islam in shaping the religious, social, and cultural context of MSAs makes these groups the dominant Muslim public on campus. Their discursive authority allows them to be guardians of the epistemic and ontological boundaries of belonging. Michael Warner argues that it is "precisely the circulation of discursive forms that has decisive power on forming the conceptual infrastructure of movements and creating modes of authority and power that are manifest in the relation of dominant publics to various types of marginal counter publics" (quoted in Hirschkind and Larkin 2008, 5–6). In this case, we can see how the dominant Muslim public on campus maintains a privileged position in relation to more marginalized members of the subculture. In a focus group with Shia students in British Columbia, we were told stories of blatant discrimination that led to these students' alienation and marginalization from the mainstream Sunni-dominated Muslim culture on campus. Adil described his encounter with a Sunni MSA member who had begun to develop more extreme sensibilities and attitudes, which led to Adil being personally threatened as a Shia:

> I remember even like a few years ago even, I was just on my lunch break, and one of the kids from the MSA came up to me, and this guy used to get along with everybody, but then gradually you started to see the changes. The beard kind of grew longer, he started to dress very, very differently. Everything about him just became really sort of extreme, and I hate using that term. He started to look like he has just stepped right out of some village back home. And you can see that the ideology coming hand-in-hand with that. And he took me aside on my lunch break and said, "There is no room for people like you here. And if you say a word about any of your beliefs, I'll end up in jail for what I'm going to do to you." I mean, it's one thing to say that, no, we don't have any sort of extremism in the Muslim community. I think we do; it is definitely highlighted, and it is blown up a bit in the media, you know, the cases with like CSIS [Canadian Security and Intelligence Service] really putting their finger down on it. But it does exist. I don't think it is as big a deal as they make it. But it does exist, I think at least.

Although being careful that his remarks about "extremism" would not be misconstrued in light of stereotypes about Muslims, Adil nonetheless was understandably troubled by this disturbing encounter and the bigotry he was subjected to from this fellow Muslim student. He went on to describe how some Sunni Muslims whom he did know would tell him that they were advised by their *shaykh* (religious scholar) to stay away from Shias:

It goes to the extent that maybe some of them who are more closer to me, they will say that, like, they will even tell me that, "We talked to our *shaykh* at the mosque, and he told us, avoid this person. Or tell him to come to me, don't talk to him directly." [Laughter.] Things like that, because I guess he has the answers, and they don't. . . . I try to avoid it altogether, but I guess at times they provoke it or invoke it. And you just want to tell them what you know or how you've been taught to follow a certain thing. And, yeah, that division will always exist, as soon as we start to discuss a little bit in depth about each sect in the religion.

Interestingly, during the focus-group interview, the students, including Ali, laughed at the story. This laughter seemed to be elicited by a sense of how ridiculous some students' chauvinistic attitudes were, though it was sad to see how the bigotry they encountered had become so normalized that their response was laughter as opposed to sadness, disappointment, or even anger. Rummana explained how the MSA constitution even stipulated that membership was exclusive to Sunnis but that Shia students fought against this stipulation and took the matter to the larger student union on campus, and as a result the constitution was changed. She and other students recounted how this move was met with acts of subterfuge against them. They reported that in their prayer space their *turba*s (small stones to rest their foreheads on while prostrating in prayer) would be stolen and Sunni students would not return their salaams. Rummana voiced her concerns about this situation and how it gestured to broader and deeper divisions among Muslims globally:

Just based on the schools of thoughts, even at the university level when I first started to become more involved even with things like the MSA, they made it very clear that any sort of Shia practices were not welcome. And it was in their constitution, and when I challenged it, they kicked me out of the club entirely, so you really lose that sense of global partnership or any, like that sense of the *ummah*, which is unfortunate. I think that we can't even resolve our own issues in the Muslim world. So it's kind of interesting for me how people outside the Muslim world think that it's a war between, you know, us and them. I think even internally we are kind of like battling it out.

Through these acts of exclusion, aversion, and bigotry, Muslim publics become fractured spaces, and the corporate basis for building solidarities and alliances to combat common oppressions such as Islamophobia and racism are diminished.

Dealing with Islamophobia on Campus

MSAs also sponsor events that cater to the wider campus community to educate it about Islam and to dispel myths, misperceptions, and Islamophobic stereotypes. This role for MSAs has become necessary to counter the backlash from the 9/11 attacks and the ongoing "war on terror" that has led to racism and Islamophobia on campuses across the country. As a response to growing Islamophobia on campuses, the Canadian Federation of Students established a task force to further study the problem and make recommendations. The Islamophobia, anti-Semitism, and antiracism campaign was originally motivated by an incident of hate at Ryerson University in Toronto in 2004, where the multifaith prayer space was defaced with graffiti on the wall stating "Die Muslim Die." In September 2006, Arab and Muslim students' associations discovered death threats slipped under their office doors, which stated, "Those who follow the Islam faith need to be killed in the worst possible way imaginable." Students experienced direct acts of hate, including accusations of being a "terrorist," of being associated with the Taliban, or of being bomb-carrying militants who were threatening physical attacks. A York University student from Toronto said, "People watch us and make certain comments, like 'Taliban.' It is dehumanizing, and they are demonizing minorities." Along with promoting racism and Islamophobia on campuses, such acts create the breeding ground for radical grievances.

As an intervention to combat the backlash Muslims have experienced since 9/11 and the "war on terror," Islamic education events are also a means by which questions surrounding Muslim practices and Islam can be discussed and deliberated in a constructive setting. Zabeda explained:

> I think there are still so many questions about 9/11 that we could easily address. . . . For example, we have Islam Awareness Week. The MSA has

been trying to get rid of the misconceptions that people have because there are many. And so, for example, one common one would be that women are inferior to men and they are subjugated. And they think that we are oppressed even though it is quite clear that we are not. Like when they see us speaking, you know talking, going to school, if you are oppressed, would we be talking this way? They still have that [view that] just because you wear a cloth over your head, because you want to cover your body, you are oppressed.

The importance of Islam awareness campaigns was a common thread for many MSAs because of the growing necessity to dispel stereotypes about Islam and Muslims. In her comments, Zabeda highlighted a common perception of Muslim women as imperiled subjects (see Razack 2008 and Zine 2009) or of Muslims as terrorists, a view that dominates popular-media portrayals, even those that predate 9/11. Operating within a dominant culture that is bombarded with negative images and portrayals of Muslims, the MSA is tasked with providing a counterimage of all Muslims on campus. MSAs can and do play an effective role as discursive actors by creating a different Muslim narrative. This counterpublic role enables counterhegemonic views about Islam and Muslims to be positioned from these subaltern sites as oppositional knowledge that helps challenge and dismantle the propaganda and jingoism that frame dominant representations of Islam in the media and indeed in some university classes.

In other studies, Muslim university students have reported that owing to the more educated, open, and diverse environment of a university setting, they experienced less overt kinds of racism or Islamophobia than outside of campus (see Peek 2003; Nasir and al-Amin 2006; Hopkins 2011). Many students found their campuses ethnically and racially diverse, which they regarded as minimizing the effect of potential Islamophobia. Although the students we interviewed reported some cases of racist and Islamophobic incidents, overall they were not harshly critical of the campus culture despite these cases. This ambivalence is surprising and troubling in the way everyday acts of racism and discrimination and microaggressions have become normalized.

As a way of dispelling myths and negative stereotypes about Islam and Muslims, long-standing MSA activities such as Islam Awareness Week, Ramadan, and Eid dinners have renewed impetus.[4] These events are also ways that religious identities are asserted within the secular sphere of university life to allow for a more visible Muslim presence on campus. As Garbi Schmidt (2002) notes, MSAs in the United States participate in global social justice causes (e.g., Israel Apartheid Week) and other forms of activism. Similarly, in Canada MSAs are active in social justice causes locally and globally. The events supported broadly by these MSAs include many charitable campaigns, such as orphan-sponsorship programs and fund-raising for relief efforts abroad. MSAs are also involved in the Pink Hijab and Purple Hijab days in support of breast cancer and domestic-violence awareness, respectively, but one Ontario university also sponsored Hijab Solidarity Day, on which non-Muslim women wore head scarves in support of Muslim women who cover but face discrimination for doing so. This effort was spearheaded by a non-Muslim professor on the campus but was also supported by the campus MSA. More politically focused events include the Peace, Not Prejudice campaign, which developed in direct response to the neoconservative Islamofascism Awareness Week.[5] In the face of competing attempts by supporters of Islamofascism Week, this event was aimed at facilitating dialogue, building bridges of solidarity with other groups on campus, and promoting a better understanding of Islam.

4. Eid in this reference refers to the festival at the end of Ramadan, the month of fasting known as Eid ul Fitr.

5. Islamofascism Awareness Week was first organized in 2007 by neoconservative critic of Islam David Horowitz and the Horowitz Freedom Center. According to the Terrorism Awareness website (www.terrorismawarness.org), 114 college campuses across America participated in its inaugural year. The central aim of the campaign has been to draw a link between Islam (Muslims and MSAs) and terrorism and to promulgate the notion of "Islamofascism" as a real threat on college campuses and to national security. In addition, David Horowitz has further claimed that faculty and students who are sympathetic to terrorism have hijacked university departments, in particular Middle East studies, women's studies, and Islamic studies (see also Bezzano 2010).

MSAs as Apolitical

Tahir Abbas (2011) notes that in the United Kingdom after 9/11, Muslim student groups on university campuses were unable to deal effectively with identity and political issues. Similarly, despite the campus-based activism and social justice activities, many students were dissatisfied with their MSAs' response to specific political issues and incidents. Zeenat was critical of her MSA's inaction in responding to an incident in which a woman pulled off a sister's *hijab* in a campus washroom and verbally attacked her. Many students echoed such concerns about the MSA not taking a strong enough stand when Islamophobic actions occurred and were critical of some MSAs' apolitical position in the face of such discrimination. For Tahir, a politically engaged student who worked with numerous social justice clubs on campus, the MSA at his university had perpetuated a culture of political illiteracy:

> MSAs are largely incompetent politically. They are mostly familiar with the day-to-day ritualistic form of our *deen* [religion]. Then they are completely unfamiliar with the political dynamics of the people they help to mold. . . . Young Muslims are largely politically illiterate. They don't have a history of political experimentation. They go to the *halaqa*s [study circles] and *jummah*s [Friday prayers] and dinners and think they've lived. My views are bleak. I have been thoroughly unimpressed by the Muslim student body because it's a pathetic attempt to organize themselves into coherent political voices . . . like they make no sense to me. . . . Don't get me wrong, I love my MSAers . . . but it's like they play on their doctrinal monopoly.

Tahir recognized that his MSA purveys a specific Islamic frame of knowledge through religious activities, which creates a particular kind of MSA subject, one he regards as politically immature and incompetent and focused exclusively on "ritualistic forms" of practice. As a critical voice, Tahir positioned himself in opposition to the dominant Muslim counterpublic on his campus. Lori Peek adds to Tahir's description of MSAs as purveyors of exclusive religious identities. She explains that the emphasis on religion is a means by which Muslim students are brought together and not segregated from their coreligionists (2005, 230). Some MSAs adopt this strategy of focusing on Islamic practices as a means to build unity among their diverse members and connect their MSA chapter to broader networks of Muslims; however, this focus can be a limiting narrative that diminishes their ability to engage in other social justice and civic activities, thus leaving some members dissatisfied.

Tahir's critique of MSAs as apolitical is not unique to his MSA chapter. Yunus, a student at another Ontario university, expressed similar concerns regarding the MSA's response to the Danish cartoon controversy:

> The MSA is . . . very, very, very inactive politically. They are very, very scared. I don't know [why]; I wasn't an executive. I couldn't understand why we're not able to put out a very strong statement against certain cartoons that were printed in Canada, and we were always trying to give statements in line with the official statement of the university . . . and that was a problem for me. . . . We're not trying to be objective. . . . If we need to fit in, we should fit in; . . . if we don't need to fit in, we should stay out, and we should be very careful because it shapes us as individuals. . . . [I]t shapes us as a community, and it shapes us as whatever we want to see ourselves.

Yunus described his MSA's behavior as apolitical and cautious and cited a fear of exclusion or reprisal from the broader university public or perhaps from the security communities that regard with suspicion the politicization of Muslim student groups around such issues as the Danish cartoons. The sense of fear and desire to "fit in" may have been brought about by the Islamophobic acts that had taken place on campuses. For example, a Canadian Federation of Students Task Force report noted in 2007 that Muslim candidates running for election in two separate campaigns repeatedly had their posters torn down (25). These candidates were either involved in the MSA or were visibly Muslim (one of the candidates wore the *hijab*). It is possible that such incidences compel some MSAs to remain apolitical as a means to avoid negative attention and harassment. However, in not taking up a role as counterpublic actors and not responding to issues of racism and Islamophobia, the MSAs shore up the dominant narratives by their silence and reinforce Muslims' subaltern position instead of actively contesting and resisting it.

Conclusion

In this chapter, we have argued that MSAs are more than just clubs. Rather, they form a subaltern Muslim counterpublic and are constituted as campus-based social movements. They assist students in aligning their faith and activism in ways that create Islamic subcultures on campus and guide students in pious living. The associations also provide awareness and education about Islam within the university and serve to mobilize their members' identities as Muslims and Canadians in order to challenge Islamophobia, imperialism, and other forms of oppression affecting Muslims in both local and transnational contexts. Far from being insular, they engage in outreach activities and have a vibrant presence on many campuses. Despite internal divisions within many MSAs based on sectarian or ideological differences, MSAs nonetheless remain the dominant student bodies representing and maintaining a Muslim presence on campuses and have served to create communities of faith, activism, and action.

References

Abbas, Tahir. 2011. *Islamic Radicalism and Multicultural Politics*. London: Routledge.

Ambrozas, Diana. 1998. "The University as Public Sphere." *Canadian Journal of Communication* 23, no. 1. At http://www.cjc-online.ca/index.php/journal/article/view/1024/930.

Asmar, Christine, Elizabeth Proude, and Lici Inge. 2004. "'Unwelcomed Sisters?' An Analysis of Findings from a Study of How Muslim Women (and Muslim Men) Experience University." *Australian Journal of Education* 48, no. 1: 47–63.

Bezzano, Elliot. 2010. "Muslim Students Associations." In *Encyclopedia of Muslim American History*, edited by Edward Curtis, 410–13. New York: Facts on File.

Calhoun, Craig, ed. 1992. *Habermas and the Public Sphere*. Cambridge, MA: MIT Press.

Canadian Federation of Students Task Force on the Needs of Muslim Students. *2007 Final Report*. Toronto: Canadian Federation of Students.

Fraser, Nancy. 1990. "Rethinking the Public Sphere: A Contribution to the Critique of Actually Existing Democracy." *Social Text* 25, no. 26: 56–80.

———. 1995. "Politics, Culture, and the Public Sphere: Toward a Post-Modern Conception." In *Social Postmodernism beyond Identity Politics*, edited by Linda J. Nicholson and Steven Seidman, 287–314. Cambridge: Cambridge Univ. Press.

Habermas, Jürgen. 1991. *The Structural Transformation of the Public Sphere: An Inquiry into a Category of Bourgeois Society*. Translated by Thomas Burger and Frederick Lawrence. Cambridge, MA: MIT Press.

Hirschkind, Charles. 2006. *The Ethical Soundscapes: Cassette Sermons and Islamic Counterpublics*. New York: Columbia Univ. Press.

Hirschkind, Charles, and Brian Larkin. 2008. "Introduction: Media and Political Forms of Religion." *Social Text* 26, no. 3: 1–9.

Hopkins, Peter. 2011. "Towards Critical Geographies of the University Campus: Understanding the Contested Experiences of Muslim Students." *Transactions of the Institute of British Geographers* 36:157–69.

Hussain, Amir, and Mahmoud M. Ayoub. 2007. "The Islamic Tradition." In *A Concise Introduction to World Religions*, edited by Willard G. Oxtoby and Alan F. Segal, 233–38. New York: Oxford Univ. Press.

Mahmood, Saba. 2011. *Politics of Piety: The Islamic Revival and the Feminist Subject*. Princeton, NJ: Princeton Univ. Press.

Maira, Sunaina. 2009. *Missing: Youth Citizenship and Empire after 9/11*. Durham, NC: Duke Univ. Press

Memon, Nadeem. 2009. "From Protest to Praxis: A History of Islamic Schools in North America." PhD diss., Univ. of Toronto.

Mir, Shabana. 2006. "Constructing Third Spaces: American Muslim Undergraduate Women's Hybrid Identity Construction." PhD diss., Indiana State Univ.

———. 2007. "American Muslim Women and Cross Gender Interaction on Campus." *American Journal of Islamic Social Science* 24, no. 3: 70–90.

———. 2009. "Not Too 'College-Like,' Not Too Normal: American Muslim Undergraduate Women's Gendered Discourses." *Anthropology & Education Quarterly* 40, no. 3: 237–58.

Nasir, Na'ilah Suad, and Jasiyah al-Amin. 2006. "Creating Identity-Safe Spaces on College Campuses for Muslim Students." *Change: The Magazine of Higher Learning* 38, no. 2: 22–27.

Peek, Lori. 2003. "Reactions and Response: Muslim Students' Experiences on New York City Campuses Post 9/11." *Journal of Muslim Minority Affairs* 23, no. 2: 271–83.

————. 2005. "Becoming Muslim: The Development of a Religious Identity." *Sociology of Religion* 66, no. 3: 215–42.

Razack, Sherene H. 2008. "Modern Women as Imperialists: Geo-politics, Culture Clash, and Gender after 9/11." In *Casting Out: The Eviction of Muslims from Western Law and Politics*, 83–106. Toronto: Univ. of Toronto Press.

Schmidt, Garbi. 2002. "Dialectics of Authenticity: Examples of Ethnification of Islam among Young Muslims in Sweden and the United States." *Muslim World* 92:1–17.

Starrett, Gregory. 2008. "Authentication and Affect: Why the Turks Don't Like Enchanted Counterpublics." *Comparative Studies in Society and History* 50, no. 4: 1036–46.

Wiktorowicz, Quintan. 2004. "Islamic Activism and Social Movement Theory." In *Islamic Activism: A Social Movement Theory Approach*, edited by Quintan Wiktorowicz, 1–34. Bloomington: Indiana Univ. Press.

Zine, Jasmin. 2009. "Unsettling the Nation: Gender, Race, and Muslim Cultural Politics in Canada." *Studies in Ethnicity and Nationalism* 9, no. 1: 146–63.

3 "No, I'm Not a Salafist"

*Salafism, Secularism, and Securitization
in the Netherlands*

MARTIJN DE KONING

In Dutch counterradicalization policies and the debates on Islam today, the focus is almost entirely on the phenomenon of foreign fighters who left the country to go to Syria to join the Islamic State or Jabhat al-Nusra. In these debates, the young men and women who traveled to Syria are often linked to Salafism: an Islamic trend. Salafism, however, is much more than the foreign-fighter phenomenon, and most Dutch Salafi preachers, in fact, denounced both the Islamic State and Jabhat al-Nusra (de Koning et al. 2014). This chapter examines the dominant factions within Dutch Salafism before 2013, when the foreign-fighter phenomenon became a contentious issue. In September 2012, I attended a meeting in Utrecht titled "Salafisme—een kennismaking" (Salafism—an Introduction), organized by a Dutch student union. At this meeting, Abu Yasin, a prominent Dutch Salafi preacher, talked about what Salafism meant to him. After a lively debate, Abu Yasin told a number of us that after a terrorist attack a journalist asked him if he was a "Salafist." "No, I'm not a Salafist," he replied. But why would a preacher who is happy to speak at a public meeting on Salafism and identify himself as "someone following the Salafi *manhaj* [method]" deny his affiliation to a journalist and then recount this story to others? Abu Yasin's reply to the journalist, the debate about Salafism, and our participation in the debate cannot be understood without a consideration of the Dutch Islam debates in which Salafism often appears as the poster boy of so-called radical Islam. The Dutch Islam debates have been

75

so pervasive that it is difficult for Muslims to avoid the politics of identity, Islamophobia, and the stigmatization that result from it. Abu Yasin apparently was attempting to elude the negative definitions of Islam and Salafism while simultaneously presenting and positioning himself in response to these imposed definitions. Abu Yasin denied being a "Salafist" because he thought the journalist equated the label with violence, terrorism, and al-Qaeda. "No, I'm not a Salafist" then becomes a mode of resistance challenging what Abu Yasin perceives as accepted and anticipated answers to questions such as "Who am I?" and "What am I supposed to be?" (Cadman 2010). It is this type of "everyday resistance" that is the central focus of this chapter, which is based on my research in the Netherlands and the United Kingdom.[1]

After a short introduction to Salafism as a utopian trend, I analyze different styles of activism—transcendence, reversal or inversion, and escape—to explain the various modes of engagement in a type of resistance Michel Foucault (1982) calls "counterconduct." This resistance is not a response to changing political and economic structures but rather an effort to evade a government's attempts to monitor and regulate Muslims as Muslims, but at the same time Salafi Muslims opt for a different mode of regulation. As I argue, this type of counterconduct is closely related to Dutch integration policies and the "Dutch Islam" debate, both as the locus

---

1. This research began in 2007 as part of the project Salafism as a Transnational Movement of the International Institute for the Study of Islam in the Modern World and Radboud University Nijmegen and the project Forces That Bind or Divide funded by the Nederlandse Organisatie voor Wetenschappelijk Onderzoek of the University of Amsterdam. Since 2007, I have spoken to and followed (on- and offline) forty-eight men and fifteen women, most of them between sixteen and twenty-five years old and from Moroccan Dutch backgrounds but also including several native Dutch converts to Islam and a number of Turkish Dutch and Somali Dutch Muslims. Most of the interviews were conducted in informal settings; the interviews with women were conducted via email and chat programs. I also spoke to ten Dutch Salafis who migrated to the United Kingdom. I thank Annelies Moors, Femke Kaulingfreks, and Stijn Sieckelink for their useful comments on earlier versions of this paper. All names have been changed to protect the interviewees' identities.

of resistance and as a method of determining the terms that make resistance possible and meaningful.

Governmentality: Securitization, Secularism, and Integration

Foucault's notion of governmentality is intimately connected to resistance.[2] Instead of reducing the mechanisms of power to repression or hierarchy, Foucault's notion of governmentality allows us to conceptualize power in a multilevel and multilayered way because it is concerned with the management and maintenance of bodies, persons, populations, and the circulation of goods and ideas (cf. Amir-Moazami 2011). Governmentality creates and targets particular social categories of people who are identified as groups requiring government intervention (Rose, O'Malley, and Valverde 2006, 87). In response to the perceived problems of integrating Muslims and signs of radicalization, new agendas, frameworks, tools, practices, and institutions of governance emerge, and new instruments of government are invented (Rose, O'Malley, and Valverde 2006, 88). Governmentality is not a top-down model of power in which the state controls all, but "an assemblage of networks, authorities, groups, individuals, and institutions [that are] enlisted [and] brought to identify their own desires and aspirations with those of others" (Rose, O'Malley, and Valverde 2006, 89; cf. Miller and Rose 1990). Foucault locates the particular techniques that a government uses to create liberal subjects in, for example, education, therapy, youth programs, and so on. In the case of young Muslims in the Netherlands, we can find such techniques in the counterradicalization efforts, public debates on Islam, and integration efforts.

In this section, I explore how Muslims have become entangled in a particular regime of governmentality that aims to produce liberal subjects through securitization. Broadly speaking, in this particular form of governmentality, particular beliefs, practices, and public manifestations

2. This section and the next are taken from and expand on my analysis of the emergence of a so-called radical network in the Netherlands between 2001 and 2004 (de Koning 2013).

of Islam are seen as a threat to national security, social cohesion, and national identity and culture. The securitization of Islam is related to the secular assumption that religion should be relegated to the private sphere and to the idea that migrants are a threat to the project of homogenizing the nation-state. The focus on Islam and Muslims as threats to social cohesion has triggered a securitization of Islam and Muslims and an "Islamization of security," which means that any debate on Islam focuses on the threat it represents. This focus puts Islam center stage in public debates and policies concerning national security (de Graaf 2011). But this equation of Islam and a threat to security is certainly not an exclusive Dutch development; several researchers throughout Europe have recently delved into the issue of the process of securitization (e.g., Fekete 2004; Cesari 2009; de Graaf 2011; Croft 2012; Edmunds 2012; Mavelli 2013). Transforming a particular group from an ordinary political issue into a security matter legitimates the adoption of exceptional measures that may go beyond (or even undo) existing legal benchmarks and rights (Edmunds 2012) but crucially at the same time allows the issue to become part of the daily political, bureaucratic security logic (Mavelli 2013).

Muslims have been transformed from a social category to a social problem through a discourse of culturalization. By the 1990s, developments had already taken place that entailed migrants being categorized primarily based on their culture or religion or both (de Koning 2010). Dutch values with respect to secular and sexual freedoms became the standard for integration: the so-called culturalization of citizenship (Mepschen, Duyvendak, and Tonkens 2010). After September 11, 2001, the focus on integration in the media and in politics shifted almost entirely to Islam, Muslims, and their alleged threat to Dutch society (Vliegenthart 2007; Buijs 2009). The attacks on that date were the starting point of a growing fear that Dutch Muslims would be recruited by foreign Muslims to engage in violent struggles, but the murder of Theo van Gogh on November 2, 2004, shifted the public's attention to so-called homegrown radicals. Mohammed Bouyeri, a Dutch Muslim, killed writer and film director van Gogh because he believed van Gogh was responsible for "insulting the prophet" (quoted in Bartels and de Koning 2011, 31). After the murder, a large project called Binding Society (Maatschappelijke

Binding) was initiated, which required all government departments to devise projects opposing radicalization and furthering social cohesion. Mainstream Muslim organizations were partners in these endeavors, but all Salafi networks were excluded (although some contact between the networks and local authorities remained) because they were seen as the main agents responsible for radicalizing Muslim youth: Bouyeri, for example, was known to have visited Salafi circles.

These counterradicalization endeavors not only were intended to prevent violence but were also presented as a way to support social cohesion and protect free speech, both of which were allegedly threatened by "radical" Muslims. This was an important topic in the Dutch debate before and certainly after the murder of Theo van Gogh. As Brian Goldstone argues, the juxtaposition between angry Muslims and free speech in the debate serves as an organizing impetus and a legitimizing logic for secular liberalism (2007, 208). The counterradicalization policy established after this murder institutionalized the separation between moderate/liberal Muslims and radical Muslims (de Koning 2010). The opposition between liberal Islam and radical Islam correlates with the opposition between "good Islam" and "bad Islam," a distinction Mahmood Mamdani (2004) makes. "Good Islam" can be relegated to specific areas in the public sphere, but when Islam is experienced as entering into the public sphere in an assertive or even aggressive way, it is frequently labeled "bad Islam." We can identify such a distinction as far back as the time of European colonization (Moors 2011)—for example, in the Dutch East Indies (Indonesia) (Kennedy and Valenta 2006). At that time, this labeling process was part of the Dutch government's attempt to counter transnational Middle Eastern influences on local Islam and to stimulate a domesticated form of local Islam that the Dutch regarded as less political and fanatical than "Arab Islam" (Maussen, Bader, and Moors 2011). In the present, the emergence of groups unwilling to comply with the framework of liberal Islam, the secular political culture, or democracy and integration is labeled as "radicalization" (Algemene Inlichtingen en Veiligheidsdienst 2004, 2007).[3]

---

3. For an extensive critique on the concept of radicalization, see Kundnani 2012.

The techniques of governmentality focus on the observation of particular developments, their classification, and the production of normality/deviance. The public debates on Islam and the counterradicalization policies are carriers and producers of symbolic references to why Muslims are a problem (for example, problems with street youth, violence, intolerance, and "fanatical" religion). These references are often regarded as the cause of current and anticipated threats to society that in turn constitutes the legitimatization of and rationalization for intervention and transformation. We can regard the public debates on Islam and the policies regarding Muslims, integration, and security politics as a surveillance of the everyday lives of Muslims. Through websites and social media, a number of specialists take part in this surveillance. But laypeople join in, too, and are encouraged to enact the accepted and expected role of the Dutch secular liberal citizen. The debates about (radical) Islam and the government's counterradicalization policies have affected Muslims' lives severely, as Stuart Croft (2012) has shown to particular effect in the United Kingdom. In the Netherlands, several studies have explored how particular debates on Islam trickle down into the daily lives of people at different levels in society and in a variety of ways, ranging from people's experiences in school (de Koning 2008) and the workplace (Siebers 2010) to, of course, their media consumption (Uitermark and Gielen 2010; Van Zoonen, Vis, and Mihelj 2010).

Counterconduct and Salafism

It is precisely in government policies devised to manage integration and radicalization that Muslims are objectified as governable targets and that the subjectification of Muslims as Muslims occurs (cf. Cadman 2010). Governmentality, however, refers not only to the surveillance of others through particular techniques but also to the governing, surveilling, and fashioning of the self. Public statements made by politicians about particular ideas and practices of Muslims not only are made out of a concern for public order but also enable citizens to reflect on their own ideals and practices and subsequently to make the "right" choices. Foucault (1977) refers to Jeremy Bentham's design for the Panopticon, a modern prison where populations were categorized and individuals were organized in a regulated space and time. No guard was needed for inmates to internalize the rules because they felt they were being watched from all angles. The core idea of this style of prison is that it imposes a system of external control but simultaneously induces inmates to internalize this new pressure to reform and to constitute themselves in terms of the norms through which they are governed.

Through the Panopticon, people reflect upon and adjust their behavior because they are aware of being constantly under surveillance by guards they cannot see. Not everyone is willing to conduct themselves by following the modes of good citizenship defined by secular liberal governance. The question of how people can and do resist hegemonic policies has always been at the forefront of social science. Studies have focused on resistance to slavery, including how people show dissatisfaction with a society's status quo by resorting to small acts of defiance. Such studies have contributed greatly to our understanding of what resistance actually means and to the related debates about agency and subjectification (cf. Seymour 2006). As both Carl Death (2011, 427) and Louiza Odysseos (2011) explain, studies of resistance often juxtapose power (of the government) and resistance (of the subaltern) by framing the former as oppressive and the latter as liberating and emancipating. Resistance, however, is not simply opposed to power in that it often overlaps with and is based on the techniques of governmentality. According to Foucault, the same mechanisms that the state uses in its efforts to "conduct the conduct" of individuals also create spaces for forms of counterconduct to develop, which enable some dissident subjects to conduct themselves differently (2007, 194–216). Whereas the governance of people makes particular identities and modes of behavior dominant, expected, and accepted, resistance questions and opposes those identities and modes of behavior by asserting "the right to be different" (Foucault 1982, 781). The term *counterconduct* refers to struggles "not to be governed like that, by that, in the name of those principles, with such and such objective in mind and by means of such procedures, not like that, not for that, not by them" (Foucault, quoted in Death 2011, 428). Applying Foucault's concept of counterconduct allows us to explore the close relationship between power and resistance and the various modes of subjectification without imposing presupposed ideas of liberation and emancipation upon the subject (Cadman 2010, 540; cf. Foucault 2007).

Counterconduct is not only about rejecting a particular way of being governed but also about opting for a different kind of governmentality. As such, Salafism provides an interesting case because it was the main target of Dutch counterradicalization efforts until 2013, when the foreign-fighters issue became dominant. Salafism is a branch of global Sunni Islam that originated in eighteenth-century Arabia. The name "Salafism" is taken from the term *al-salaf al-salih*, "pious forefathers," which is used to describe the first three generations of Muslims who personally experienced the rise of Islam and who are regarded as exemplifying the correct way that all Muslims should live (Meijer 2009b). Here, I regard Salafism as a utopian movement (Price, Nonini, and Fox Tree 2008) that aims to revitalize Islam based on an idealized vision of the lives of the first Muslims, a vision that its followers find more just and satisfying than present forms of Islam. Salafi preachers claim not only that they spread a message of the eternal, universal, and authentic Islam but also that only the people who follow their version of "true" Islam belong to *al-firqa al-najiya*, the saved sect, and to *al-ta'ifa al-mansura*, the victorious group that will enter paradise. A "true" Muslim, therefore, is someone whose knowledge, intention, and practice unite in the correct (according to Salafi principles) dedication to and worship of the unique and one God (Meijer 2009b). The crucial dimension that sets Salafism apart from other branches of Islam is that for Salafists the Qur'an, the hadith, and the practices and statements of the *salaf* are all-encompassing ideals that one (and others) should conform to as closely and as strictly as possible (de Koning, Wagemakers, and Becker 2014).

The Salafi trend has been able to establish itself as a global movement that has been remarkably successful in adapting itself to local circumstances, albeit remaining a minority almost everywhere.[4] The first Dutch branches of Salafism were established in the 1980s. In 1986, the Saudi nongovernment organization al-Haramain established the El Tawheed

4. For a good overview of the global spread of Salafism, see Meijer 2009a.

mosque in Amsterdam, and in 1989 another Saudi nongovernment organization, al-Waqf, created the al-Fourqaan mosque in Eindhoven, in the
southern Netherlands. In 1990, the as-Soennah mosque in The Hague
completed the list of what still counts as the main centers of Salafism in
the Netherlands, although the network belonging to al-Fourqaan later
split into three mosques. Since 2001, all of the main networks have experienced several episodes of fusion and fission (see de Koning 2012a).

An important part of the activities of the Salafi movement in the Netherlands is directed toward establishing a good, harmonious, and united
moral community of Muslims by convincing and educating Muslims to
share a common life and a common vision and to take part in the practices
that constitute a good life. The movement's courses, lectures, and conferences have become the primary loci of a moral rehabilitation of Muslim
youth in a "morally corrupt" Dutch society. In particular, the Internet has
been of great use to Salafi Muslims to disseminate their message and to
attract a wide range of Muslims (Becker 2009).

Salafist imams, preachers, and activists try to reconfigure participants' everyday practices, routines, and orientations by allowing them
to focus on what matters in (the Salafi version of) Islam. In this way,
they aim to produce committed subjects with daily routines, attire,
and (political) attitudes that differ from others, both Muslim and non-
Muslim (cf. Tuğal 2009).

It is precisely this ethnopolitical resistance that distinguishes counterconduct from other modes of resistance (Davidson 2011, 28; Chrulew
2014). There is no evidence that the Salafi networks in the Netherlands
are seeking to implement sharia or to prepare for an Islamic revolution to
create an Islamic state in the Netherlands. They do not engage in demonstrations, and they refrain from being active in political parties and Parliament.[5] Nevertheless, besides being a religious trend, Salafism is political
in the sense that it tries to evade and sometimes to go against the current
tide of Dutch politics and policies that emphasize secular values and freedoms, sexual freedoms, and loyalty to the Dutch nation-state.

---

5. Except for a few militant groups that are beyond this chapter's scope.

Modes of Counterconduct: Transcendence, Reversal, and Escape

Utopian movements' capacity to create alternative utopias is precisely what makes political institutions and elites so wary of them. It is also the reason they are presented as a threat to social cohesion, security, and existing social and political arrangements in society (cf. Price, Nonini, and Fox Tree 2008). This does not immediately make clear, however, what kind of tactics Salafi Muslims deploy to avoid or change the range of legitimate conduct and to challenge the government's ability to reproduce the hold of government (Davidson 2011). Several studies outside of the field of Muslim studies have already analyzed different types of tactics, such as violent confrontation (Imre and Jose 2010) and reversal (turning the rules and regulations of the state against the state itself) (Prakash 2012), or they have tried to incorporate the perspectives of counterconduct within social movement theory (Death 2010). Others have applied the concept of counterconduct to modes of activism in the Arab world (Mamvig 2012). In the remainder of this chapter, I explore the three tactics of counterconduct that I encountered most frequently among Dutch Salafis: transcendence, reversal or inversion, and escape.[6] These tactics illustrate the different ways of engaging with the governmentalities of Islam in the Netherlands, the intimate relationship between the modes of political resistance against these governmentalities, and the relationship between resistance and governmentality, on the one hand, and the technologies of self-fashioning among Salafis, on the other.

Transcendence: Performing Arts, Politics, and Islam

In November 2007, the Dutch newspaper *De Telegraaf* published an article about radical anti-Islam politician Geert Wilders's intention to release his film *Fitna*. At the same time, one of the young visitors to the El Tawheed

---

6. In the remainder of this section, I expand on a previous brief analysis of styles of Salafi activism in de Koning 2012b.

mosque in Amsterdam, Abu Dujana,[7] released a music video on YouTube singing the song "Het paradijs bevindt zich in mijn hart" (Paradise Is Present in My Heart):

Paradise is present in my heart and I'm prepared to die on this path.
  This sweet taste is anchored in my soul and no one is able to
  overcome my *deen* [religion].
You can do what you want to oppose [*bestrijden*] me, but I will always
  practice my faith.
But do what you want to seduce me, I will always avoid disbelief.
[Voice-over by Wilders:]
"Stop the immigration from Muslim countries
Do not allow any new mosques anymore
Close Islamic schools
Forbid the burqa
Forbid the Qur'an
Expel criminal Muslims, like those Moroccan street terrorists who
  drive people in the country completely insane, expel them from
  the country
Take responsibility."

Always negative in the newspapers, on TV, all those hypocrites
  participate in that war but despite this conspiracy we hold onto the
  two: the noble Qur'an and the doctrine of the Prophet.
Write whatever you want about our religion, but I will not defect from
  my methodology.
This is our path, and the struggle is our duty, and don't think I will also
  sing for your plans.
Because paradise is present in my heart and I am prepared to die on
  this path.
This sweet taste is anchored in my soul, and no one is able to overcome
  my *deen*.
You can do what you want . . .[8]

---

7. For reasons of anonymity, the name "Abu Dujana" is a pseudonym.
8. Printed by permission of the song's author.

Singing in Dutch, Abu Dujana mixes Islamic *anashid* (sing. *nashid*, religious music, usually acapella) with hip-hop and samples from the Dutch news featuring Wilders's anti-Islam statements. Abu Dujana not only attacks Wilders but also indicates that there is a particular place where Wilders's attacks and state policies in general have no bearing: Abu Dujana's heart. Here he clearly carves out a space where he rejects the governmentalities of the Dutch state and at the same time opts for a different type of discipline, that of Islam. He also denounces mainstream Muslim organizations (referring to their members as "hypocrites" who have "sold" themselves and Islam to the Dutch state, which has co-opted them). Abu Dujana made this video precisely when the securitization of Islam was at its highest, according to some researchers (de Graaf 2011).

Abu Dujana told me that with such *anashid* he tried to raise political awareness among Muslims, focusing on a particular issue he said was very clear: the fight against Islam. According to him, many Muslims do not fight injustice "because it is easier that way" or "because one is ignorant as to what is going on."[9] His reference to the faith in his heart can therefore also be seen as a call for Muslims to "return" to the "true" Islam. In the text of this song, he also states that part of the fight against Islam has been to "seduce" people into losing their faith, evidencing his recognition that the policies and debates are not only about state power as a form of repression but also about power in its more subtle forms. His Dutch rhymes, his way of singing the *nashid*, and the sampling of Wilders's statements reveals Abu Dujana's past as a rapper. Like many young people who engage with the Salafi movement, he did not completely abandon his old hobby but transformed it into a way of performing that conformed with Salafi restrictions on music and musical instruments. Nevertheless, he did receive some criticism from fellow Salafi Muslims, who questioned the religious appropriateness of the *nashid* form because of the song's political message, the sampling, and especially his choice to use Dutch instead of Arabic.

9. Personal communication with Abu Dujana, November 22, 2010.

At one point, Abu Dujana decided to delete his videos on YouTube, in particular "Paradise Is Present in My Heart," "Blanke tirannie" (White Tyranny, about the oppression of Muslims by white people), and "De Bezetting" (The Occupation, which refers to the Israeli occupation of Palestine). In the first two cases, the critique of Muslims played a role in his decision, but his main reason for withdrawing all three was that he was afraid of coming under the scrutiny of Dutch intelligence and security services. With the murder of Theo van Gogh as well as the increased activities and reports of the Dutch General Intelligence and Security Services, his fear was not off the mark. There is no evidence that he was actually monitored by the Security Services, but here we clearly see how the Panopticon serves to regulate the actions of citizens, especially in a case of resistance. In recent years, however, Abu Dujana has returned to being the head of a small but vocal network of Salafi-oriented activists, but he is not producing any *anashid* anymore.

Reversal and Inversion: Political and Societal Engagement

After the announcement of Wilders's film *Fitna*, the youth chapter of the Salafi Tawheed mosque in Amsterdam also joined in the growing debate, presenting an open letter to the Dutch Parliament claiming that Wilders's film violated the right to freedom of religion for Muslims and was detrimental to the integration of Muslims in society. It called upon Parliament to take action and to explain the negative consequences of this film to Wilders. Both of these examples, Abu Dujana's songs and the Tawheed mosque's petition, bring together the secular and religious but do so in different ways. The petition is a nonreligious discursive form that appeals to secular concepts of democracy and rights, yet it also affirms the claim that Salafis are the defenders of the Muslim minority. Abu Dujana employs an Islamic music style, mixes it with elements from hip-hop, and infuses it with a political message that is partly secular and partly religious. Both in form and in content, the petition and the *nashid* are examples of how Salafi Muslims partake in the secular arrangements of the public sphere. These acts of protest blur the boundaries between the religious and the secular, a discursive merging that is necessary for Islamic voices to be heard in the secular public domain (de Koning 2012a).

Other examples of the blurring of boundaries between the secular and religious pertain to social outreach tactics. In recent years, several Salafi mosques have engaged in low-level neighborhood activities, ranging from barbecues during national feasts to neighborhood-watch schemes on New Year's Eve. Such styles of activism are, however, also contested by different actors. There is an ongoing discussion, for example, among Dutch Salafis about whether the use of petitions is Islamically acceptable or not because they are considered to be a form of participating in secular democracy. A similar discussion pertains to social outreach. Becoming a part of and participating in the structures of society means that Salafis have to play according to sets of rules that are devised by and benefit existing power holders. This accommodation creates a fear among Salafis that they will become much easier to co-opt through the normal channels of political representations and negotiation and forced to make compromises and "dilute" Islam (de Koning 2012a). Others within Salafi circles, however, propose that these forms of activism could be seen as examples of proselytizing by defending Islam and Muslims in public (such as in the case of the petition) or by promoting a friendly and inviting image of Islam.

On New Year's Eve in The Hague in 2011, the as-Soennah mosque announced on its website that it intended to participate in the local neighborhood-watch project, saying that the mosque would be open all night and that there would be patrols on the streets (in collaboration with other mosques and the police):

> In this way we not only guarantee the safety of our neighborhood, our homes, and our families, but at the same time we show how strong our Community is. By demonstrating that we, as a Community, can keep our neighborhood safe, we show the politicians of The Hague that they have to cooperate with us if they want to get anything accomplished. The current political climate dictates exactly the opposite. Most politicians shy away from cooperating with us. Instead of being a solution,

people experience us as a threat. This New Year's activity provides an opportunity to show a different side of us.[10]

In the case of the Tawheed mosque's petition, we can speak of a reversal of techniques of governmentality. Muslims are usually urged to comply with secular democratic rule and democratic rights, but the Tawheed mosque reversed the situation and asked politicians to uphold and to live up to their own ideals of democracy, freedom, and emancipation. In the case of the neighborhood-watch scheme, it is probably better to speak of an inversion. The as-Soennah mosque participated in the neighborhood-watch project not because it was asked to, as often occurs when politicians and opinion leaders invite Muslim organizations to take responsibility for the actions of others, but because it recognized the problems with fireworks, unrest, and violence on New Year's Eve in The Hague[11] and because it saw the project as an opportunity to enhance its public profile.

One could argue that the initiative showed how by taking responsibility and the initiative to maintain the peace in their neighborhood the members of the as-Soennah mosque had internalized the state's attempt to create liberal citizens. However, it was something they did based on their own ideas about what is good and bad behavior and to present themselves as crucial to the state's attempt to maintain the neighborhood's social peace. The latter clearly informed the public debate when the mosque's statement was immediately taken up by journalists, who labeled this initiative "sharia police" and "creeping sharia," regarding it as a tactic of infiltration. Politicians also voiced their concerns because they often considered the Salafi use of secular forms of governmentality as window dressing or a smokescreen. Earlier, in 2009, the Dutch Home Office had published the so-called facade brochure, which warned against a Salafi

10. From the As-Soennah mosque website, Al Yaqeen, at http://al-yaqeen.com/nieuws/nieuws.php?id=2056, posted Dec. 28, 2011, Dutch, my translation. This website is not available anymore, but this text can also be found in a report by the municipality of The Hague: sv 2011.662, RIS 182188, Regnr. BSD/2012.4.

11. The Hague has one of the most notorious New Year celebrations in the Netherlands, including small riots and arson.

secret agenda, in which all kinds of seemingly friendly and transparent activities organized in neighborhoods would really be used as a means of proselytizing. The brochure contained "case descriptions" illustrating such practices and offering clues for municipalities to recognize such forms of window dressing. The current state governance of Islam pushes at least some Salafi networks and individuals to partake in public activities and debate, but as soon as Salafis go public and employ secular forms of activism, state authorities distrust their intentions because they believe the Salafis become less recognizable as Salafis in these public activities and hence become more difficult to control.

What the debates following the neighborhood-watch project tell us, among other things, is how difficult it is for Salafis to escape the negative definitions of Islam in general and of Salafism in particular. Not only do these negative definitions trigger different styles of activism, but as soon as they do, rigid classifications reemerge in public to reestablish the boundaries between the secular and the religious. The distinctions between the secular and the religious as well as between moderate and liberal Islam (and/or Muslim) operate as forms of macro-, meso-, and microsurveillance. As a mode of microsurveillance, these distinctions mean that an individual Muslim is continuously reflecting upon himself or herself with respect to the dichotomies. Abu Dujana, given his reference to ignorant people, appears to suggest that people have to take up a position as Salafi if they do not want to be labeled "hypocrites" (his version of the outsiders' distinction between moderate and radical Islam). In the case of the as-Soennah mosque's participation in the neighborhood-watch scheme, the media imposed the opposition with its reference to "sharia police," and the state did the same with the government's "facade brochure." At a macrolevel and mesolevel, the distinctions have become a powerful tool to delegitimize Salafi practices and to mobilize politicians to act. At the same time, however, they trigger, inform, and shape religiopolitical mobilization among Salafis.

Escape: Dutch Salafis in the United Kingdom

Considering different styles of activism that are in themselves neither clearly religious nor secular also indicates how individual people, religious networks, and state actors "do things" with categories such as "Islamic," "non-Islamic," and "secular." Such a perspective allows for a different appraisal of the so-called Salafi facade. The Tawheed mosque's petition to Parliament was not simply a means of criticizing Wilders and Dutch politicians but also an argument for the state's noninterference in religion. By using nonreligious styles of activism, the mosque intended not only to become more politically acceptable and to proselytize but also to escape the negative valuation of Salafi Islam and the religious and secular divide that in practice works to subordinate religion to the state.

Another way of escaping from the Dutch religious-secular opposition is literally to leave the Netherlands for the United Kingdom, a movement that in Islamic terms is defined as "doing *hijra* [migration]." Interviews and Internet chats indicate that Muslims consider life in the United Kingdom to be "easier." Living in cities such as Birmingham, Manchester, and Leicester, where there are many more migrants from similar backgrounds, they feel less targeted or under surveillance as "Muslims," "radicals," "foreigners," and "allochthonous" beings than in the Netherlands, where they experience both a lack of recognition and the prospect of being treated as foreigners forever.

However, there appears to be something more in this choice to escape. In recent research, an increase in self-identification as a Muslim is seen as a possible reaction to stigmatization. To some extent, this may be the case, but there is something more to this self-identification. As Rogers Brubaker has noted, for example, this reaction may also be a response to the experience of being singled out, categorized, analyzed, surveyed, and surveilled in policies, media, and research and of being held accountable not only for one's individual actions but also for the (in)actions of others who are labeled Muslims. Furthermore, as the intra-Salafi debates over Abu Dujana's *nashid* and over the inversion/reversion tactics of the Tawheed and as-Soennah mosques show, a similar process also occurs among the Salafis themselves. When old Salafi networks fall apart and new networks arise, it is at these moments in particular that internal surveillance among and between Salafis heightens, often combined with a use of powerful labels such as *hypocrite* and *apostate.*

Many Salafis view migration as a way of escaping the pressures emanating from these processes of categorization. Other reasons to migrate are the desire to live in an "Islamic" country (often in the Middle East), which some Salafis regard as a necessity according to Islamic rulings (although some Salafi scholars now approve of Muslims staying in Europe as long as they actively engage in *da'wa* [mission]). But it was after the victories of the nativist anti-Islam Freedom Party during municipal (2010), national (2010), and European (2009) elections that some Muslims openly speculated about how long it would be before they were stopped from practicing their religion in the Netherlands or before their safety was threatened. This safety issue was related to a fear about the lack of protection from violent attacks more than to a fear of open persecution. Migrating to the Middle East, however, appears to be more difficult than many expect, and among Dutch Salafis the United Kingdom has a very positive image of being a tolerant country with a large and advanced Muslim community. It would therefore be "easier to live as a practicing Muslim" in the United Kingdom. In some Salafi circles, the impression of Birmingham is so positive that one Salafi scholar I communicated with designated it a place for *hijra*. This impression is underscored by the fact that an organization run by a married couple living in Birmingham offers help to Dutch Muslims wanting to migrate to the United Kingdom, using the website Hijra2Birmingham.nl. In almost all accounts given by Dutch Salafis in the United Kingdom, the pressure of being categorized and held accountable (by non-Muslims and Muslims) was mentioned as either one of the reasons to migrate or (more often) as the main difference between the Netherlands and the United Kingdom. In particular, the Salafis who had a public profile in the Netherlands appeared to enjoy the anonymity that life in the United Kingdom grants them as well as the benefits of a stronger infrastructure of Salafi circles in the United Kingdom (compared to in the Netherlands). They also feel more protected against racism and Islamophobia in the United Kingdom because of the strict antiracism laws.

Simultaneously, however, some give a positive evaluation of the Netherlands after they have lived in the United Kingdom for some time, regarding the Netherlands as better organized and cleaner but their "migrant neighborhood" (for example, Small Heath in Birmingham) as "dirty and run down." Many still keep in contact with their families and fellow Salafi "brothers and sisters" in the Netherlands and state that they still identify themselves as Dutch. After some time, most of them appear to realize that intra-Salafi struggles and the ensuing social pressures occur in the United Kingdom as well. Furthermore, the Salafis who are associated with sympathizing with (or engaging in) armed struggle are very aware of the fact that they are under counterterrorism surveillance, a reality they find much more intrusive than anything they experienced in the Netherlands. Most Salafis in the United Kingdom, however, spend their lives in relatively isolated neighborhoods in London, Manchester, and Birmingham, which appears to shield them from the situations they experienced in the Netherlands.

Conclusion

Abu Yasin's denial of the reporter's use of the label *Salafist* to describe him can be seen as one example of a Salafi preacher trying to conduct himself in a manner other than that prescribed by the Dutch integration and counterradicalization policies. By denying the negative connotations attributed to the term, he challenged the reporter's assumptions, and as a preacher he advocated his own highly idealized version of Islam. This example also shows we cannot take for granted how the label *Salafi* is used among Muslims in interactions between Muslims and the state or between Muslims and the media. In this chapter, I have highlighted the different modes of counterconduct that show not only how Salafis are affected by and respond to the securitization of Islam but also how they are able to transcend, reverse or inverse, and escape that securitization.

The intra-Salafi debates and the responses in media and politics about these different forms of resistance illustrate the intimate relationship between ethics and politics. Abu Yasin's attempt to deny the imposed definition of Salafism and the fact that he made this denial public challenged the journalist's preconceptions and established Abu Yasin as a savvy preacher who was well aware of the Dutch debates. At the same, however, his denial may also have fueled the distrust of Salafi Muslims that lies at the heart of much of the debate.

In refusing to be governed according to a model of securitization, Salafis like Abu Yasin destabilize existing modalities of surveillance.

However, when they go public with their grievances and claims, Salafism becomes more diffuse, which triggers both internal Salafi debates and attempts by the Dutch state to police and reaffirm the boundary between the secular and the religious. Ongoing attempts by Salafi Muslims to resist dissent through music, petitions, and societal participation mean that they continue to be targets of governmental intervention policies that aim to channel Islam into forms that are more acceptable by the state. Salafis themselves thus play a huge role in legitimizing the moderate-radical dichotomy and the counterradicalization policies. At the same time, certainly in the case of petitions and the neighborhood-watch schemes, Salafi Muslims have clearly thought a great deal about what forms of dissent will be considered acceptable in Dutch society. These cases illustrate not only how the Salafi community is problematized as a target of governmental intervention but also how governmentality involves using modes of subjectification: "a subject's ethical relation to itself as a governed subject" (Cadman 2010, 553).

Among Salafis, the different styles of activism also provoke debate, mainly about whether these actions are compatible with "true" Islam or not. Therefore, although the different modes of counterconduct are carried out in an attempt to escape the securitization of Islam, at the actual time that this resistance is shown and in its aftermath these modes simultaneously produce a reinstatement and reinforcement of securitization and a confirmation of the Salafi doctrines and debates associated with them.

When we take into account the intimate relationship between ethics and politics (in a Foucauldian sense) and overcome the binary opposition of power and resistance, the Foucauldian counterconduct approach allows us to appreciate the fact that the Dutch state, media, researchers, and Salafis are all part of the same political context. The Salafi movement's resistance responds to, relies upon, and is implicated in the different strategies, techniques, and power relationships that it opposes (cf. Death 2010). Although political governmentality can never fully force citizens to submit, Salafism, notwithstanding its ideas of isolation and of being a shield against the temptations of life, can never be fully immune to the state's influence.

References

Algemene Inlichtingen en Veiligheidsdienst. 2004. *Saoedische invloeden in Nederland*. The Hague: Ministerie van Binnenlandse Zaken and Koninkrijksrelaties.
————. 2007. *Radicale dawa in verandering, de opkomst van islamitisch neoradicalisme in Nederland*. The Hague: Ministerie van Binnenlandse Zaken and Koninkrijksrelaties.

Amir-Moazami, Schirin. 2011. "Dialogue as a Governmental Technique: Managing Gendered Islam in Germany." *Feminist Review* 98, no. 1: 9–27.

Bartels, Edien, and Martijn De Koning. 2011. "Submission and a Ritual Murder: The Transnational Aspects of a Local Conflict and Protest." In *Local Battles—Global Stakes: The Globalisation of Local Conflicts and the Localisation of Global Interests*, edited by Ton Salman and Marjo De Theije, 21–41. Amsterdam: VU Univ. Press.

Becker, Carmen. 2009. "'Gaining Knowledge': Salafi Activism in German and Dutch Online Forums." *Masaryk University Journal of Law and Technology* 3, no. 1: 80–98.

Brubaker, Rogers. 2013. "Categories of Analysis and Categories of Practice: A Note on the Study of Muslims in European Countries of Immigration." *Ethnic and Racial Studies* 36, no. 1: 1–8.

Buijs, Frank J. 2009. "Muslims in the Netherlands: Social and Political Developments after 9/11." *Journal of Ethnic and Migration Studies* 35, no. 3: 421–38

Cadman, Louisa. 2010. "How (Not) to Be Governed: Foucault, Critique, and the Political." *Environment and Planning D: Society and Space* 28, no. 3: 539–56.

Cesari, Jocelyne. 2009. *The Securitisation of Islam in Europe*. Paris: Centre for European Policy Studies.

Chrulew, Matthew. 2014. "Pastoral Counter-Conducts: Religious Resistance in Foucault's Genealogy of Christianity." *Critical Research on Religion* 2, no. 1: 55–65.

Croft, Stuart. 2012. *Securitising Islam: Identity and the Search for Security*. Cambridge: Cambridge Univ. Press.

Davidson, Arnold I. 2011. "In Praise of Counter-Conduct." *History of the Human Sciences* 24, no. 4: 25–41.

Death, Carl. 2010. "Counter-Conducts: A Foucauldian Analytics of Protest." *Social Movement Studies* 9, no. 3: 235–51.
————. 2011. "Counter-Conducts in South Africa: Power, Government, and Dissent at the World Summit." *Globalisations* 8, no. 4: 425–38.

De Graaf, Beatrice. 2011. "Religion Bites: Religieuze orthodoxie op de nationale veiligheidsagenda." *Tijdschrift voor Religie, Recht, and Beleid* 2, no. 2: 62–81.

De Koning, Martijn. 2008. *Zoeken naar een "zuivere" Islam: Geloofsbeleving and identiteitsvorming van jonge Marokkaans-Nederlandse Moslims.* Amsterdam: Bert Bakker.

———. 2010. "Understanding Dutch Islam: Exploring the Relationship of Muslims with the State and the Public Sphere in the Netherlands." In *Muslim Diaspora in the West: Negotiating Gender, Home, and Belonging,* edited by Haideh Moghissi and Halleh Ghorashi, 181–97. Burlington, VT: Ashgate.

———. 2012a. "The 'Other' Political Islam: Understanding Salafi Politics." In *Whatever Happened to the Islamists? Salafis, Heavy Metal Muslims, and the Lure of Consumerist Islam,* edited by Amel Boubekeur and Olivier Roy, 153–76. New York: Columbia Univ. Press; London: Hurst.

———. 2012b. "Styles of Salafi Activism: Escaping the Divide." *Material Religion: The Journal of Objects, Art, and Belief* 8, no. 3: 400–401.

———. 2013. "'We Reject You'—'Counter Conduct' and Radicalisation of the Dutch Hofstad Network." In *Radikaler Islam im Jugendalter: Erscheinungsformen, Ursachen, und Kontexte,* edited by Maruta Herding, 92–109. Halle, Germany: Deutsches Jugendinstitut.

De Koning, Martijn, Ineke Roex, Carmen Becker, and Pim Aarns. 2014. *Eilanden in een zee van ongeloof: Het verzet van de activistische da'wa in België, Nederland en Duitsland.* Institute for Migration and Ethnic Studies (IMES) Report Series. Amsterdam: Radboud Universiteit.

De Koning, Martijn, Joas Wagemakers, and Carmen Becker. 2014. *Salafisme: Utopische idealen in een weerbarstige praktijk.* Almere, Netherlands: Uitgeverij Parthenon.

Edmunds, June. 2012. "The 'New' Barbarians: Governmentality, Securitisation, and Islam in Western Europe." *Contemporary Islam* 6, no. 1: 67–84.

Fekete, Liz. 2004. "Anti-Muslim Racism and the European Security State." *Race & Class* 46, no. 1: 3–29.

Foucault, Michel. 1977. *Discipline and Punish: The Birth of the Prison.* Translated by Alan Sheridan. Harmondsworth, UK: Penguin.

———. 1982. "The Subject and Power." *Critical Inquiry* 8, no. 4: 777–95.

———. 2007. *Security, Territory, Population: Lectures at the Collège de France, 1977–78.* Translated by Graham Burchell. New York: Palgrave Macmillan.

Goldstone, Brian. 2007. "Violence and the Profane: Islam, Liberal Democracy, and the Limits of Secular Discipline." *Anthropological Quarterly* 80, no. 1: 207–37.

Imre, Rob, and Jim Jose. 2010. "Religious and Political Violence: Globalising Syncretism and the Governance State." *Religion, State, and Society* 38, no. 2: 153–68.

Kennedy, James C., and Markha Valenta. 2006. "Religious Pluralism and the Dutch State: Reflections on the Future of Article 23." In *Geloven in het publieke domein: Verkenningen van een dubbele transformatie*, edited by Wim van de Donk, Petra Jonkers, Gerrit Kronjee, and Rob Plum, 337–53. Amsterdam: Amsterdam Univ. Press.

Kundnani, Arun. 2012. "Radicalisation: The Journey of a Concept." *Race & Class* 54, no. 2: 3–25.

Mamdani, Mahmood. 2004. *Good Muslim, Bad Muslim: America, the Cold War, and the Roots of Terror.* New York: Pantheon.

Mamvig, Helle. 2012. *Governing Arab Reform: Governmentality and Counter-Conduct in European Democracy Promotion in the Arab World.* Danish Institute for International Studies (DIIS) Working Paper, vol. 14. Copenhagen: DIIS. At http://www.diis.dk/sw125654.asp.

Maussen, Marcel, Veit Bader, and Annelies Moors, eds. 2011. *Colonial and Post-colonial Governance of Islam Continuities and Ruptures.* Amsterdam: Amsterdam Univ. Press.

Mavelli, Luca. 2013. "Between Normalisation and Exception: The Securitisation of Islam and the Construction of the Secular Subject." *Millennium: Journal of International Studies* 41, no. 2: 159–81.

Meijer, Roel, ed. 2009a. *Global Salafism: Islam's New Religious Movement.* New York: Columbia Univ. Press.

———. 2009b. "Introduction: Genealogies of Salafism." In *Global Salafism: Islam's New Religious Movement*, edited by Roel Meijer, 1–32. London: Hurst.

Mepschen, Paul, Jan-Willem Duyvendak, and Evelien Tonkens. 2010. "Sexual Politics, Orientalism, and Multicultural Citizenship in the Netherlands." *Sociology* 44, no. 5: 962–79.

Miller, Peter, and Nikolas Rose. 1990. "Governing Economic Life." *Economy and Society* 19, no. 1: 1–31.

Moors, Annelies. 2011. "Colonial Traces? The (Post-)Colonial Governance of Islamic Dress: Gender and the Public Presence of Islam." In *The Colonial and*

Post-colonial Governance of Islam, edited by Marcel Maussen, Veit Bader, and Annelies Moors, 135–55. Amsterdam: Amsterdam Univ. Press.

Odysseos, Louiza. 2011. "Governing Dissent in the Central Kalahari Game Reserve: 'Development,' Governmentality, and Subjectification amongst Botswana's Bushmen." *Globalisations* 8, no. 4: 439–55.

Prakash, Amit. 2012. "Governance, Governmentality, and the Study of Conflicts." In *Norms and Premises of Peace Governance: Socio-cultural Commonalities and Differences in Europe and India*, edited by Janel B. Galvanek, Hans J. Giessmann, and Mir Mubashir, 50–57. Berlin: Berghof Foundation.

Price, Charles, Donald Nonini, and Erich Fox Tree. 2008. "Grounded Utopian Movements: Subjects of Neglect." *Anthropological Quarterly* 81, no. 1: 127–59.

Rose, Nikolas, Pat O'Malley, and Mariana Valverde. 2006. "Governmentality." *Annual Review of Law and Social Science* 2, no. 1: 83–104.

Seymour, Susan. 2006. "Resistance." *Anthropological Theory* 6, no. 3: 303–21.

Siebers, Hans. 2010. "The Impact of Migrant-Hostile Discourse in the Media and Politics on Racioethnic Closure in Career Development in the Netherlands." *International Sociology* 25, no. 4: 475–500.

Tuğal, Cihan. 2009. "Transforming Everyday Life: Islamism and Social Movement Theory." *Theoretical Sociology* 38, no. 5: 423–58.

Uitermark, Justus, and Amy-Jane Gielen. 2010. "Islam in the Spotlight: The Mediatisation of Politics in an Amsterdam Neighbourhood." *Urban Studies* 47, no. 6: 1325–42.

Van Zoonen, Liesbet, Farida Vis, and Sabina Mihelj. 2010. "Performing Citizenship on YouTube: Activism, Satire, and Online Debate around the Anti-Islam Video *Fitna*." *Critical Discourse Studies* 7, no. 4: 249–62.

Vliegenthart, Rens. 2007. "Framing Immigration and Integration: Facts, Parliament, Media, and Anti-Immigrant Party Support in the Netherlands." PhD diss., Vrije Universiteit Amsterdam.

4

The Construction of a Multifaceted British Islamic Identity

*Third-Generation British-Born
Bangladeshis from East London*

AMINUL HOQUE

This chapter examines the lives and multifaceted identities of six third-generation British-born Bangladeshi teenagers from Tower Hamlets, East London: Akbar, Azad, Saeed, Sanjida, Taiba, and Zeyba.[1] By adopting an ethnographic narrative approach to research, I retell some of the complex stories of these individuals to illustrate how the complexity and fluidity of identity are crucial in understanding their life experiences. I argue that they find it hard to be both British and Bangladeshi and face difficult identity choices. Many young Bangladeshis contest, reject, and reconstruct national (British) and ethnic (Bangladeshi) identity categories to make them meaningful. In many ways, they are embroiled in the common migrant story of nonbelonging. Marginalized by some sections of mainstream British society owing to ethnocultural differences, many are also excluded from the Bangladeshi community because of their adoption of a seemingly Western lifestyle. They are also dismissed by their kin when they visit Bangladesh and told that they are "British" or "Londonis." They are part of a "ping-pong generation," neither here

---

1. Pseudonyms have been used to protect the identities of the six individuals.

nor there, rejected by others around them, and not fully grasping a sense of belonging.

Taiba (age seventeen) and Zeyba (age fifteen) have painfully experienced this tension around cultural and racial exclusion and the blurred meaning of nation, home, and sense of belonging. Born and raised in Britain, possessing a commanding grasp of the mainstream British culture and language, and situated in a community where her friends and family reside and to which she affectionately refers as "home," Zeyba asks rhetorically, "I was born here. I am 100 percent British. Where is it exactly that I am supposed to go back to?" Taiba reiterates this feeling of exclusion: "I wanted to be white just so I wouldn't hear things as 'Go back to your own country, you don't belong here.'" This complex situation brings into sharp focus the question of identity or identities. Are these teenagers Bangladeshi or British or Muslim or Londoners, none of these, or a fusion of all of them? The central argument of this chapter is that this dual exclusion from both wider British society and Bangladeshi culture has forced many third-generation Bangladeshis to seek alternative religiously oriented identities. In modern geopolitics, the emergence of Islam as a powerful mobilizing entity for its followers has led to the growth of religiously oriented identities in the younger generations across the Muslim diaspora. Numerous young Bangladeshis have syncretized their Bangladeshi culture with their Western socialization in an Islamic framework. The result is the construction of a form of British Islamic identity. This "new Islam" is a strong, modern, assertive, and positive public identity and represents a critique both of Western society and of a "backward" traditional Bangladeshi culture (Kibria 2008). Enabling the subjects to identify comfortably with their multifaceted identities, British Islam challenges traditional Bangladeshi norms, values, and rituals and contests the complex notion of what it means to be British. British Islam allows many to be British, Bangladeshi, and Muslim all at the same time, thus occupying more of a sociopolitical rather than theological space in wider society. Furthermore, as a dynamic and complex postmodern identity, British Islam requires a constantly changing view of self, responding to rapid social, economic, and technological changes in modern society. British Islam is a fluid response to this crisis. It is a hybrid concept negotiating the complexities of modern society and providing its members with the voice, visibility, belonging, representation, and confidence to partake in the wider political process. It is important to note that despite the dominant media and political narrative, the vast majority of young Bangladeshis from East London are concerned with questions of social and economic justice rather than preoccupied with violent revolutions and an alternative Islamic state (DeHanas 2016).

Methodology

Although a triangulation of methods was used throughout the study (questionnaires, participant observations, focus groups), the predominant research method utilized to gather the data was an in-depth, one-on-one interview with each participant. The locations for the recorded interviews varied among youth-club settings, cafes, college canteens, family homes, community and training centers, and public parks. The interviews followed a semistructured thematic format and were predominantly conversational in tone. I attempted to enter the young interviewees' world and to view that world from their perspective. I deliberately spent much time getting to know each participant. I wanted them to feel comfortable with me. The decision to focus on the life stories of only six individuals was deliberate. My research was governed by an ethnographic inquisitive desire and a phenomenological philosophy, and the benefit of having such a small sample size was that I was able to spend much in-depth time with the participants, which allowed me to build trust and rapport as well as to gain deeper insight into and understanding of their lives, feelings, experiences, and aspirations (Denscombe 2010).

The six individuals took me on many journeys and told me many stories about themselves. They introduced me to their friends, invited me into the warmth of their homes to meet their families, and walked me through landmarks important to their identities. These landmarks included the estates where they grew up, the parks where they had their first fight, the mosques where they go to pray every Friday, the *shisha* (flavored tobacco) bars where they congregate routinely on a Saturday evening, and the battered fence they climbed to play truant from school. This humanistic approach allowed for authentic and honest conversation to take place between the participants and me. It also enabled me to capture the complexity, messiness, and fluidity of identity. Although the central question of identity guided the interviews, the themes covered within the conversations were designed with the participants' life-history narrative in mind and with a focus on areas such as childhood memories, family, and school.

One of the key findings from my multiple conversations with the participants was the centrality of Islam in their lives—whether in a political, symbolic, or spiritual guise. The remainder of this chapter explores in detail three components of this British Islamic identity. In particular, I examine why and how Islam has emerged as a political identity for many, explore some of the physical manifestations of a British Islamic identity in East London, and discuss the positive interpretation of Islam and the *hijab* (head scarf) for many young women as a triple resistance to racial exclusion from British society, internal Bangladeshi patriarchy, and wider everyday sexism. I also explore the complexity of "Britishness" and "identity" because they are crucial concepts in understanding young Bangladeshis' multifaceted identities. However, before I discuss my findings in greater detail, it is important to outline a brief overview of Islam in Britain and of the Bangladeshi community of East London because doing so will provide a useful sociopolitical context and history for the narratives and analysis that follow.

Islam in Britain: Depth, Diversity, and Controversy

There is evidence of a Muslim presence in Britain as far back as Tudor and Stuart times, from the late fifteenth century to the early eighteenth (Matar 1998, 45–49). There is a common misconception that Islam is a monolith—that there is a singular British Muslim community as opposed to plural communities. This view is erroneous. British Islam is a complex mosaic of people divided along lines of class, sect, clan, caste, ideology, levels of religiosity, and ethnonationality (Abbas 2005; Peach 2005; Lewis 2007; Modood 2010; Bowen 2014). Although an "imagined identity" links global Muslims together in a deterritorialized world (Roy 2004, 18–19), the reality is that no domestic or global *ummah* (Muslim community) exists. According to the UK census of 2011, there were 2.7 million Muslims in England and Wales (UK Office for National Statistics 2012), of which around 1.6 million were from South Asia (Sedghi 2013). Furthermore, nearly half of this Muslim population was younger than twenty-five, and 88 percent was younger than fifty (Sedghi 2013). Followed by around 5 percent of the total population, Islam was by 2012 the second-largest organized religion in Britain after Christianity (UK Office for National Statistics 2012).

It has been and continues to be difficult to be a Muslim in Britain. The construction of the Orientalist negative gaze aimed toward Muslims has intensified with the international "war on terror" waged as a backlash to the attacks on the World Trade Center in New York and the Pentagon in Washington, DC, on September 11, 2001 (9/11), the London Underground bombings on July 7, 2005 (7/7), the *Charlie Hebdo* murders in France in 2015, the terror attacks in Manchester and London in 2017, and the ongoing crisis in the Middle East. These international incidents have influenced the evolving identification of British Muslims as Muslims from particular ethnoracial groups (e.g., "Pakis") to a religious group ("Bin Ladens"), from peaceful neighbors to global threat (Marranci 2005), and from a "passive" to a "troubled" community, especially after 9/11 (Hai 2008). We have also witnessed the emergence of a "new" type of racism (Barker 1981) that has replaced skin color and race as markers of separateness with differences in the "other's" culture, way of life, and religious values (Allen 2005, 2010).

Although domestic factors such as inequality, poverty, and social cohesion are important in the question of a British Muslim identity (Institute of Race Relations 2016), the international political climate has also pushed many Muslims into siding with an imagined Islamic *ummah* against a perceived and antagonistic British state. The international geopolitical climate has fostered Islamophobia in Britain. *Islamophobia*, used as a term and as a form of unconscious—and in some cases conscious— "fear or dread" of Muslims (Abbas 2005, 11), has crept into British political and public debate. The recent Runnymede Trust report (Elahi and Khan 2017) confirms that "fear" and "dread" of Muslims have become naturalized and normalized in many segments of British society. Fear and

dread of Muslims are steeped in history as western Europe fought to prevent conversion to Islam and mounted political resistance to the powerful
Abbasid, Moghul, and Ottoman Islamic Empires (Armstrong 2004). John
Esposito (1999) argues that despite the Islamic world's many positive contributions to Western science and culture, successive western European
governments have characterized Muslims from the East as barbaric and
intolerant religious zealots.

Tahir Abbas argues that the "otherization" of Muslims—the construction and reduction of a people to be "less" than what they are (Ameli et
al. 2006)—is still prevalent today (2005, 11). For instance, much research
suggests that since 9/11 more low-level abuse has been aimed at Muslims,
who became the objects of the negative alteration of the "gaze" (Geaves
2005, 67),[2] were stared at, were called "Osama" because of their beards
(N. Ahmed 2005, 203) and "terrorist" because of their Muslim clothing
(Ansari 2005), and were spat at (Birt 2005). Much of the rhetoric that came
from racist groups after 9/11 was highly inflammatory, encouraged insult
and provocation, and employed language and images designed to foster
hatred (Allen 2005, 55–60). And violence—often fatal—toward European
Muslims has intensified in the aftermath of the *Charlie Hebdo* and Bata-
clan murders in France in 2015 (Sabin 2015). Recent statistics highlight that
hate crimes against Muslims in London rose by 70 percent in 2015, from
478 to 816, according to the Metropolitan Police (Adesina and Marocico
2015). Furthermore, in the immediate days after the London Bridge terror
attack in June 2017, figures released by the mayor of London, Sadiq Khan,
showed a fivefold increase in Islamophobic anti-Muslim hate crime (Dodd

2. The negative alteration of the "gaze" refers to a critical "gaze" from many segments
of wider mainstream British society that oversimplifies and essentializes British Muslims as a threat and as a problem. The "gaze" must be situated and contextualized within
a wider historical backdrop of power, Orientalism, and colonialism, and must also be
viewed within the prism of racism and an environment of suspicion and mistrust toward
the Muslim community. Central to the "gaze" is the question of Britishness and whether
British Muslims can claim "Britishness" and whether they have integrated or assimilated
into the British "way of life."

and Marsh 2017). In extreme cases, individuals have been killed for wearing Muslim dress (Federation of Student Islamic Societies 2014).

Geopolitics has also become entangled with the national identity question, asking British Muslims to choose whether they are British or Muslim. Among a lengthy backdrop of examples, recent controversies such as the "Trojan Horse" inquiry into the Islamification of Birmingham schools and a letter by Communities Secretary Eric Pickles in 2015 to more than a thousand Muslim leaders in Britain in which he asked them to "explain and demonstrate how faith in Islam can be part of British identity" appeared both to single out the British Muslim community for not being British enough and to blame the radicalization of youth on the British Muslim community as opposed to the Internet, social media, global geopolitics, and wider issues of social injustice (Wintour 2015). This somewhat hostile attitude toward Islam and Muslims and its tendency to associate Islam with intolerance and extremism effectively ask British Muslims yet again to decide whether they are Muslim or British by constructing these two facets of identity as oppositional and incompatible.

The Bangladeshis of East London

Against the wider sociopolitics of Islam in Britain, this chapter focuses on Bangladeshi Muslims from the London borough of Tower Hamlets, East London. Two important statistics provide a sense of perspective. First, with 32 percent of its resident population Bangladeshi (81,000) (UK Office for National Statistics 2012), the borough of Tower Hamlets has the highest global concentration of Bangladeshis (predominantly from the region of Sylhet) outside of Bangladesh itself. Second, out of the 513,000 estimated Bangladeshis living in England and Wales in 2011, 90 percent identified themselves as Muslims (Sedghi 2013), so the terms *Bangladeshi* and *Muslim* have largely become synonymous. For some of my participants, Islam plays a functional, practical, and spiritual role in their lives, and for others it plays a nominal and symbolic one. Some of them wear the *hijab*, go to the mosque, and pray routinely, whereas others lead a seemingly Westernized lifestyle and pray only during the weekly Friday prayers or during the annual fasting month (Ramadan). Some do not pray at all. Among my respondents, it is natural for Akbar and Sanjida to be both "Bangladeshi" and "Islamic" because they consider being a "Muslim" an "important" part of everyday Bangladeshi culture. Islam and the many symbols associated with the religion, such as the *hijab*, are "normal" and "important" to Zeyba, Sanjida, Saeed, and Azad. For Taiba, Islam is her "main identity," and Akbar wants to be identified as a "Muslim Bengali boy." Because the majority of third-generation Bangladeshis are born into the religion of Islam and because the practice of Islam and the heritage of many South Asian cultures have become inextricably intertwined (Storry and Childs 2002), being devoted to the religion is fairly normal and natural for this group. They are culturally Muslim.

This religious and cultural homogeneity reinforces a sense of oneness and community in Tower Hamlets. The similarity in ideology, physical attributes of skin color and dress, and habits of prayer and diet among the third-generation Bangladeshis unites them under a broad Bangladeshi Muslim culture. This is a pivotal way identities are formed. We construct our identity through a complex prism of "sameness" and "difference" (Lawler 2013). And as Kath Woodward observes, "We present ourselves to others through everyday interactions, through the way we speak and dress, marking ourselves as the same as those with whom we share an identity and different from those with whom we do not" (2004, 39). The similarities mark out the differences between "us" and "them" and contribute to the "othering" process.

The story of Sylheti emigration goes as far back as the late seventeenth century, when Sylhetis, along with people from Noahkali, Chittagong, and elsewhere, performed menial tasks as seamen (lascars) on British ships (Visram 1986). The lascars tended to slip ashore illegally when docked in either Britain or New York. Most resided in guesthouses, such as the aptly named Strangers Home located in Tower Hamlets. Sylheti migration into Britain peaked in the 1950s and 1960s through a process of "chain migration" (Desai 1963, 1–67; Begum and Eade 2005, 184)—a complex system where primary settlers brought over other men from their village and provided them with work and accommodation (Adams 1987). This explains the high concentration in London of Bangladeshis from one particular region of Bangladesh (Gardner 1998). Migration was initially by men (Davison 1964), until their families started to come over in the 1970s and 1980s.

In many ways, the Bangladeshi immigrant story in Britain is more about poverty and class than about race (Rahman 2007), although all three are inextricably interlinked. The Bangladeshi first-generation settlers in Britain were located in some of the most disadvantaged areas in Britain. They were likely to be living in inferior and overcrowded housing conditions, to have low literacy and educational achievement, and to have the poorest health, with exceptionally high rates of diabetes and heart disease. They also suffered high unemployment owing to deindustrialization and the decline of the manufacturing, textiles, and catering sectors (Tinker 1977). Nearly sixty years on, British Bangladeshis are still in a position of social and economic deprivation and alienation. Like their pioneer forefathers, many British-born, third-generation Bangladeshis occupy the lower echelons in modern society and are likely to be positioned at the bottom of the labor market. Poor social housing, low income (Babb et al. 2006, 80), poor health, high unemployment, and underachievement in education are still widespread. In 2009, 70 percent of British Bangladeshis lived in low-income households (Poverty Site 2010); in 2015, they were most likely to be in the "persistent poverty" group; and in 2013, 38.5 percent of them were eligible for free school meals, and around 33 percent were living in overcrowded housing conditions (Institute of Race Relations 2016). Although there have been recent advances in educational attainment resulting in the emergence of a professional class among young Bangladeshis (UK Department for Education 2014), they still continue to experience unequal outcomes at university and in employment (Runnymede Trust 2012). Wider systemic and structural issues centered on racism, discrimination, and Islamophobia still exist and contribute further to the cycle of poverty and deprivation.

The Construction of a British Islamic Identity

In summary, with increased hostility toward young Bangladeshi Muslims since 9/11 and 7/7, they

- Are one of the most socially and economically marginalized groups in Britain;
- Are no longer depicted as hardworking, respectful, and law-abiding but rather as a "problem group" (Alexander 2006, 258) and have become constructed as active participants in street rioting (Amin 2003);
- Have become engulfed in the global "war on terror" and viewed as potential violent terrorists;
- Have become constructed as a "threat" and an "enemy within" (Sian 2015, 184);
- Have become the target of negative media, state, and societal responses and representations depicting them as backward, oppositional, antimodern, un-British, and culturally different from mainstream society.

British-born third-generation Bangladeshis are negotiating their national, ethnic, and religious identities within this geo/sociopolitical context and grappling with the broader academic and political debate of what it means to be a "British Muslim" (Bunting 2004; Lewis 2007). Religious identities are complex and not fixed; they are fluid, multiple, hybrid, syncretic, and often contradictory. Identities are socially constructed through modalities of discourse, representation, power, and the exclusionary practice of "othering" (Hall 1996, 4; Burr 2003). The concept of the "other" was central in the stories the six participants told to me. The "non-Muslim," "the white man," "Bangladesh," "British culture," among many other categories, represented notions of otherness to the participants. Equally, a negative and racialized representation of the immigrant and Muslim "other" has also revived notions of "in"-group and "out"-group status (Hagendoorn 1993). The practice of "othering," therefore, is a complex two-way process. Stuart Hall (1996) and others, such as Michel Foucault (1980) and Judith Butler (1990), argue that it is only through the relation to the "other"—the representable, the symbolic, and the powerful—the relation to what it is not, that identity is constructed. Identities are consequently "constructed through, not outside, difference" (Hall 1996, 4).

British Islam is a postmodern identity—dynamic, fluid, diverse, open to change, and often contested by its members. Islam, for many, helps negate the complexities of identity. By definition, British Islam enables many third-generation Bangladeshis to comfortably identify with and fuse the many segments of their multifaceted identities: national, linguistic, ethnic, racial, cultural, religious, and gendered. Sanjida (age sixteen) notes that "along with my Bangladeshi heritage, my religion, Islam, is also important to me. These are two important parts of my identity. These are parts of who I am." Saeed (age nineteen) is adamant that "I am a Muslim. That is the way I view myself and the way I want others to view me as." The Swiss academic Tariq Ramadan reinforces the notion of this all-encompassing European Islamic identity, asserting that he is "Muslim by religion, Swiss by nationality, European by culture, Egyptian by memory and universalist by principle" (quoted in Lewis 2007, 143).

There are clear examples of the physical manifestation of this multifaceted and dynamic British Islamic identity in my participants' everyday practices. This iteration of Islam allows its members to take elements from their Bangladeshi, Muslim, and British-born identities and fuse them with the everyday urban traits of East Londoners. This fusion entails a skillful and complex process of what the American Islamic scholar Hamza Yusuf terms "discernment" (quoted in Lewis 2007, 36–39). Yusuf offers a notion of a multicultural Britishness, arguing that Islam allows for the expressions of local customs, so a Scottish Muslim can still enjoy haggis, albeit from halal (Islamically permissible) ingredients. The purpose of Islam is not to obliterate local customs. Homi K. Bhabha argues that many post-colonial migrants have developed a culture that is "in-between" cultures as they grapple with the inner struggles of trying to blend in with the norms and values of their new culture while maintaining the traditions and rituals of their ancestors (1996, 54). It appears that British Islam is "in between" Bangladeshi, British, and Muslim cultures as it takes the best from all its cultural influences and fuses them together.

This complex process of discernment has helped many of my participants negotiate their identities. Akbar (age nineteen) tells me how his family celebrates Christmas every year with a halal turkey; Sanjida tells me her family celebrates the New Year by going to the fireworks display at Tower Bridge each year; and Azad (age eighteen) admits to going to the "pub" to watch football (soccer) on a large-screen television and feeling comfortable drinking "Coca-Cola." Many have found a space for religious expression within their everyday lives. For example, when Saeed plays for his local football team, and the game coincides with the midafternoon daily prayers, he and some of his team pray publicly during halftime. These examples of discernment illustrate the participants' construction of a dynamic and fluid postmodern British Islamic identity. Despite physical and ideological differences, young Bangladeshis are representative of the general youth of Britain—they face uncertainty, difficulties, and a precarious future. Although many are frustrated and angry, they are not radical Islamists espousing change and violent revolutions. They are merely enmeshed in the everyday fabric of life, worrying about routine issues affecting everybody, such as rent or mortgage payments and childcare provision. They experience problems similar to those that their non-Muslim peers experience, problems connected with drugs, mental health, relationships, careers, jobs training, and sexuality. In essence, they are "normal" despite the climate of fear and moral panic generated by wider Islamophobia.

Young Bangladeshis are also part of a modern, literate, trendy, globalized, Islamically conscious, and technological—MTV, iPhone, and Facebook—generation and are actively constructing a "new Islam" for themselves. This new British Muslim religiosity acts as a bridge between tradition and modernity. It has theoretical, political, and theological credence in part owing to the influence of scholars such as Hamza Yusuf, Tariq Ramadan, and Abdul Hakim Murad, whose messages of equality, discernment, human rights, democracy, and the exertion of civil responsibility are assisting young British Muslims to come to terms with the riddle of their identity and nonbelonging. Through internal debate, self-criticism, and articulate advocacy, many young Bangladeshis are translating anger into argument and shaping the future of British Islam in East London alongside a model compatible with a Western British culture, albeit within a "halal" context. As such, they have evolved from being "migrants" to being "citizens" (Baxter 2006). A brief survey of this new British Islamic culture suggests the "complementarity" (Malik 2004a, 1) of Islam with Western concepts and lifestyle as opposed to their stark opposition. With its emphasis on banking, education, entertainment, smaller families, individualism, women's rights, engagement with media and civil society, professionalism, and dining out, British Islamic culture looks like "halal capitalism." A whole new syncretic infrastructure (banking, insurance, restaurants, tourism, fashion, social entertainment, music, bookshops, advice and advocacy, sports services, and so on) has emerged in East London catering to the personal, cultural, social, and economic needs of third- and fourth-generation British-born Bangladeshi Muslims. British articulations of Islam clearly play a pivotal and dynamic role in the lives of many young Bangladeshis. Importantly, religion helps to fill the identity void of feeling like a tourist in both the country of their birth and the country of their ancestors. Faith offers a sense of spiritual and political acceptance and belonging: "I am proud to be a Muslim. Let them call me a terrorist. I don't care," claims Saeed. The chapter turns next to this message of defiance and youthful bravado as well as to the emergence of Islam as a political identity.

The Emergence of Islam as a Political Identity

The religion of Islam has become an integral part of many young Bangladeshis' personal identities. This visible "religiosity" (Akhtar 2005, 164) has become more evident among the younger generations of British Bangladeshi Muslims, many of whom are religiously more devout and assertive of the Muslim faith than their parents. So why is there a spiritual, ideological, and practical revival of Islam in the lives of many young British Muslims? One key explanation revolves around the idea of victimhood. As a consequence of intense political scrutiny and of the public and media reaction to recent domestic and global events that depict the monolithic and Orientalist view that Muslims are anti-Western, violent, and barbaric, many British Muslims in contemporary society have developed a "victim" mentality (Marranci 2005). Madan Sarup (1994) and others (Abbas 2005;

Kibria 2008) argue that when a minority group is faced with hostility, one of its first responses is to become more insulated and display a strong collective and reactive identity to those who oppose it, which can lead some members of the group into deliberate disassociation from the host society—a form of "insulation" against the "isolation" of being the migrant "other" (N. Ahmed 2005, 194). This sense of victimhood is evident in Saeed's words: "This is a testing time for Muslims. Everybody is against us. But we will pass this test, and, *inshaAllah* [God willing], everybody will realize one day that Islam is the only truth. . . . Islam is very important for me."

One consequence of this sense of victimhood is the emergence of many who are ideologically and spiritually engaged with a revival of Islam in the sociopolitical arena—in essence, Muslims by name and identity although not by practice (Akhtar 2005) as well as Muslims who actively practice their faith through symbolic acts such as performing the daily prayer, growing a beard or wearing a *hijab*, observing Ramadan, learning Arabic, and making the annual pilgrimage to Mecca. As Stephen Castles and Mark Miller (1993) note, for some minorities living in the West, their "difference" has become a mechanism of resistance against Western ideology and culture. This feeling of persecution, victimhood, and "symbolic exclusion" (Akhtar 2005, 168) by and from mainstream society has contributed to the development of a political identity for many of the young people I spoke with. Jonathan Birt (2005) argues that many young Muslims have developed a more politicized identity and are intent on absolving Islam of the charge of inherent violence and barbaric terror. It is important to make a distinction between the political Islam that has risen within the Muslim world and the politicized Bangladeshi from Tower Hamlets. Underpinned by the radical philosophies of Islamic thinkers such as Qutb, Mawdudi, and Khomeini, Islamism has developed largely as a response to despotic regimes and an American-backed imperialism in the Islamic world and is governed by terrorist violence, military coups, and revolutions (Kepel 2003, 30–42). The politicized third-generation Bangladeshi of Tower Hamlets, in contrast, is frustrated and angry about local and global issues of marginalization and has a sense of injustice. Zeyba echoes this frustration:

ZEYBA: In the airport, they took you aside, and they had to call the manager just so that you could come through. It just made you feel like, I don't know, a different species or something.

AH: Do you think this was because you and your family were religiously dressed?

ZEYBA: Well, they didn't stop anyone else.

Saeed angrily tells me that in order to get the police to respond to a disturbance in their neighborhood, they have to lie and "say that a white boy is getting beaten up because if we say Asian they take their time in coming over." A British Islamic identity provides a vehicle for protest against people's social conditions, offering alternative programs of social and political action. Islam appeals to young Bangladeshis in that it offers structure, hope, order, stability, and confidence at a time when they feel powerless because their life chances are determined largely by external structures over which they have no control. Certainly, you can sense a high level of disillusionment in Zeyba's and Saeed's narratives.

Religion for many young people in this generation offers two incentives. The first is empowerment. Islam affords them a neutral space where race, social alienation, and poverty become less significant, allowing them to engage in a journey from the "periphery" to the "center" of British society (Malik 2004b) via a system of what Ron Geaves calls "contest" and "protest" (2005, 70). It empowers them to fight for their rights. For example, Saeed states, "I don't take shit from no one. I respect my parents and some of the older boys from my area. But Islam has given me the confidence to fight against injustice. . . . If something is wrong, then I must speak out." And Azad reaffirms this sense of empowerment by claiming that Islam has provided him with the "mental and spiritual tools" to focus on his "career, family, education, and health." This confidence has also allowed many to reclaim Britishness: "I have a right to be British," Saeed asserts. "I was born and raised here. No one can take that right away from me."

The second incentive offered by religion is a sense of belonging. In a context where Britishness and British values remain complex, exclusive, racialized, and fuzzy (Gilroy 1987; Ward 2004) and where British

Bangladeshis are also marginalized from traditional Bangladeshi culture because of their adoption of a seemingly Western lifestyle, Islam has afforded the participants in my research membership in an imagined Islamic global community—the *ummah*—in which race, nationality, citizenship, and the color of passport are ignored in a transnational global brotherhood and sisterhood of faith. Zeyba believes in this imagined community: "I don't just have three sisters. Even though they are strangers, I feel connected to the many millions of Muslims around the world. Sometimes I feel as if I have millions of brothers and sisters . . . like one big family." This imagined community of believers, however, remains an ideal. In practice, ethnic, class, and national affiliations remain a barrier to this utopian ideal of *ummah*. However, it is not the reality but rather the metaphor of the *ummah* that is attractive to its members (Malik 2004b). The ideology of *ummah* is immensely powerful and provides not only membership in a movement that is the second largest in the world and the fastest growing but also connection to fourteen hundred years of history and a romantic past (Ansari 2004, 19).

From a theoretical perspective, it can be argued that the revival of Islam for many young Bangladeshis is a direct result of years of misrecognition of their identity. Therefore, the politicization of the participants in my research is in many ways a struggle for "recognition." For many minority communities living in contemporary Western liberal multicultural societies, there is a demand for "recognition" (Taylor 1994). The Canadian philosopher Charles Taylor (1994) argues that nonrecognition or misrecognition can inflict harm and can be a form of oppression, imposing on someone a false, distorted, and reduced mode of being. Within this context, exerting a British Islamic identity should be viewed as an "equality seeking movement" (Modood 2005, x) for the participants of this study. Public space is essentially created through ongoing discursive contestation and political struggles for recognition by differing groups, especially those groups who are experiencing multiple levels of deprivation, disadvantage, and discrimination and who are therefore engaged in a struggle for social and economic justice, visibility, and representation. The claiming of an identity, therefore, is a political act: an attempt to readdress the social structure of modern society that positions young Bangladeshis at the periphery in subordinate and undesirable positions (Giddens 1984).

Ultimately, a British Islamic identity is a politicized sense of self. Members of this vibrant and dynamic social movement are governed less by a call to violent action, it seems, and more by membership in a symbolic Islam that affords them a sense of acceptance, belonging, and recognition and makes them visible in wider society. This visibility has been accelerated by many British Muslims' involvement in the antiwar movement, which has brought younger Muslims into local and national politics and social justice campaigns. Perhaps one of the most visible examples of this vibrant, confident, syncretic, and politicized British Islamic identity can be found in the stories of the three female participants in this study, all of whom put forward a dynamic, multifaceted, and positive interpretation of Islam and the *hijab*. The final part of this chapter examines the construction of a distinct gendered British Islamic identity.

The Hijabi Barbie

A distinctive new Islamic fashion industry underpins the social and political ethos of British Islamic culture, imbuing it with a positive sense of community and sisterhood. The *hijab* has become mainstream—a cool, fashionable "accessory" (Iqbal 2010) for a young and trendy generation. Catwalk models wear the *hijab* (M. Ahmed 2004); websites and blogs are dedicated to the *hijab*; and many retail outlets cater to the new Muslim woman looking for colorful and trendy clothes in a female-only environment. Take the self-labeled "Hijabi Barbies" (Fanshawe 2006). Generally, we see a fusion of Western dress, technology, and concepts with Muslim attire and etiquette. The Hijabi Barbies are young women wearing head scarves with jeans and expensive trainers or high heels, on social media and listening to their iPods, eating out in restaurants that have segregated gendered seating and do not serve alcohol. They exemplify the constant negotiation between the different layers of British, Bangladeshi, Muslim, and feminine identities. As Zeyba says, "I don't like the disgusting clothes my mum wears. I like wearing baggy jeans and baggy tops. I mainly shop in H&M. I have many colored *hijab*s to match the color of my clothes."

Sanjida (age sixteen) looks forward "to weddings. It's an excuse to dress up. . . . I don't mind wearing the head scarf. Actually, I have some really bright funky ones that match my sarees." Taiba also tells me of her *hijabi* friend Lipi, who is very religious but drives a sports car with "blacked-out" windows so that she can maintain a sense of separation from men and play loud hip-hop. They frequent *shisha* bars together, which can be considered controversial in Sylheti–Bangladeshi culture because it is a departure from the traditional behavior of Bangladeshi women and entails smoking in an arena associated with men. These examples illustrate the increased religiosity and co-creation of a trendy and modern British Islam that sometimes is in friction with more conservative understandings of the faith.

Dressed in brightly colored *hijab*, flowing skirts, and jeweled shoes, the Hijabi Barbies do not claim to be "perfect Muslims" and are much like other girls and women. They are fed up with being painted by the brush of fanaticism, extremism, and oppression and are increasingly choosing to express their identities and faith through their clothing. Zeyba illustrates this defiance: "Either we are terrorists, or we don't like Britain. Like I said earlier, I am British because I was born here, and our fathers don't beat us up . . . or force us to wear the *hijab*, and, er, I personally don't know anyone who is a terrorist. . . . I can do and be whatever I want. I am not oppressed."

These "visibly Muslim" (Tarlo 2009) women are engaged in internal self-criticism and have combined elements of religion with fashion. Modern, trendy, religiously conscious, they are negotiating their femininities within patriarchal practices (Sanghera and Thapur-Björkert 2007, 187) and constructing new syncretic meanings of what it means to be British, Bangladeshi, Muslim, and female (Contractor 2012).

Rapid social and economic generational change has taken place between the British-born females of this study and their mothers and grandmothers—for example, enhancement in educational attainment, higher literacy levels, and diversification in employment patterns. These sociopolitical changes have contributed to a more confident, vocal, visible, and politically active younger generation of women. And despite relentless negative critique emanating from many mainstream political, media, and feminist circles (see, e.g., Mernissi [1975] 2003), Islam and the symbolism of the *hijab* have also instilled a sense of visibility, sisterhood, and self-consciousness among my participants, helping them cope with the ambiguities and contradictions they experience in British society. The act of veiling as a concept therefore performs a political role—it represents a symbol of resistance and helps forge a minority identity within Western society that has constructed Muslims as the invisible "other" (Bullock 2007, 191). Whether these women are veiled or not, their position as members of an actual, imagined, and ideological British Islamic identity enables them to construct a positive minority Muslim identity in British society. A female Muslim identity evoked through the symbolism of the *hijab* has become a public expression of personal identity and must be located within the wider politics of "recognition" discussed earlier.

Young Bangladeshi women are engaged in a positive interpretation of Islam that enables them to further their gender interests and challenge traditional Bangladeshi patriarchal norms. Although gender equality remains an uncompleted and complex project, British Islam is steadily allowing women to counter the traditional image of Bangladeshi women as no more than childbearers and homemakers and to claim public spaces as gender-neutral zones. Zeyba makes this same point: "My mum always walks behind my dad whenever they go out in public. I hate that about Bangladeshi culture. It's as if us women are inferior to men. Me and my sisters are always telling my mum off for doing it. Islam teaches us that we are equal to men. My mum should learn to stand up for herself more like my sisters do with their husbands."

British Islam allows women to feel part of a local and global community of sisterhood and has countered the identity conundrum that they belong to neither a Bangladeshi ethnic community nor a British national community. For women who choose to cover themselves in a head scarf or face veil, the act of veiling has a triple significance. First, for the vast majority of these women, the *hijab* represents a spiritual journey that provides them with dignity and respect. Second, the veil has become a symbol of "resistance" and "rejection" of the West (L. Ahmed 1992, 235). And third, it enables women to resist and reject traditional patriarchal Bangladeshi cultural practices and parental regimes (El Guindi 2000; Shain 2003; Gupta 2009). Many women have, as a result, become visible in public spaces dominated by men (Mule and Barthel 1992) as well as vocal and

confident members of British society (Shain 2003)—far from the dominant Orientalist view of them as passive, docile, and subjugated.

Conclusion

British-born, third-generation Bangladeshis from East London are part
of many overlapping and interwoven discourses and narratives. They are
also part of multiple representations and social constructions. They have
been constructed as "Westernized" by their Bangladeshi elders and community, as "un-British" by many sections of the wider British society, as
"British" by fellow kin in Bangladesh, as "radicalized Muslims" by sections
of the tabloid press and the Far Right, and as welfare scammers, gangsters, hoodies, and criminals. Their dynamic identities must be viewed
within these competing sets of complex representations. Amid this identity conundrum of nonbelonging, Islam offers these young people a sense
of belonging and acceptance as they struggle against years of systemic and
institutional isolation, racism, and poverty. Islam also provides a safety
net against a Bangladeshi culture and way of life that is becoming increasingly alien and irrelevant to the everyday lives of young members of this
community. For these youth, their grandparents' and parents' country of
origin has little emotional or even cultural meaning, and its place has been
taken by religion (Parekh 2006). The struggle for the third generation in
Britain has shifted from striving for racial and ethnic equality, as the first
and second generations did, to searching for a globally oriented religious
identity (Samad 1992).

British Islam has been reclaimed as a progressive, modern, and publicly expressed identity and is a space where young people can engage in
a process of syncretism and discernment—picking and choosing different
elements and taking the best out of the multiple cultures they are a part
of. Importantly, a British Islamic identity performs a political role—membership in a fluid and dynamic Islamic identity provokes the desire for
"recognition, visibility, acknowledgement, association" and "protection"
that Cornel West refers to in his discussion of identity (1995, 15–16). As
a consequence, their multifaceted British Islamic identity continues to be

the way they identify themselves and how way they want to be identified by others.

References

Abbas, Tahir. 2005. "British South Asian Muslims: State and Multicultural Society." In *Muslim Britain: Communities under Pressure*, edited by Tahir Abbas, 3–17. London: Zed Books.

Adams, Caroline. 1987. *Across Seven Seas and Thirteen Rivers*. London: Tower Hamlets Art Project Books.

Adesina, Zack, and Oana Marocico. 2015. "Islamophobic Crime in London 'up by 70%.'" *BBC News*, Sept. 7. At http://www.bbc.co.uk/news/uk-england-london-34138127.

Ahmed, Leila. 1992. *Women and Gender in Islam: Historical Roots of a Modern Debate*. New Haven, CT: Yale Univ. Press.

Ahmed, Maria. 2004. "Islam's New Followers: How Teens and Trendies Are Being Drawn to the Muslim Faith." *Eastern Eye*, Mar. 12.

Ahmed, Nilufar. 2005. "Tower Hamlets—Insulation in Isolation." In *Muslim Britain: Communities under Pressure*, edited by Tahir Abbas, 194–207. London: Zed Books.

Akhtar, Parveen. 2005. "'Re(turn) to Religion' and Radical Islam." In *Muslim Britain: Communities under Pressure*, edited by Tahir Abbas, 164–76. London: Zed Books.

Alexander, Claire. 2006. "Imagining the Politics of BrAsian Youth." In *A Postcolonial People: South Asians in Britain*, edited by Nasreen Ali, Virinder S. Kalra, and Salman Sayyid, 258–71. London: Hurst.

Allen, Chris. 2005. "From Race to Religion: The New Face of Discrimination." In *Muslim Britain: Communities under Pressure*, edited by Tahir Abbas, 49–65. London: Zed Books.

———. 2010. *Islamophobia*. Farnham, UK: Ashgate.

Ameli, Saied R., Syed Mohammed Marandi, Sameera Ahmed, Seyfeddin Kara, and Arzu Merali. 2006. *British Muslims' Expectations of the Government: Hijab, Meaning, Identity, Otherization, and Politics: British Muslim Women*. London: Islamic Human Rights Commission.

Amin, Ash. 2003. "Unruly Strangers? The 2001 Urban Riots in Britain." *International Journal of Urban and Regional Research* 27, no. 2: 460–63.

Ansari, Humayun. 2004. *"The Infidel Within": Muslims in Britain since 1800.* London: Hurst.

———. 2005. "Attitudes to Jihad, Martyrdom, and Terrorism among British Muslims." In *Muslim Britain: Communities under Pressure*, edited by Tahir Abbas, 144–63. London: Zed Books.

Armstrong, Karen. 2004. *Islam: A Short History.* London: Phoenix.

Babb, P., H. Butcher, J. Church, and L. Zealey. 2006. *Social Trends.* No. 36. London: Office for National Statistics.

Barker, Martin. 1981. *The New Racism: Conservatives and the Ideology of the Tribe.* London: Junction.

Baxter, Kylie. 2006. "From Migrants to Citizens: Muslims in Britain 1950s–1990s." *Immigrants and Minorities: Historical Studies in Ethnicity, Migration, and Diaspora* 24, no. 2: 164–92. At http://dx.doi.org/10.1080/02619280600863663.

Begum, Halima, and John Eade. 2005. "All Quiet on the Eastern Front? Bangladeshi Reactions in Tower Hamlets." In *Muslim Britain: Communities under Pressure*, edited by Tahir Abbas, 179–93. London: Zed Books.

Bhabha, Homi K. 1996. "Culture's In-Between." In *Questions of Cultural Identity*, edited by Stuart Hall and Paul du Gay, 53–60. London: Sage.

Birt, Jonathan. 2005. "Lobbying and Marching: British Muslims and the State." In *Muslim Britain: Communities under Pressure*, edited by Tahir Abbas, 92–106. London: Zed Books.

Bowen, Innes. 2014. *Medina in Birmingham, Najaf in Brent: Inside British Islam.* London: Hurst.

Bullock, Katherine. 2007. *Rethinking Muslim Women and the Veil: Challenging Historical and Modern Stereotypes.* 2nd ed. London: International Institute of Islamic Thought.

Bunting, Madeleine. 2004. "Young, Muslim, and British." *Guardian*, Nov. 30. At https://www.theguardian.com/uk/2004/nov/30/islamandbritain.madeleinebunting.

Burr, Vivien. 2003. *Social Constructionism.* 2nd ed. Hove, UK: Routledge.

Butler, Judith. 1990. *Gender Trouble: Feminism and the Subversion of Identity.* London: Routledge Classics.

Castles, Stephen, and Mark J. Miller. 1993. *The Age of Migration: International Population Movements in the Modern World.* London: Macmillan.

Contractor, Sariyah. 2012. *Muslim Women in Britain: De-mystifying the Muslimah.* London: Routledge.

Davison, Robert B. 1964. *Commonwealth Immigrants*. Oxford: Oxford Univ. Press.

DeHanas, Daniel Nilsson. 2016. *London Youth, Religion, and Politics: Engagement and Activism from Brixton to Brick Lane*. Oxford: Oxford Univ. Press.

Denscombe, Martyn. 2010. *The Good Research Guide: For Small-Scale Social Research Projects*. 4th ed. Maidenhead, UK: Open Univ. Press.

Desai, Rashmi. 1963. *Indian Immigrants in Britain*. Oxford: Oxford Univ. Press.

Dodd, Vikram, and Sarah Marsh. 2017. "Anti-Muslim Hate Crimes Increase Fivefold since London Bridge Attacks." *Guardian*, June 7.

Elahi, Farah, and Omar Khan. 2017. *Islamophobia: Still a Challenge for Us All—A 20th Anniversary Report*. London: Runnymede Trust.

Esposito, John L. 1999. "Clash of Civilizations? Contemporary Images of Islam in the West." In *Islam, Modernism, and the West: Cultural and Political Relations at the End of the Millennium*, edited by Gemma Martin Muñoz, 94–108. London: I. B. Tauris.

Fanshawe, Simon. 2006. "The Millions of Reasons to See Islam in a New Light." *Guardian*, Nov. 15. At http://www.theguardian.com/society/2006/nov/15/comment.guardiansocietysupplement.

Federation of Student Islamic Societies (FOSIS). 2014. "FOSIS Horrified by Murder of Female Muslim Student." Press release, June 18. At http://media.fosis.org.uk/press-releases/1596-fosis-condemns-horrific-murder-of-female-muslim-student.

Foucault, Michel. 1980. *Power/Knowledge: Selected Interviews and Other Writings, 1972–1977*. Brighton, UK: Harvester Press.

Gardner, Katy. 1998. "Women and Islamic Revivalism in a Bangladeshi Community." In *Appropriating Gender: Women's Activism and Politicized Religion in South Asia*, edited by Amrita Basu and Patricia Jeffery, 203–20. London: Routledge.

Geaves, Ron. 2005. "Negotiating British Citizenship and Muslim Identity." In *Muslim Britain: Communities under Pressure*, edited by Tahir Abbas, 66–77. London: Zed Books.

Giddens, Anthony. 1984. *The Constitution of Society: Outline of the Theory of Structuration*. Berkeley: Univ. of California Press.

Gilroy, Paul. 1987. *There Ain't No Black in the Union Jack: The Cultural Politics of Race and Nation*. London: Hutchinson.

El Guindi, Fadwa. 2000. *Veil: Modesty, Privacy, and Resistance*. New York: Berg.

Gupta, Atiha Sen. 2009. *What Fatima Did*. London: Oberon Books.

Hagendoorn, Louk. 1993. "Ethnic Categorization and Outgroup Exclusion: Cultural Values and Social Stereotypes in the Construction of Ethnic Hierarchies." *Ethnic and Racial Studies* 16, no. 1: 26–51.

Hai, Yasmin. 2008. "First Person." *Guardian*, Apr. 5. At http://www.theguardian.com/lifeandstyle/2008/apr/05/familyandrelationships.family1.

Hall, Stuart. 1996. "Who Needs 'Identity'?" In *Questions of Cultural Identity*, edited by Stuart Hall and Paul du Gay, 1–17. London: Sage.

Institute of Race Relations. 2016. "Inequality, Housing, and Employment Statistics." At http://www.irr.org.uk/research/statistics/poverty/.

Iqbal, Nosheen. 2010. "Beyond the Veil." *London Evening Standard*, Nov. 5.

Kepel, Gilles. 2003. *Jihad: The Trial of Political Islam*. London: I. B. Tauris.

Kibria, Nazli. 2008. "The 'New Islam' and Bangladeshi Youth in Britain and the US." *Ethnic and Racial Studies* 31, no. 2: 243–66.

Lawler, Steph. 2013. *Identity: Sociological Perspectives*. 2nd ed. Cambridge: Polity Press.

Lewis, Philip. 2007. *Young, British, and Muslim*. London: Continuum.

Malik, Jamal. 2004a. Introduction to *Muslims in Europe: From the Margin to the Centre*, edited by Jamal Malik, 1–18. Berlin: LIT.

———, ed. 2004b. *Muslims in Europe: From the Margin to the Centre*. Berlin: LIT.

Marranci, Gabriele. 2005. "Pakistanis in Northern Ireland in the Aftermath of September 11." In *Muslim Britain: Communities under Pressure*, edited by Tahir Abbas, 222–33. London: Zed Books.

Matar, Nabil. 1998. *Islam in Britain: 1558–1685*. Cambridge: Cambridge Univ. Press.

Mernissi, Fatima. [1975] 2003. *Beyond the Veil: Male–Female Dynamics in Modern Muslim Society*. London: Saqi Books.

Modood, Tariq. 2005. Foreword to *Muslim Britain: Communities under Pressure*, edited by Tahir Abbas, viii–xii. London: Zed Books.

———. 2010. *Still Not Easy Being British: Struggles for a Multicultural Citizenship*. Stoke-on-Trent, UK: Trentham Books.

Mule, Pat, and Diane Barthel. 1992. "The Return to the Veil: Individual Autonomy vs. Social Esteem." *Sociological Forum* 7, no. 2: 323–32.

Parekh, Bhikhu. 2006. "Europe, Liberalism, and the 'Muslim Question.'" In *Multiculturalism, Muslims, and Citizenship: A European Approach*, edited by

Tariq Modood, Anna Triandafyllidou, and Ricard Zapata-Barrero, 179–203. London: Routledge.

Peach, Ceri. 2005. "Britain's Muslim Population: An Overview." In *Muslim Britain: Communities under Pressure*, edited by Tahir Abbas, 18–30. London: Zed Books.

Poverty Site. 2010. "Low Income and Ethnicity." At http://www.poverty.org.uk /06/index.shtml.

Rahman, Z. H. 2007. "We Need to Ask Difficult Questions." *East London Advertiser*, May 10.

Roy, Olivier. 2004. *Globalised Islam: The Search for a New Ummah*. London: Hurst.

Runnymede Trust. 2012. "Briefing on Ethnicity and Educational Attainment." June. At https://www.runnymedetrust.org/uploads/Parliamentary%20briefings /EducationWHdebateJune2012.pdf.

Sabin, Lamiat. 2015. "Moroccan Man Killed at Home in Front of Wife in 'Horrible Islamophobic Attack.'" *Independent*, Jan. 17. At http://www.independent .co.uk/news/world/europe/moroccan-man-in-france-killed-at-home-in-front -of-wife-by-intruder-shouting-about-islam-9985072.html.

Samad, Younas. 1992. "Book Burning and Race Relations: Political Mobilisation of Asians in Bradford." *New Community* 18, no. 4: 507–19.

Sanghera, Gurchathen, and Suruchi Thapur-Björkert. 2007. "'Because I Am Pakistani . . . and I Am Muslim . . . I Am Political'—Gendering Political Radicalism: Young Femininities in Bradford." In *Islamic Political Radicalism: A European Perspective*, edited by Tahir Abbas, 173–91. Edinburgh: Edinburgh Univ. Press.

Sarup, Madan. 1994. "Home and Identity." In *Travellers' Tales: Narratives of Home and Displacement*, edited by Jon Bird, Barry Curtis, Melinda Mash, Tim Putnam, George Robertson, and Lisa Tickner, 89–101. London: Routledge.

Sedghi, Ami. 2013. "UK Census: Religion by Age, Ethnicity, and Country of Birth." *Guardian*, May 16. At https://www.theguardian.com/news/datablog/2013/may /16/uk-census-religion-age-ethnicity-country-of-birth.

Shain, Farzana. 2003. *The Schooling and Identity of Asian Girls*. Stoke-on-Trent, UK: Trentham Books.

Sian, Katy Pal. 2015. "Spies, Surveillance, and Stakeouts: Monitoring Muslim Moves in British State Schools." *Race Ethnicity and Education* 18, no. 2: 183–201. doi:10.1080/13613324.2013.830099.

Storry, Mike, and Peter Childs, eds. 2002. *British Cultural Identities*. 2nd ed. London: Routledge.

Tarlo, Emma. 2009. *Visibly Muslim: Fashion, Politics, and Faith*. Oxford: Berg.

Taylor, Charles. 1994. "The Politics of Recognition." In *Multiculturalism: Examining the Politics of Recognition*, edited by Amy Gutmann, 25–74. Princeton, NJ: Princeton Univ. Press.

Tinker, Hugh. 1977. *The Banyan Tree: Overseas Emigrants from India, Pakistan, and Bangladesh*. Oxford: Oxford Univ. Press.

UK Department for Education. 2014. "GCSE and Equivalent Attainment by Pupil Characteristics in England, 2012/13." SFR 05/2014. At https://www.gov.uk/government/uploads/system/uploads/attachment_data/file/280689/SFR05_2014_Text_FINAL.pdf.

UK Office for National Statistics. 2012. "Religion in England and Wales 2011." At http://www.ons.gov.uk/ons/dcp171776_290510.pdf.

Visram, Rozina. 1986. *Ayahs, Lascars, and Princes: Indians in Britain, 1700–1947*. London: Pluto Press.

Ward, Paul. 2004. *Britishness since 1870*. London: Routledge.

West, Cornel. 1995. "A Matter of Life and Death." In *The Identity in Question*, edited by John Rajchman, 15–32. London: Routledge.

Wintour, Patrick. 2015. "Cameron Backs Pickles' Letter to Muslim Leaders." *Guardian*, Jan. 19. At http://www.theguardian.com/uk-news/2015/jan/19/david-cameron-backs-eric-pickles-letter-muslim-leaders.

Woodward, Kath. 2004. "Questions of Identity." In *Questioning Identity: Gender, Class, Ethnicity*, edited by Kath Woodward, 5–42. 2nd ed. London: Routledge and Open Univ. Press.

5

Scouts in Rough Terrain

Collective Strategies of Muslim Youth
in Switzerland for Coping with Exclusion

ANDREAS TUNGER-ZANETTI
and JÜRGEN ENDRES

In June 2011, the main railway station in Lucerne became the scene of a quite unusual but perhaps trailblazing event. In the station restaurant, normally the place where travelers have a cup of coffee or tea between two trains, young and middle-aged men with beards and women with head scarves and Swiss flags gathered, soon joined by private security staff with green armlets. The Association of Islamic Youth Switzerland had called for a demonstration against discrimination and Islamophobia after its search for a seminar room had ended up in a series of refusals with sometimes questionable justifications and cancellations. About one hundred Muslims from Switzerland, mostly young adolescents, answered the call. Banners were raised, saying, "No to Islamophobia and yes to tolerance," declaring that "Muslim youth belong to Switzerland," and proclaiming that showing "a lot of skin is not the liberty we want." The event had its own very special history, but various forms of boundary making, exclusion, and discrimination are—as shown in this chapter—part of the daily experiences of Muslim youth and adolescents in Switzerland.

This chapter sets out to show that open protest is only one way—and not the most frequent one—by which members of Muslim youth groups try to cope with their difficult situations in Switzerland and their ability to interact as Muslims with the non-Muslim majority of Swiss society. It highlights the wide range of activities Muslim youth groups offer as well as the functions these groups have for their members and the society. Furthermore, it discusses the different strategies employed by individuals and groups who face discrimination and marginalization owing to their religious affiliation.

This study employs as its conceptual framework the *civic social capital* approach developed by Alex Stepick and his colleagues Terry Rey and Sarah Mahler (Stepick, Rey, and Mahler 2009a; Stepick and Rey 2011). Based on the *social capital* concepts of Pierre Bourdieu (1983), James Coleman (1988), and Robert Putnam (2000), in the introduction to their collected volume *Churches and Charity in the Immigrant City* Stepick, Rey, and Mahler utilize the term *civic social capital* "largely to shift focus away from social capital's emphasis on economic benefits to individuals and towards activities that are also civil" (2009b, 14). Studying immigrant religious communities in Miami, Florida, these researchers focus "on how religious organizations enable or deter social relationships with the broader civic society" (14). To employ the concept analytically, Stepick, Rey, and Mahler, in line with previous distinctions of social capital theorists, differentiate civic social capital along forms of bonding, bridging, and linking social capital. According to them, *bonding social capital* "emerges from networks where people share perceived identity relations. It reflects social ties among people defined as socially homogeneous or similar in race, ethnicity, gender, class, and/or religion" (15). Bonding social capital provides emotional support and mutual help to likeminded people. By contrast, *bridging social capital* "ties together people who are socially different" (15)—that is, it goes beyond the limited range of likeminded and similar people. Bridging social capital is concerned "with bridging social ties that link immigrants to the broader civic society" (15). Stepick, Rey, and Mahler argue that bridging activities may "promote a sense of civic responsibility, overcome divisiveness and insularity, and encourage not only tolerance but co-operation" (15). Bridging social capital strives to achieve the common good and strengthen the larger society. *Linking social capital* establishes ties between "people who are not only different, but also unequal in power and access to resources. . . . [It] spans vertical arrangements of power, influence, wealth, and prestige" (16). Importantly, this form of civic capital links people and organizations of different levels of power. For example, a leader of a marginalized group may establish ties to spokespersons in influential pressure groups, elected politicians, and appointed officials. Linking is thus status-bridging social capital and may open doors to new resources and a secure, acknowledged place in society.

In our research, we found that bonding activities and bonding ties are predominant among the various activities and relations of Muslim youth groups, whereas bridging activities and relations are less frequent and often secondary to bonding activities. Linking activities are practically absent. Our data stem from the research project Muslim Youth Groups and Engendering Civic Social Capital in Swiss Society, conducted from January 2011 to February 2013 in the German- and French-speaking parts of Switzerland under the supervision of Professor Martin Baumann and with our colleague Samuel M. Behloul.[1] The data consist mainly of field protocols, interview transcripts, photos, screenshots from websites and social media sites, and leaflets (Endres et al. 2013). Because the Swiss case is marked by some peculiarities, it seems appropriate to start with some salient features of the Swiss "landscape" as far as Islam is concerned.

The Terrain and Its New Settlers: Rough and Inhospitable

Muslim Migration

In 1970, 16,353 individuals, or 0.26 percent of the total population, identified themselves as Muslim according to Switzerland's national census.[2]

1. Despite the number of young Muslims living in Switzerland and the public discourse on them, conspicuously no in-depth study about them and their organizations existed. Therefore, our project had an essentially exploratory character. Nonetheless, we tried to map with our sample the existing diversity in the landscape of Muslim youth groups in Switzerland (country of origin, religious orientation, geographic distribution, etc.). We conducted semistructured interviews with Muslim youth group leaders, group members, and sporadic visitors to events organized by these groups. Participant observation and observation of relevant websites and social media platforms completed our mixed methods. Unless otherwise noted, quotations from youth are from our interviews.

2. The period 1970–2000 is conveniently presented in Bovay 2004, and the most recent years are covered in Schneuwly Purdie and Tunger-Zanetti 2017. Official census

By 2014, the number had risen to some 450,000 individuals, representing 5.5 percent of the population. The increase occurred for several reasons. During the 1960s and early 1970s, the demand for workers in Switzerland encouraged young men from Turkey and Yugoslavia to join the Italian guest workers already present there. The wives and children of these workers were admitted in the 1970s and 1980s. From the 1980s on, political crisis in several Middle Eastern countries brought political refugees and victims of repression and civil wars as additional groups. The biggest single cause of the increased number of Muslims, however, was the breaking up of Yugoslavia during the 1990s and early 2000s, doubling the census figures from 152,217 in 1990 to 310,807 in 2000. During the past decade, the increase has considerably slowed and is now owing mainly to a new generation born in Switzerland.

As can be conjectured from this background, the vast majority of first-generation Muslim immigrants were and still are not very well-off. They have struggled to make a decent living for themselves and their children. Immigrants as well as the receiving Swiss society have been slow to acknowledge the fact that the future for most of these immigrants remains bound to Switzerland. Nationality figures show this clearly. In 2000, 56 percent of Muslims in Switzerland held citizenship in one of the former Yugoslavia's successor states, 20 percent in Turkey, but less than 12 percent had a Swiss passport. By 2015, the portion of Swiss citizens among Muslims living in Switzerland was rapidly approaching 40 percent.[3] Another indicator of the will to stay is the increasing number of Islamic (and other) associations founded since the 1990s. The main reason for the existence of many of these associations is the running of an estimated 260 mosques and prayer rooms with connected services (Qur'an schooling, hajj travels,

---

data can be found on the homepage of the Swiss Federal Statistical Office at http://www.bfs.admin.ch.

3. As of 2015, 34 percent of all Muslim residents in Switzerland age fifteen years and older were of Swiss nationality (Schneuwly Purdie and Tunger-Zanetti 2017, 674). The percentage of those age fourteen and younger is not surveyed but is certainly higher because parents applying for Swiss nationality usually include their minors in the procedure.

language courses, etc.). The vast majority of Swiss Muslims are Sunni. Only a minority observe Islamic precepts on a regular basis.[4]

What make the Swiss case peculiar in comparison to that of other western European countries are the political system and the incorporative regime. The Swiss naturalization rules are among some of the more restrictive in Europe (Achermann et al. 2010; Migrant Integration Policy Index 2013). Application for Swiss citizenship can be filed only after twelve years of residence, but each year of residence between the ages of ten and twenty counts for two years (i.e., is doubled). However, there is no guarantee of being approved because the application is submitted to a communal vote in most municipalities or to representative bodies in the bigger cities. This mechanism stems from the constitutional framework of direct democracy marked by frequent referendums on the most diverse facets of public interest, be it taxes, laws on waste deposal, limitation of managers' salaries, or the erection of minarets. Political parties thus profit from the opportunity of constant campaigning in their preferred playground.

Forms of Exclusion and Discrimination in the Public Sphere

One such theme of constant campaigning since the 1960s is immigration politics (Skenderovic 2007). Strict limitation of immigration and a harsh line toward foreign workers and other foreign residents have increasingly dominated the political agenda and permeated large parts of society, including leftist elements. The discourse, drawing on earlier xenophobic tendencies, was first directed against Italian and other southern European workers but subsequently included or shifted to asylum seekers (e.g., Tamils in the early 1980s) and in the recent past even to highly skilled Germans.

Religion was not a significant aspect of this issue until 2001. Certainly, "foreign" religions adhered to by old but small communities such as the Swiss Jews or imported by immigrants (Salvation Army, theosophism,

---

4. Twenty-three percent attend a service at least six times a year, and 30 percent perform prayer at least "nearly every day" (Flaugergues 2016, 9, 12).

neo-Hinduism) had faced waves of hostility in the past. The general suspicion toward Islam had grown since the Iranian Revolution in 1979 and the Rushdie affair in 1989 and was further nurtured because of the large influx of Muslims from the former Yugoslavia as a result of the Balkan wars. However, as in other western European countries, in Switzerland it was the attacks in the United States on September 11, 2001, followed by the Madrid and London bombings in 2004 and 2005 as well as by the Danish cartoon crisis in 2005 that made "Islam" a problem for many native Swiss citizens. The same people from the former Yugoslavia and Turkey with whom they had worked for years in factories or hospitals were now identified as Muslims (Behloul 2009) or Orthodox Christians, for that matter.[5]

These stimuli from outside the country met with a general crisis of Swiss identity, caused by rapid modernization, large-scale structural economic changes, and increased mobility with the concomitant breakup of social structures. One consequence of modernization and high secularization was large-scale religious illiteracy: irrespective of one's own religious affiliation, many citizens were no longer able to grasp religious phenomena in adequate categories or to recognize the internal diversity of large religious traditions and the role context plays in shaping and modifying those traditions. This form of illiteracy is not restricted to groups with low education but is common also among elite groups such as politicians and journalists.[6]

Thus, Muslims were and still are easily identified as the paradigmatic "Other": many are first-generation immigrants and still hold—as shown earlier—foreign citizenship. Although the proportions of those

5. Orthodox Christians have been facing suspicion and opposition as being part of "problematic people from the Balkans," who allegedly are inclined to drive too fast (one tabloid recurrently calls them "Balkan-Raser," or "Balkan speedsters"—because a number of drivers with a Balkan background had caused grave traffic accidents from speeding) and to use violence. Thus, anonymous perpetrators on two occasions in 2009 destroyed the poles marking the future position of a Serbian Orthodox church in Belp, canton of Bern (Ruef 2015).

6. Grace Davie ([2000] 2002) was an early observer of this phenomenon in Great Britain. On Swiss journalists, see U. Dahinden 2009.

naturalized, especially among the young generation, continues to rise rapidly, these naturalized Swiss citizens are not recognized as "really Swiss" by nationally minded fellow countrymen. Furthermore, although the vast majority of Muslims handle Islam in the same "secularized" way as most Swiss Christians handle Christianity, it is the minority of practicing Muslims who are socially visible. In the eyes of the highly secularized and religiously illiterate Swiss majority, visible religious practices are irritating. They appear to exceed the strictly private realm commonly associated with religion. At the same time, these Islamic practices do not count among the folklore-like traditional Christian rites (e.g. Corpus Christi processions) that the Swiss majority are used to seeing in public. Visibly practiced religion thus appears as a "strict" version of a religion that tends to be seen as "problematic."

As to the public and media discourse, reporting about Muslims and Islam in the Swiss media is mostly poorly informed, inadequate, and often unfair. There is little comfort in knowing that the quality of reporting about other religions is no better (U. Dahinden 2009). In the Swiss media, Islam is the most profiled among all non-Christian religions and, what is more, the one most associated with—real or hypothetical—problems and dangers. For example, the constant use of the formulaic phrase "radical Islamic Taliban" in news pieces about Afghanistan and Pakistan supports this association. Even stating that X is *not* a threat connects X with the idea of "threat" and leaves behind the possibility that others of the same group might still be a threat (cf. Lakoff and Wehling 2009). It is thus no wonder that most Muslims in Switzerland reject the general picture of Islam they find in the media and try to show themselves in a favorable light (Behloul 2012; see also Behloul, Leuenberger, and Tunger-Zanetti 2013). Poor training among spokespersons for Muslim associations in turn results in inadequate reactions to inadequate media reports and thus generates further events for reporting and helps to perpetuate the dynamics.

Damaging media reporting creates occasions for new political episodes related to Islam in Switzerland, be it spectacular moves such as the national referendum to ban minarets in 2009 or minor ones such as an interpellation in a cantonal parliament. These moves offer further occasion for reporting in the media. Conspicuously, Muslim voices are largely absent in these debates. To date, there are no members of federal and cantonal parliaments with a Muslim background. Muslim associations or umbrella organizations are aspiring to legal recognition as public corporations in several cantons but will have to go a long way for this recognition and may have to wait for changes in legislation.

All of these features of the Swiss version of direct democracy create obstacles for religious and other minorities to put down roots in Swiss society. A case in point is the lack of Islamic religious education in state schools. Such an education exists only in half a dozen districts, although cantonal legislation allows it in many more. Discussions about founding a department of Islamic theology in one of the Swiss universities have been dragging on for years, and even the newly realized state-funded Swiss Centre for Islam and Society at the University of Fribourg met with right-wing political opposition. Politicians are very reluctant to engage in projects of this type because they have nothing to gain from them and know the inertia of the political system. Although not all features of the Swiss public sphere enumerated so far stem from an anti-Muslim attitude, they combine to create a high level of structural exclusion of Muslim individuals and associations from participation in Swiss society.

Forms of Exclusion and Discrimination in the Private Sphere

In parallel to their experiences at the societal and political level, Muslims in Switzerland face various boundaries, exclusion, and discrimination at the individual level, too. Limits drawn in the public and political discourse are also drawn in the individual sphere. In their study on practices of boundary making between adolescents in Switzerland, Janine Dahinden, Kerstin Duemmler, and Joëlle Moret show that Muslims—together with people from Kosovo—form "the outgroup par excellence" (2010, 6). In a survey of Swiss youths in two cities asking what they would think if their brother or sister were to marry a foreigner, the results were quite clear: a marriage with someone coming from Kosovo or with someone with an Islamic background would be least accepted (6). The authors characterize the situation in Switzerland as having "bright boundaries" allowing for no ambiguity in membership issues vis-à-vis Muslim inhabitants

(7; see also Alba 2005). As a consequence, various forms of exclusion and discrimination based on religious affiliation are reported, ranging from difficulties in obtaining an apprenticeship or entering the labor market because of visible signs of religiosity (head scarf, Islamic forms of clothing) to daily—less obvious but nonetheless long-ranging—forms of exclusion. Some examples include:

In the summer of 2013, two Muslim girls of Somali origin were suspended from school in Heerbrugg because they wore head scarves. After the case gained media attention and was extensively reported, the responsible school commission gave in and allowed the two girls to return to school with their head scarves. The controversy only calmed down after the Swiss Federal Supreme Court ruled in 2015 that the head scarf is admissible in public schools (Schneuwly Purdie and Tunger-Zanetti 2017, 668).

In autumn the same year, in Ittigen, a suburban municipality of the Swiss capital Berne, a landlord requested a Muslim family to move out of their apartment because the mother (a convert of Swiss origin) wore a head scarf. According to the landlord, neighbors had complained about the head scarf and asked him why he had let the apartment to a Muslim family. The "friendly family" (as the landlord described them) acquiesced to the request and moved to another flat (Kammermann 2013).

Other forms of exclusion affect the sphere of leisure activities and thus an important area of life, especially for adolescents. In many public baths, the so-called burkini—a swimming costume that completely covers the body, which enables Muslim women to obey Islamic norms of clothing while swimming in public—is forbidden. The result is that some women are excluded from using the baths.

At the level of citizenship rights, even applicants meeting the very high requirements experience discrimination on religious grounds. In a well-documented case, the application process for a family of Turkish origin was purposely protracted, and the application was finally turned down because the woman wore a head scarf and her husband had been active in a local mosque (Müller 2012).

Furthermore, forms of self-imposed exclusion by Muslim youth and adolescents can be observed. This exclusion includes not playing football (soccer) in football associations (because of alcohol use and collective showering) and not participating in social events with non-Muslim friends and colleagues. Just the fact of being different (following the ritual prayers, not consuming alcohol, etc.) and being repeatedly asked to justify their choices sometimes leads to self-exclusion. Gezim, a twenty-five-year-old Swiss with a Muslim Albanian background explains: "In Switzerland, football tournaments, Grümpelturniere, as they are called, are often events where the local population comes together. Thus, there is social control there, too. As a Muslim, if you go to pray during the tournament, if you wear only long trousers and so on, you automatically attract attention. . . . Thus, the various mechanisms of pressure, which come together, make it hard to resist and stay resolute.

Gezim's short statement highlights a mechanism that can be observed among practicing young Muslims in Switzerland. The will to adhere to Islamic norms and regulations (and to do this openly) often results in irritation and alienation among their non-Muslim peers and thus can be an obstacle to social participation.

The Scouts: Muslim Youth Groups in Switzerland

According to our definition, more than one hundred Muslim youth groups exist in Switzerland. We define Muslim youth groups as those at which Muslim youth (ages fourteen to twenty-nine years) regularly gather by characterizing themselves as a "Muslim group" (e.g., in the group's name) or those whose activities are determined by their members' religious affiliation to Islam (a group of young Muslims simply playing football together would not match the criteria of our definition). Such groups can be part of the structure of a mosque association but not necessarily. Nonetheless, an overwhelming number of youth groups do belong to a mosque association. In these cases, the imam or a member delegated by the mosque association board organizes the group and leads its activities. Most of these mosque-associated youth groups—like the vast majority of mosque associations—are quite homogeneous with respect to their members' nationality, ethnicity, and language of origin.

In the past few years, a new type of Muslim youth group has appeared. This type of group is not or is only loosely attached to one of the existing mosque associations and is characterized by a heterogeneous member-ship, crossing national or ethnic characteristics. What unifies the mem-bers most is the common affiliation to Islam and the self-identification of being "Swiss Muslims" rather than "Muslims in Switzerland." Often in contrast to most of their mosque-associated counterparts, members of this type of group use one of the Swiss languages as a colloquial language during their meetings and show a high degree of self-organization and self-responsibility. These groups include Ummah—Muslim Youth of Swit-zerland, FRislam (consisting of Muslim citizens of Fribourg), the Mus-lim Students Association Zurich, and the Association of Islamic Youth Switzerland.

The activities offered to regular members or sporadic visitors by mosque-associated as well as unattached groups vary. They include reli-gious activities in the strict sense (Qur'an reading and interpretation, workshops on the life of the Prophet Muhammad, etc.) as well as forms of civic engagement (blood donations, litter cleanup, etc.) and a wide range of leisure activities (canoeing, hiking, paintball, skiing, football, etc.). Most of the leisure activities show an Islamic framing, which can include, among other things, gender separation, opportunities for prayer, and halal food. Both the religious and theological emphasis as well as the Islamic framing of essentially nonreligious leisure-time activities underline the often intended bonding character of the vast majority of the Muslim youth group activities and the social ties arising from them. In this regard, Mus-lim youth groups very much correspond to their Christian counterparts.

Bridging activities can also be observed in these groups even though they are rare. Some of the groups, for instance, try to engage in dialogue with the non-Muslim majority. They organize public lectures on Islamic topics (e.g., "The Role of Women in Islam," "Between Golden Age and Decline: A Critical Analysis of the History of Muslim Peoples"), take part in interreligious dialogue initiatives, and organize information booths on Islam in pedestrian areas. Revealingly, these opportunities for opening communication and bridging are only rarely taken advantage of by the non-Muslim majority. Information desks are often sparsely frequented, and lectures on Islamic topics organized by Muslim youth groups receive little attention from non-Muslims. Sadiq, a twenty-seven-year-old Muslim,

reports: "We want to play a part in the society of Switzerland. For this reason we participate with our youth group in charity walks, visit homes for
old people, help social institutions, or invite non-Muslim youth groups or
school classes to our mosque. . . . Unfortunately, the series of lectures in
our mosque was poorly attended."

Until now, public demonstrations against discrimination and Islamophobia are extremely rare. The question of their usefulness and strategic
value is often discussed among young Muslims. Some tend to argue that
protest rallies are counterproductive because they worsen public opinion
about Islam and Muslims in Switzerland. Others in turn highlight their
Swiss identity and their societal affiliation and claim the same rights as
all other Swiss. Remarkably, the current protests focus not only on the
situation of Muslims in Switzerland but also on the situation of Muslims
abroad—for example, in Syria and Egypt.

In parallel to activities in the "real world," Swiss Muslim youth-group
activities can also be observed on the Internet. This is especially true for
unattached Muslim youth groups, which not only maintain their own
quite professional home pages but are also active on Facebook, Twitter,
and YouTube. The Internet is used for diverse aims, mostly (1) to present
the young Muslims in the group to other young Muslims as well as to the
non-Muslim majority of Switzerland; (2) to promote and document events;
(3) to participate in and to comment on the societal and political discourse
on Islam and Muslims in Switzerland and Europe; (4) to broadcast and
comment on news from the Islamic world; (5) to spread and discuss passages from the Qur'an or the traditions of the Prophet Muhammad; and
(6) to remind their users of important religious obligations and feasts. The
Internet is sometimes used to promote a consumer boycott—for example,
against products manufactured in the Israeli-occupied territories and sold
under the label "made in Israel."

Managing Inhospitality: Functions and Strategies
of Muslim Youth Groups

On this rough and inhospitable terrain, Muslim youth groups, as actors
or networks that produce bonding social capital, have become vitally

important for their young regular members and for their sporadic visitors. This importance has a religious dimension as well as a social and societal one.

Functions

At least eight sometimes overlapping functions fulfilled by Muslim youth groups on the individual level can be distinguished. In most of these functions, except for the fifth, the bonding element is obvious.

1. Muslim youth groups offer shelter without need for explanation and justification. On top of the daily experiences of exclusion and discrimination, young Muslims in Switzerland often have to justify their religious belief and practice. In school, in sports clubs, at workplaces, they are asked why they do not go to parties, why they do not consume alcohol, why women do not have the same rights as men, why they wear the head scarf, and why they pray so frequently. In this context, Muslim youth groups gain importance for their members and visitors by offering them a protected space without exclusion and without the continuous need to justify being Muslim and therefore different. In Muslim youth groups, what separates young Muslims from the rest of society—the Muslim parts of their identity—can be practiced and lived out without comment and without being perceived as being different and exotic. These groups create an environment where young Muslims can perceive themselves as "normal" and belonging. Accordingly, a young Muslim woman of Turkish origin, Inci, age twenty-nine, describes the advantages of taking part in leisure activities organized by Muslim youth groups in the following way: "I like going to events of Muslim youth groups, like the 'snow get-together,' because there I can be as I am. I don't have to explain myself again and again. There, it is normal to pray and I don't have to withdraw from the group to pray."

Those attributes that differentiate young Muslims from their non-Muslim contemporaries and that can generate a steady challenge to their social identity and affiliation fulfill a unifying and community-building function within the context of Muslim youth groups. This function leads to an undisputed social affiliation to the community of Muslims. This function applies also to the virtual spaces Muslim youth groups maintain.

As Kai-Uwe Hugger and Ferdal Özcelik (2010) show, these virtual spaces offer their users the opportunity to construct and negotiate their identity. Here, they can find the acceptance they commonly do not get in the Swiss offline world.

2. Muslim youth groups offer their members the possibility of digesting negative encounters within Swiss majority society. Hence, they can be described as spaces for handling experiences of being different, of being excluded, and of being discriminated against. Young people who share similar experiences discuss these experiences within the groups and develop and share strategies for managing such situations and overcoming the feelings and issues they generate.

3. Young Muslims consistently find that social recognition and acceptance as well as social affiliation are refused to them or at least challenged. The more they manifest their Muslim identity (through their outward appearance or their behavior), the more frequently they are confronted with a refusal of acceptance. Thus, a shortage of social recognition is characteristic for not all but for many young Muslims in Switzerland. In this context, Muslim youth groups become important. Within such groups, religious attributes, features, and orientations that cause exclusion and nonacceptance in the outer, non-Muslim world are highly valued and result in social recognition. Criteria of exclusion, such as wearing a head scarf, become within the Muslim context criteria of inclusion and social recognition.

4. Muslim youth groups function as important places for their members to learn and to practice diverse social skills and competences. Being a member of a Muslim youth group often results in learning soft skills, such as the ability to organize events, to take on responsibility, to lobby for one's own interests, to state one's own positions, and to contribute to the group. Learning these skills is especially important for young Muslims who are incorporated only seldomly in other structures, such as sports clubs and other associations.

5. There is no doubt that the vast majority of young Muslims in Switzerland are integrated in Swiss society and interact in many forms with its non-Muslim members. School, sports clubs, professional training positions, and so on play an important role in the process of everyday

incorporation. In these spheres, however, the question of religion, of religious affiliation, is factored out. A young Muslim interviewee, twenty-five-year-old Gezim, reports:

> I'm happy to talk with anybody about my religious affiliation, with my boss and with the other employees. But I ask myself, "When is it useful?" Recently, we had a business event including dinner and wine tasting. [As a practicing Muslim,] I couldn't go. If someone asks me [for the reasons], I just say that I can't come, so I don't have to explain about the prohibition of alcohol in Islam. In public, I don't always mention my religious affiliation as reasons. . . . I have had jobs in which religion was never a topic. They don't know at all that I am a Muslim. I would not have a problem explaining or justifying it, but I don't provoke it.

In contrast, Muslim youth groups serve to encourage their members to stress their Muslim identity and to interact with the non-Muslim Swiss majority as a Muslim religious subject. Thus, the bonding social relations within Muslim youth groups also encourage religious identity and context-bridging activities by providing the necessary practical opportunities and structures as well as emotional support. This happens in many ways—for example, in the form of interreligious-dialogue events that are organized by Muslim youth groups; in the form of information booths in pedestrian areas where Muslim youths and adolescents inform non-Muslims about Islam, their groups, and the challenges of living as a practicing Muslim in Switzerland; and in the form of public protests criticizing exclusion and discrimination because of their religious affiliation. All these forms have in common the fact that they offer young Muslims the possibility to act as Muslims and hence to introduce an important part of their identity into their daily forms of interaction with non-Muslims. The bridging character of this function is clearly different from the bonding character of the other functions. Contrary to the examples studied by Stepick and his team, this function is a direct consequence of societal behavior toward the group under study. Most Muslim youth groups, especially those not connected to a mosque, feel the necessity of presenting themselves to the public in one way or the other.

6. For young Muslims wanting to practice their faith and to observe its religious commands and prohibitions, participating in youth-oriented leisure activities can be a real challenge. Not consuming alcohol, respecting Islamic "dress codes," avoiding contact with the other sex, not listening to profane music, and endeavoring to fulfill their prayer obligations are difficult to harmonize with the normality of youth culture in Switzerland. For some young Muslims, reconciling these different parts of their lives might be even impossible. As shown earlier, the inability to do so often leads to being stigmatized as different and outside of society. This challenge can result in forms of self-exclusion and the inability to live the life of a juvenile.

Here, Muslim youth groups offer alternative forms of youth leisure activities. These alternatives are often characterized by an "Islamic framing" of everyday youth activities. The activities themselves are the same as those provided in the larger society (skiing, football, hiking, etc.), but the framework differs. For example, once a year the Association of Islamic Youth Switzerland organizes a football tournament for young Muslims in Switzerland. Most of the teams participating have an Islamic background, but not all players can be described as practicing their faith. From a sporting point of view, there are nearly no differences between this tournament and a "normal," non-Muslim football tournament. The game is in the foreground, every ball is hard fought, and a cup is awarded to the winner. But there are in fact differences: every player has to wear long trousers; female visitors are invited only for the evening program; only nonalcoholic beverages are served; the food is halal; religious books are sold; a Muslim preacher delivers a sermon; Arabic *anashid* (Islamic vocal music) are presented; and the daily ritual prayers are part of the program.

Thus, bonding activities such as the football tournament described enable young Muslims to link their identity as youths with their religious identity. Furthermore, the Islamic framing of sporting and other youth activities enables them to participate in juvenile spheres of life, even those from which they would otherwise be excluded. Thus, the Islamic framing extends scopes and prevents social exclusion.

7. The high value of religious and secular knowledge has a long tradition in Islam. Mosques, as the proper places to acquire religious knowledge,

perform an important role in their children's classes: they offer classes for learning the basics of the *'ibadat* (ritual obligations) and some *ayat* (Qur'an verses) for prayer. The situation, however, becomes more difficult for adolescents because very few imams combine a thorough theological training with a sense for the questions of young people and a good knowledge of the mechanics of Swiss society. Moreover, as mentioned earlier, there is no systematic Islamic education in state schools.

All this makes Muslim youth groups a natural place for religious learning. This learning can take the form of occasional classes with one of the rare imams who is able to understand the unique position of young people. It can also take the form of a small informal study group that regularly meets for classes in Qur'an interpretation; in one case, such a group was run by a young adult who followed a German distance-learning course. A third format is the seminar, sometimes publicly advertised on websites, in newsletters, and in the social media, with prominent guest speakers taking on topics such as the life of the Prophet, the aspects of a glorious Islamic civilization, and individual conduct in life.

Typically, one question underlies almost all of these learning activities: "What does this mean for our lives as Muslims in Switzerland today?" Discussing possible approaches to the Qur'an, the sunna, the relevance of the Muslim community, as well as the implications of Islam for one's own life is a core function of Muslim youth groups.

8. Finally, the mosque-based youth groups of Bosnian and Turkish background especially offer a frame in which religion is more or less intimately tied to an ethnic or cultural tradition. Several Bosnian mosques, for example, have folklore groups for children and young people. The singing of religious songs is practiced together with nonreligious folk dance in traditional garb. Turkish groups tend to tie religious considerations to Islamic history and especially Ottoman history. The ethnic folklore is much less prominent as a feature of Albanian mosques because aspirations for an independent "Greater Albania" were based more on language than on religion. Arab mosques, in contrast, do not distinguish one specific Arab culture from (universal) Islam but rather tend to accept Arab Islam without question as the natural and correct expression of Islam.

Even if "bonding" activities and ties prevail, Muslim youth groups do have potential for bridging the gap between themselves and the non-Muslim majority of society. At least three qualifications for and features of such bridging are worth mentioning:

First, as a more or less organized entity, a Muslim youth group by its very existence expresses some commonality of interest among its members and can be addressed as a group by other groups, authorities, or the media, which would not happen to individuals. Members of the core group or a spokesperson is able to articulate the group's goals. This articulation helps to identify and distinguish different tendencies in a field otherwise difficult to read.

Second, members of Muslim youth groups are personally involved in the religion, whereas many of their coreligionists adhere to Islam only through an inherited family tradition. Apart from the experience of practicing their faith, they sometimes have considerable religious knowledge and are capable of explaining it to others. When addressing this pool of experts, society gets a more informed comment from them than from nonpracticing adherents of the tradition.

Finally, because Muslim youth groups have some self-conscious although critical views of society, they are potential partners for civic engagement. Some groups become active in this field by their own initiative, and others will probably not refuse to participate when approached by non-Muslim actors regarding issues of common interest.

Strategies

The perspective of this chapter is that of young Muslims rather than that of society. We complete our overview by distinguishing strategies for how Muslim youth groups try to cope with their situation in an often inhospitable environment.

1. *Courting or struggling for sympathy.* Young (and older) Muslims identify the negative image of Islam as a source of difficulty, so one coping strategy consists of creating and diffusing positive counterimages. Civic engagement is one form this endeavor can take: donating blood, cleaning up public space, distributing food packages among needy people in

collaboration with the social welfare office, bringing cookies into class-rooms at the end of Ramadan, and organizing a walk with elderly people. In some cases, the youth groups do not limit their target audience to those reached by direct interaction but try to enhance the positive effect of their activity by inviting the media to report on it.

Winning sympathy is also a goal of individual behavior. Staying polite in response to insults and slights, patiently answering the same questions, showing readiness to help and provide hospitality are probably needed in contexts outside the group. Such attitudes are certainly already part of family education. Nevertheless, the group reaffirms the validity of these attitudes and their basis in Islamic tradition, especially in the role model of the Prophet.

2. *Drawing boundaries with other Muslim groups.* Although unity within the Muslim community, the *ummah*, is highly valued, fundamental differences sometimes arise within it. The main boundary that can be observed runs between some organizations of the mosque-bound type and those with strong ties to the Islamic Central Council Switzerland, such as the Association of Islamic Youth Switzerland. The central dichotomy is "European" Islam versus "original" Islam. One party presents itself as "European," implying thereby that it represents an unproblematic form of Islam that fits in the Swiss context and labels the other side as "Arab." The opposing party sees itself as oriented toward "pure" and "original" Islam and criticizes Islamic cultures from a European background (e.g., the Balkans) for their local traditions. It considers them no more acceptable than a too compromising "Euro-Islam" designed to please the majority society.

However, the opposition plays a role only at the level of umbrella organizations, where real ambitions to represent as many Muslims as possible vis-à-vis the authorities are at stake. Matters are much less fixed ideologically among young people, many of whom participate in activities of both camps as long as they feel at ease. Gathering huge followings is difficult in the highly differentiated Muslim community within a country that is already segmented (three local languages, twenty-six federal states) and marked at the same time by extremely high physical mobility.

3. *Harmonizing Islam and Switzerland.* Although boundary drawing within a community under pressure is not very attractive, another

strategy seems more promising. It tries to demonstrate allegiance to the country by showing that "Islamic values" and "Swiss values" are compatible. One way of doing this is by participating in the annual Federal Day of Thanksgiving, Lent, and Prayer designated to reaffirm the cooperation between the state and religious communities for the common interest. Another way is to identify values enshrined in the Swiss Constitution with values expressed in the Qur'an or the Sunna. The youth camp organized by the group Ummah in June 2012 under the general theme "ways toward Swiss identity" offered a range of workshops treating topics such as Swiss law, Swiss history, and "cleanliness and recycling."

There can be no doubt that all but very few practicing young Muslims living in Switzerland consider religious freedom in the country sufficient to perform the essential obligations of their religion. They complain about discrimination in practice rather than in legislation, although some grievances exist there as well (e.g., the ban on minarets, the ban on slaughtering animals without prior anaesthetization, the lack of religious education in state schools, the lack of recognition of Muslim associations as public corporation).

4. *Public protest.* Speaking up against discrimination in the media is still another way of coping with this situation. The Association of Islamic Youth Switzerland chose this strategy in the example mentioned at the beginning of this chapter. It took this action after having been let down several times by contractors for its summer seminar, who canceled room agreements at the last minute. In this case, as in others, public protest can be seen as a specific reaction and contribution to public discourse. It is an option demanding considerable organizational skills as well as a firm hand in handling the controversial situation. The Association of Islamic Youth Switzerland was supported in this protest by the Islamic Central Council Switzerland, which has several native Swiss converts in key positions.

Protest or resistance can take other, more subtle forms, as in the more frequent cases wherein members of youth groups mobilize their "brothers and sisters" through social media for online votes on questions such as "Burqa ban—yes or no?" These forms as well as individual postings in online forums or participation in demonstrations are among the choices available to most Muslim youth.

5. *Information.* Finally, information should be considered. Information booths with copies of the Qur'an and brochures, open days in local mosques, public lectures about "the Muslim woman," and so on are clearly aimed at a larger public, although the response to them is generally small. Such efforts to disseminate information rarely take the (self-)critical stance of independent academic scrutiny but tend to emphasize the positive and to forget the negative. Typically, however, information is mixed into one of the other four strategies mentioned.

Conclusion and a Way Ahead

Members of Muslim youth groups in Switzerland are exploring ways to live in an environment characterized by rough terrain (structural obstacles) and often inhospitable weather (media "storms" and individual discrimination). They are learning how to make life bearable and even enjoyable by joining their forces and talents. Although such metaphors must not be strained too much, several points have become clear in our research.

Even though Muslim youth groups certainly involve only a small part of all young people with a Muslim background living in Switzerland, they are important actors for at least the larger portion of those who try to live up to most ritualistic and social obligations of their religion. As shown, their religious practices and visibility often lead to situations where their self-image as "Swiss Muslims" and their claim of being full members of Swiss society are disputed or denied. Thus, bonding activities offered by Muslim youth groups are a response to such situations. Muslim youth groups are a source of social recognition and undisputed social affiliation for Muslim young people who are confronted with various forms of stigmatization and social exclusion, building and strengthening their identity and thus providing the emotional support and solidarity that Stepick, Rey, and Mahler ascribe to bonding social capital (2009b, 15).

Aspects of bridging are not completely absent in such groups. Some groups from time to time engage in charitable activities of common public interest. Information activities and even public protest may also be categorized as bridging. Bridging becomes possible, however, only after bonding has helped to form a common ground that can serve as a bridgehead. At the same time, some groups feel that building some sort of a communicative bridge to the larger society—be it by charity or by protest—is necessary.

There is fluidity in the landscape of Muslim youth groups in Switzerland. As is typical for anything to do with youth, groups emerge and collapse, shifting their orientation and program of action. We expect this to continue for quite some time. Nevertheless, we expect Muslim youth groups to evolve into clearer and more stable profiles and to professionalize further over time. One does not need to be a prophet to assume that such groups will persist, very much like Christian and Jewish youth organizations, and become what they are already in their own view—a natural element of Swiss society.

References

Achermann, Alberto, Christin Achermann, Gianni D'Amato, Martina Kamm, and Barbara von Rütte. 2010. *Country Report: Switzerland*. Florence: European University Institute. At http://eudo-citizenship.eu/docs/CountryReports/Switzerland.pdf.

Alba, Richard. 2005. "Bright vs. Blurred Boundaries: Second-Generation Assimilation and Exclusion in France, Germany, and the United States." *Ethnic and Racial Studies* 28, no. 1: 20–49. doi:10.1080/0141987042000280003.

Behloul, Samuel-Martin. 2009. "Discours total! Le débat sur l'islam en Suisse et le positionnement de l'islam comme religion publique." In *Musulmans d'aujourd'hui: Identités plurielles en Suisse*, edited by Mallory Schneuwly Purdie, Matteo Gianni, and Magali Jenny, 53–72. Religions et modernités. Geneva: Labor et Fides.

———. 2012. "Negotiating the 'Genuine' Religion: Muslim Diaspora Communities in the Context of the Western Understanding of Religion." *Journal of Muslims in Europe* 1, no. 1: 7–26.

Behloul, Samuel-Martin, Susanne Leuenberger, and Andreas Tunger-Zanetti, eds. 2013. *Debating Islam: Negotiating Religion, Europe, and the Self.* Globaler-lokaler Islam. Bielefeld, Germany: Transcript.

Bourdieu, Pierre. 1983. "The Forms of Capital." In *Handbook of Theory and Research for the Sociology of Education*, edited by J. G. Richardson, 241–58. New York: Greenwood Press.

Bovay, Claude. 2004. "Religionslandschaft in der Schweiz: Eidgenössische Volkszählung 2000." At https://www.bfs.admin.ch/bfsstatic/dam/assets/341873/master.

Coleman, James S. 1988. "Social Capital in the Creation of Human Capital." *American Journal of Sociology* 94:95–121.

Dahinden, Janine, Kerstin Duemmler, and Joëlle Moret. 2010. "Religion und Ethnizität: Welche Praktiken, Identitäten, und Grenzziehungen? Eine Untersuchung mit jungen Erwachsenen." Schlussbericht. At http://www.snf.ch/SiteCollectionDocuments/nfp/nfp58/NFP58_Schlussbericht_Dahinden Janine.pdf.

Dahinden, Urs. 2009. "Die Darstellung von Religionen in Schweizer Massenmedien: Zusammenprall der Kulturen oder Förderung des Dialogs?" Schlussbericht. Ein Projekt im Rahmen des Nationalen Forschungsprogramms "Religionsgemeinschaften, Staat und Gesellschaft" (NFP 58). At http://www.snf.ch/SiteCollectionDocuments/nfp/nfp58/NFP58_Schlussbericht_DahindenU.pdf.

Davie, Grace. [2000] 2002. *Religion in Britain since 1945: Believing without Belonging.* Oxford: Blackwell.

Endres, Jürgen, Andreas Tunger-Zanetti, Samuel-Martin Behloul, and Martin Baumann. 2013. *Jung, muslimisch, schweizerisch: Muslimische Jugendgruppen, islamische Lebensführung, und Schweizer Gesellschaft: Forschungsbericht zum Projekt "Muslimische Jugendgruppen und Bildung von zivilgesellschaftlichem Sozialkapital in der Schweizer Gesellschaft."* Lucerne, Switzerland: Universität Luzern, Zentrum Religionsforschung.

Flaugergues, Amélie de. 2016. "Religiöse und spirituelle Praktiken und Glaubensformen in der Schweiz: Erste Ergebnisse der Erhebung zur Sprache, Religion und Kultur 2014." Statistik der Schweiz. Nauchâtel 2016. At https://www.bfs.admin.ch/bfsstatic/dam/assets/350455/master.

Hugger, Kai-Uwe, and Ferdal Özcelik. 2010. "Intraethnische Jugendgesellungen im Internet als Ressource." In *Digitale Jugendkulturen,* edited by Kai-Uwe Hugger, 119–47. Wiesbaden: Verlag für Sozialwissenschaften.

Kammermann, Tanja. 2013. "Vermieter will Familie loswerden—wegen Kopftuch." *Berner Zeitung,* Oct. 10. At http://www.bernerzeitung.ch/region/bern/Vermieter-will-Familie-loswerden-wegen-Kopftuch/story/29372535.

Lakoff, George, and Elisabeth Wehling. 2009. *Auf leisen Sohlen ins Gehirn: Politische Sprache und ihre heimliche Macht.* 2nd rev. ed. Heidelberg: Auer.

Migrant Integration Policy Index. 2013. "Switzerland." At http://www.mipex.eu /switzerland.

Müller, Martin. 2012. "Kein Pass wegen Kopftuch." *Beobachter*, Feb. 29. At http://www.beobachter.ch/justiz-behoerde/auslaender/artikel/buergerrecht _kein-pass-wegen-kopftuch/#.

Putnam, Robert D. 2000. *Bowling Alone: The Collapse and Revival of American Community*. New York: Simon & Schuster.

Ruef, Naomi. 2015. *Kirche der Heiligen Kyrill und Methodius*. Lucerne: Univ. of Lucerne. At https://www.unilu.ch/fakultaeten/ksf/institute/zentrum-religions forschung/religionen-schweiz/forschung/kuppel-tempel-minarett/gebaeude /kirche-kyrill-und-methodius/#c31980.

Schneuwly Purdie, Mallory, and Andreas Tunger-Zanetti. 2017. "Switzerland." In *Yearbook of Muslims in Europe*, vol. 9, edited by Oliver Scharbrodt, Jørgen S. Nielsen, Samim Akgönül, Ahmet Alibašıc, and Egdūnas Račius, 659–78. Leiden: Brill.

Skenderovic, Damir. 2007. "Immigration and the Radical Right in Switzerland: Ideology, Discourse, and Opportunities." *Patterns of Prejudice* 41, no. 2: 155– 76. doi:10.1080/00313220701265528.

Stepick, Alex, and Terry Rey. 2011. "Civic Social Capital: A Theory for the Relationships between Religion and Civic Engagement." In *Religionspolitik– Öffentlichkeit–Wissenschaft: Studien zur Neuformierung von Religion in der Gegenwart*, edited by Martin Baumann and Frank Neubert, 189–215. CULTuREL 1. Zurich: Pano-Verlag.

Stepick, Alex, Terry Rey, and Sarah J. Mahler, eds. 2009a. *Churches and Charity in the Immigrant City: Religion, Immigration, and Civic Engagement in Miami*. New Brunswick, NJ: Rutgers Univ. Press.

———. 2009b. "Religion, Immigration, and Civic Engagement." In *Churches and Charity in the Immigrant City: Religion, Immigration, and Civic Engagement in Miami*, edited by Alex Stepick, Terry Rey, and Sarah J. Mahler, 1–39. New Brunswick, NJ: Rutgers Univ. Press.

6 Challenging Hegemony

Voices of Dissent from the Islamic Left in Turkey

YUSUF SARFATI

Discussions on Islamic identity politics in Turkey most often focus on the Justice and Development Party (Adalet ve Kalkınma Partisi, AKP) because of the party's hegemonic position in Turkish politics in the past decade. This overemphasis on the AKP glosses over the diversity of groups with an explicit Muslim identity and gives the false impression of a univocal Islamic public sphere in Turkey. This chapter instead examines what I call the "new Islamic Left": the ideologies and practices of the Labor and Justice Platform (Emek ve Adalet Platformu, hereafter "the Platform") and Anticapitalist Muslims (Antikapitalist Müslümanlar) as alternate Islamic formations that emphasize an egalitarian, pluralist, and socially conscious Islamic politics in Turkey. These alternate Islamic movements are led by urban Muslim youth who practice resistance against AKP's hegemonic brand of Islamism and negotiate Islamic identity in novel ways in the polarized sociopolitical context of Turkey.

On the one hand, the Labor and Justice Platform and the Anticapitalist Muslims wage an intra-Islamic struggle against what they deem an interpretation of Islam corrupted by too close an engagement with state power. Thus, these groups demonstrate pockets of resistance to AKP's hegemony and construct alternate religious discourses to AKP's brand of neoliberal authoritarian Islamism. In a political climate of secular-religious tribalism and AKP's co-option of most Islamic civil society organizations, the Platform and the Anticapitalist Muslims propose alternative conceptions of morality, citizenship, and social and economic relations from an Islamic

149

perspective, showing that the Islamic public sphere in Turkey is not univocal. In this regard, these groups are constituents of a counterpublic (Fraser 1990), where Muslim youth invent counterdiscourses and formulate oppositional interpretations of their Muslim identities. The counterdiscourses formulated by these groups emphasize deliberation rather than discipline and therefore diverge from the larger Islamic sphere in Turkey (Hirschkind 2001). On the other hand, the Platform and the Anticapitalist Muslims consciously aim to create intercultural spaces where secular and religious, Turkish and Kurdish identities can be forged around common agendas, practices, and struggles.

An examination of these groups' claims, practices, and organizational structures also highlights a significant novelty in the parameters of political contestation in Turkey as it relates to Islamic politics. The Labor and Justice Platform and Anticapitalist Muslims exhibit the characteristics of new social movements (Johnston, Larana, and Gusfield 1994; Melucci 1996; della Porta and Diani 2006; Castells 2012) and thereby distinguish themselves from conventional social movements, such as the mainstream Islamist movements. Both of these grassroots organizations are composed primarily of Muslim youth, embrace horizontal forms of organization, eschew hierarchy, emphasize democratizing everyday practices, and maintain their distance from formal politics, albeit to differing degrees. In this regard, they pose a contrast with the vertically organized, formal, hierarchical movement parties contesting in elections, such as the National Outlook Movement (Milli Görüş Hareketi, MGH) and the AKP. This type of new activism indicates a transformation in Muslim identity politics in Turkey, although the extent of this transformation is thus far limited. To contextualize the political claims and organizational structures of the Platform and Anticapitalist Muslims, it is essential to briefly describe the evolution of mainstream Islamism in Turkey, particularly in the AKP period.

Ideological Background: Transformations in Mainstream Political Islam

Islamism entered Turkish politics with Necmettin Erbakan and the MGH in 1970 and became a force to be reckoned with in the 1990s with the rise of the Welfare Party (WP, Refah Partisi). The WP created pride around a Muslim identity neglected by republican secular nationalism, emphasized the significance of state-led religious education, and proposed a "new civilizational" project by reimagining an Ottomanist Golden Age. On the economic front, it emphasized the development of peripheral business interests vis-à-vis big capital and promised a "just economic order" to marginalized groups. When the WP successfully forged a coalition between a rising Islamic bourgeoisie and the urban poor around this eclectic ideology, it rose to power in 1996.

When the secular state establishment forced the WP out of office in 1997 and eventually closed down the WP and its successor, the Virtue Party (Fazilet Partisi), a reformist group backed by the Islamic bourgeoisie separated from the MGH and formed the AKP. The AKP represented a major ideological break within the MGH and fashioned itself after the conservative parties in the United States and the United Kingdom, trying to create a synthesis between universal liberal values, neoliberal economics, and Turkish Islam (Akdoğan 2006, 57; Hale and Özbudun 2011). The AKP initially secured the public support of liberal intellectuals, who would see in the AKP an ally in their fight against the illiberal secularist and nationalist tenets of Kemalism (Dagi 2006). The AKP also broke with the MGH's anti-Western foreign policy by actively pursuing Turkey's membership in the European Union (EU). The EU accession bid was instrumental for the AKP because democratization reforms would weaken the power of the military over civilians in Turkish politics. Six "harmonization packages" were passed in Parliament in 2002–4 to bring Turkish law in harmony with the EU's political democratic accountability criterion. No matter whether one described the AKP's new ideological change as the moderation of mainstream Islamism or as a turn toward post-Islamism (Bayat 2013; Dagi 2013), few doubted that the AKP represented an ideological transformation of Islamism, attempting to intermesh Islam with liberal and democratic values. Some even presented AKP-run Turkey as a successful model for weaving Islam and democracy for the Arab world (Dede 2011).

However, these optimistic analyses changed dramatically when the AKP increasingly turned toward authoritarian policies, particularly after its third term in office. The party's leadership became intolerant of legitimate oppositional voices, undermined mechanisms of democratic accountability, broke ranks with its liberal allies, brashly cultivated cronyism in state institutions, and did not refrain from cracking down on groups it deemed threatening. Hence, with the AKP sitting too long at the helm of the Turkish state, its brand of Islamic politics also became statist and lost its democratic, civic qualities.

The AKP government heavy-handedly responded to protests in Gezi Park in 2013, where the police killed eleven protesters and injured thousands. Without addressing the protestors' democratic demands regarding shrinking freedoms and restriction of urban living spaces, the government and pro-government media securitized the protests and framed the protesters as vandals, terrorists, vagabonds, and simple tools of an international conspiracy (Sarfati 2015).

In the following years, the AKP's policies significantly undermined the institution of the free press by using public institutions as a means to discipline oppositional voices. Media groups were heavily fined under bogus charges; many media critics of the AKP were fired because of government pressure on media outlets to discipline their personnel; and laws were passed to censor and monitor online social media. The AKP government also used the failed coup attempt in the summer of 2016 as a pretext to establish a state of emergency and intensify its crackdown. Since July 15, 2016, through governmental decrees the AKP has shut down 187 media outlets, jailed 130 journalists, and detained numerous civil society activists on baseless and bogus terror charges (Bağımsız Gazetecilik Platformu 2017). As a result, Turkey's Freedom of the Press score on the Freedom in the World Index deteriorated from "partly free" to "not free" (Freedom House 2015). Ten pro-Kurdish members of Parliament, including the pro-Kurdish cochairs of the Peoples' Democratic Party (Halkların Demokratik Partisi), have been jailed; ninety-seven elected mayors were removed from their posts, and trustees were appointed in their places. More than 113,000 civil servants, including 5,717 academics, were dismissed from their jobs with no recourse to appeal (İnsan Hakları Ortak Platformu 2017).

In addition to moving toward authoritarianism, AKP policies also undermined the critical and deliberative qualities of the Islamic public sphere by co-opting Islamic civil society. Many Islamic civil society

organizations and nongovernmental organizations became heavily dependent on public funds and developed rent-seeking relations with the AKP.
For instance, AKP officials would encourage groups that made bids for
public contracts to give donations to government-friendly religious foundations (Yildirim 2015). Owing to these financial arrangements, many of
these civil society organizations became mouthpieces for the AKP. Once
sources of vibrant public discussion, religious newspapers lost their critical quality by forging organic, clientelistic relations with the AKP-led
governments. In recent years, numerous Islamic civil society organizations, foundations, and associations have formed the National Will Platform, which declares a full commitment to the AKP's political ideology in
widely circulated press releases. These types of practices are reminiscent
of corporatist authoritarian regimes and strip Islamic public sphere of its
civic and democratic functions. One observer accurately maintained that
it would be more appropriate to label these organizations "civil state organizations" instead of "civil society organizations" because they have internalized the state's ideology and reflexes (Bulaç 2014). Hence, the youth-led
formations of the Islamic Left discussed in the following sections emerged
in a context where mainstream Islamism embraced illiberal and authoritarian tendencies, and most Islamic civil society was co-opted by the state.

The Labor and Justice Platform

The Labor and Justice Platform is a social justice–oriented grassroots organization formed in January 2011 after a number of meetings in December 2010 among various individuals from Islamist and leftist networks.
The group is composed primarily of young people, approximately evenly
divided between university students and employed people, although most
of the new members are university students. The members of the Platform
have regular administrative meetings once every two weeks in its main
office in Fatih, Istanbul. The group focuses primarily on labor and urban
issues and organizes actions that highlight injustices faced by underprivileged populations, such as unsecured workers and the homeless.

The Platform's initial statement of principles, written in 2011, claimed
that the group aimed "to create an intellectual and practical course that

would break the otherization between socialists and Islamists" (Emek ve Adalet Platformu 2011).[1] Although these direct references to Islamism and socialism are scrapped from the new statement of principles, updated in 2014, the Platform still defines itself as "localist" and predicates "today's societal struggles on our geography's historical and societal experiences." Thus, the group believes that a "strong struggle is built by creating a genuine connection with local dynamics and tradition" (Emek ve Adalet Platformu 2014b). Therefore, it tries to create social justice by embracing local, Muslim values without explicitly referring to "Islam" in its own foundational document. The texts of Turkish Islamic leftists, such as works by İhsan Eliaçık, Mehmet Bekaroğlu, and Hayri Kırbaşoğlu, as well as texts on Islam by Turkish socialists play a formative role in the Platform's ideological self-reference.[2]

Taking these intellectuals as sources of inspiration, group members regularly meet in various small reading groups to discuss socioreligious issues, such as Quranic exegesis, Islamic economy, and women's roles in the classical period of Islam. These discussions inform contemporary problems and current-day practices. The attempt to forge a synthesis between Muslim identity and leftist progressive politics in a deliberative setting highlights the formation of a counterpublic within the larger Islamic sphere in Turkey. These group meetings constitute an "institutionalized arena of discursive interaction" (Fraser 1990, 57), where alternative Islamic validity claims are developed, oppositional interpretations of interests are formulated, and novel cultural identities are constructed (Palczewski 2001, 166–67).

The Platform's adoption of the terms *labor*, used primarily by the Left, and *justice*, utilized mostly by the Islamists, in its name is a conscious choice that indicates a willingness to create a synthesis between Islam and the Left. In the Platform's logo, the word *labor* is written in red and the word *justice* in green, symbolizing an attempt to bring the Left closer to Islam and to pull Islamism toward the Left. The phrasing of the platform's

1. All translations are mine unless otherwise noted.
2. For a full bibliography of these texts, see Emek ve Adalet Platformu 2012a, 6–9.

motto, "Against serving the servant and exploitation" ("Kula kulluğa ve sömürüye karşı"), is also indicative of this attempted synthesis in its use of an Islamic term (i.e., being a servant to God) together with the leftist term *exploitation*. One activist defined the Labor and Justice Platform as "a space where Muslims and leftists seek answers to the questions whether they can live together and whether they can work together" (Büşra,[3] interviewed by the author, June 15, 2017). Another activist recalled how members coming from both Islamist and leftist circles engaged in an ideological self-critique:

> We are coming from a heterodox left, from a position that says the Left [in Turkey] has certain complexes on Islam and that these need to be resolved. Similarly, the Islamists [in the Platform] claimed that Islamism [in Turkey] didn't focus on labor issues, unnecessarily opposed communism, and got scared from the left. . . . Therefore, we said, "Let's experiment with this third way." . . . [We say,] "Come, whoever you are, come, but make sure to do a critique of the [intellectual] baggage you have." (Ekrem, interviewed by the author, June 2, 2017)

Although members are quite aware of this goal, some are hesitant to define the Labor and Justice Platform as the "Islamic Left." Rather, they claim that members of the platform create common cause on certain values and principles rather than on an ideology. Therefore, the group can also be seen as a pluralist organization open to people from different ideological and ideational backgrounds as long as they are willing to work on certain principles.

Along these lines, the Platform published a list of principles in 2011, which it revised in 2014 after redeliberation. According to its statement of principles, the group prioritizes "the right of labor" and claims that everyone "needs to take the right of their labor in order to live as dignified human beings" (Emek ve Adalet Platformu 2014b). Although the group

---

3. The names of the interviewees are pseudonyms unless the first and last name of the interviewee is provided. In the latter case, the first and last name are the interviewee's real name because the interviewee consented to having his or her identity disclosed.

prioritizes labor issues, it also engages with other forms of injustices, such as "the Kurdish question, gender inequality, shelter policies and ecological problems" (Emek ve Adalet Platformu 2014b). In its political protest activities, the Platform tries to provide support to (rather than claiming leadership of) the main subjects of these struggles against injustice—for example, by supporting neighborhood organizations in urban-renewal matters or women's organizations on gender issues.

The Labor and Justice Platform as a New Social Movement

The Labor and Justice Platform shows striking similarities to new social movements (NSMs) in its claim-making and organizational strategies and therefore differs significantly from the mainstream Islamist movements, such as the MGH and the AKP, which have more in common with conventional social movements.

Unlike cadre-led hierarchical structures of conventional social movements, the NSMs have a leaderless, diffused, and decentralized character (Melluci 1996, 103; della Porta and Diani 2006, 130–31; Castells 2012). The Islamist political formations in Turkey have always had a rigid hierarchical movement structure. Surrounded by party old-timers, Necmettin Erbakan and Recep Tayyip Erdoğan have been the uncontested leaders of their respective movements (MGH and the AKP), even at times when they were not able to serve formally as party leaders. In great contrast, the Platform is horizontally organized, with meetings carried out in a participatory setting and equality between participants emphasized. A secretariat composed of five active members is tasked to coordinate activities, but these members are replaced every three months to prevent the creation of a hierarchy (Emek ve Adalet Platformu 2012a, 3). Many of the political activists I interviewed claimed that the deliberative character of the decision-making processes constituted an important factor in their choice to join the Platform, giving them a sense of self-efficacy. One activist emphasized that the Platform adopts a deliberative, nonelitist view not only in its decision-making structure but also in its work with allies and communities: "For a political organization to be democratic, it needs to build an organic relationship by foregrounding solidarity and deliberation. The

Labor and Justice Platform is not the one who educates, but the one who learns; it is not the one who explains, but the one who communicates" (Bedri Soylu, interviewed by the author, May 15, 2017).

In line with its horizontal organization structure, the group defines itself as a platform, where different ideas are exchanged and deliberated. Hence, it would be inaccurate to attribute a concrete ideology to the group. As an activist claimed, "The reason we called it a platform was to define something that is loose rather than strict" (Ekrem, interviewed by the author, June 2, 2017). Another activist pointed to the similarities between the Platform and the worldwide youth uprisings in the past decade: "The spirit of the platform is similar to dynamic and horizontally organized formations that bloomed after 2010 in the world. I feel that [it is] similar to youth organizations behind the Gezi resistance, the Arab Spring, Occupy uprising, Los Indignados, and Syriza" (Bedri Soylu, interviewed by the author, May 15, 2017).

The second similarity of the Platform to NSMs is its attempts to democratize everyday practices. Rather than targeting formal institutions and seizing political power, NSMs aim to broaden participation in the civil society and democratize everyday practices (Melucci 1996, 102). Hence, the Platform's efforts aim to "challenge dominant cultural codes and create networks of shared meaning about the proper functions of society" (Melluci 1996; cf. Wiktorowicz 2004, 16) rather than to capture state power as mainstream Islamist movements have historically aimed to do.

Accordingly, the group organizes various events in which it puts its pluralist and justice-oriented interpretation of Islam into practice. During the month of Ramadan in 2011, the Platform planned simple *iftar*s,[4] where participants sat on the ground and shared food in front of luxury hotels in order to protest against the expensive *iftar*s held in these hotels by conservative elites. According to the group members, the elites' fast-breaking dinners represented the objectification and corruption of Ramadan and turned the holiday into a wasteful indulgence (Emek ve Adalet Platformu 2012b). As one of the platform members put it, "We don't want Ramadan

---

4. *Iftar* is the meal with which Muslims break their fast at sunset.

tents to become cultural events reproducing poverty" (Saim 2012, 16). One of the creative banners written during the *iftar* stated: "Fasting violates capitalism, and capitalism violates fasting" ("Oruç kapitalizmi, kapitalizm de orucu bozar"). This statement indicated that fasting and breaking the fast were to be treated as spiritual practices, where one engages in a struggle with one's will (*nefs*) and reforms oneself in one's relations with nature and with others (Cizreli 2012). This view is in sharp tension with the increased food prices during Ramadan, the limitless consumption promoted in *iftar*s held in restaurants, and the profit-seeking logic of capitalism that instrumentalizes religious holidays.

In the following year, the Platform continued to target these luxury venues by hosting fast-breaking events for various underprivileged populations, such as minimum-wage workers, African immigrants, and homeless people (Emek ve Adalet Platformu 2012b). Above all, these *iftar*s aimed to create a democratic, egalitarian praxis among participants and to erode social boundaries between different social strata.

The Platform also aims to form linkages with lower classes by other means. For instance, during one Ramadan Platform members went to a factory with Ihsan Eliaçık, a famous religious scholar close to the group, in order to break the fast together with the workers. One of the activists recalled this visit: "One of our foot [*sic*] is in these social things. . . . We took Ihsan Hoca[5] to a factory during a Ramadan and broke fast together . . . [then] you bring someone there who speaks their language. Ihsan Hoca talks to them, this and that. . . . [The workers say,] 'Let him lead us in prayer'" (Ekrem, interviewed by the author, June 2, 2017).

Similarly, when Platform members supported the resistance organized by workers of the Teksim company, they tried to create organic ties with them—for instance, by providing tutoring to the workers' children and holding sales with the workers' families (Yalçın 2015, 16). One of the activists called these efforts "beautiful and truthful work . . . work that touched the workers, where we stood by them" (Yalçın 2015, 16).

---

5. The word *hoca* refers to a religious teacher or someone learned in religion.

The Platform's Critique of the AKP's Neoliberal Authoritarian Islamism

The challenge that the Platform poses to the AKP's hegemony in religious discourse became more pronounced during several political developments in recent years, when platform members opposed the AKP's neoliberalism from a Muslim perspective. The Gezi Park protests, arguably the most significant political upheaval in modern Turkey, was a watershed political event, where the Platform strongly criticized the AKP-led government. During the protests, the Platform organized a deliberation in the Istanbul headquarters of Mazlum-Der, Turkey's oldest Islamic human rights organization, and issued a press statement with signatures from influential Islamist intellectuals, including Halil Ibrahim Yenigün, Ali Bulaç, Fatma Akdokur, Yıldız Ramazanoğlu, Ahmet Faruk Ünsal, and Cihan Aktaş, condemning the government's policies and reaction to the protesters. The statement indicated that the plans to build a mall in Taksim Gezi Park stemmed from "perceiving the city as a source of rent." Moreover, "urban transformation does not improve the urban poor's and other urban residents' lives; to the contrary, it makes them furious" (*T24 Bağımsız İnternet Gazetesi* 2013). This statement highlighted the grievances shared by many Gezi protesters that neoliberal urban projects implemented by Istanbul's municipality without resident input would transform the urban space and shrink livable spaces and therefore should be considered unjust. It suggested that a just, lasting, and by extension democratic urban transformation was possible only by incorporating urban residents, in particular the urban poor, in the decision-making structures (*T24 Bağımsız İnternet Gazetesi* 2013). The signatories also criticized President Erdoğan's exclusionary, polarizing, and threatening language toward mainly secular protesters: "If we want to reform the city, we should not forget that we cannot achieve it by obliterating, banishing, belittling, but by sitting in people's tables who are not like us, by instituting justice, by respecting their life cultures. Let's remember that prophets went to everyone with nice words. If we don't attend to other people's rights, how can we think that Islam guides our morality?" (*T24 Bağımsız İnternet Gazetesi* 2013). Although the public statement also recognized the oppression faced by Islamic circles in Turkey, particularly during the February 28th Process, it condemned the AKP government for using this past as a pretext to crack down on and vilify the opposition: "To be victims in the past does not require us to become oppressors today or to side with the oppressor" (*T24 Bağımsız İnternet Gazetesi* 2013).

The Soma coal mine disaster, which led to the death of 301 miners in May 2014, constituted another watershed event when the AKP government's policies were harshly criticized by the Platform. Worker safety and workers' health constitute an issue on which the group has always been active. For instance, the Platform participates in "conscience and justice watches" held on the first Sunday of each month, highlighting the victims of work accidents and demanding the passage of legislation outlining tighter safety measures for workers and better enforcement regulations. After the Soma disaster, the June meeting was dedicated to the Soma victims and included the Respect [for Victims] and Rage against Those Who Are Responsible March. A Platform member also held the government's neoliberal economic policies responsible for the "destruction in the mining and construction sectors" (Altıntaş 2014). This member also stated that the Soma Corporation, the owner of the Soma mines, was able to significantly decrease the cost of coal extraction by cutting work-safety measures as a direct result of neoliberal government policies (Altıntaş 2014).

The Platform also deliberately frames work-related deaths as "work murders" instead of "work accidents." In its words, "Believing in God's fate (and knowing that workers' deaths cannot be pushed one day earlier or later) doesn't prevent us from damning the responsible ones and seeing this as a problem of political understanding" (Emek ve Adalet Platformu 2014a). This view is sharply contrasted to Erdoğan's religious framing of worker deaths as "fate" on multiple occasions and of the Soma disaster as part of the mining sector's "nature." One of the younger Platform members stated how Soma was the tipping point for him to decide to join the Labor and Justice Platform: "The Soma event was a big breaking point for me. After the Soma event, I realized that engaging in organized struggle was very important" (Samet, interviewed by the author, June 15, 2017).

Another line of critique directed toward the AKP is the way the party's actions in government have affected the image of Islamism in particular and Muslim identity in general. Although the Labor and Justice Platform does not define itself as Islamist, many members joined the group from Islamist circles, and it is these members who are the biggest critics of the AKP on this issue. As one political activist stated,

> Islamists who acquired or bear the hope to find a position in media, in bureaucracy, in associations or Islamists who—while avoiding any status—tied their fate to these Islamists through friend circles and prioritize their friends' sake to truth and justice became the agents of a disastrous corruption. Unfortunately, Islamism, which was a call to morals and justice, is turned to a ruthless instrument of tyranny by these carriers and proponents. People, who revolt against oppression and raise the voice of dignity, came to a point where they cannot think of Islam as independent from the corrupt language of the powerful. (Kızılkaya 2014)

Here, Sinan Kızılkaya points to the increasing patronage relations formed between AKP governments and Islamic business circles, civil society organizations, and media outlets. Although Islamic business organizations and the flourishing Islamic civil society organizations were key drivers of Turkey's democratization in the 1990s and early 2000s, especially during early AKP governments, these organizations eventually became dependent on state funds, developed clientelistic relations with the government, were co-opted by the governing party, and lost their autonomous, civic qualities (Sarfati 2017). Similarly, Islamic media organizations became AKP mouthpieces through corporate and personal relations, thereby losing their independent, critical qualities. In this political atmosphere, where an Islamist government became increasingly authoritarian and its actions were legitimized by most Islamic social actors, Islamism became "a cursed identity," according to one activist (Serdar, interviewed by the author, May 23, 2017).

Another activist explained how the AKP's corrupt practices undermined the appeal of Islam to the youth: "Particularly this theft issue, the issue of not standing trial after [the events of] December 17–25 alienated a segment of Turkish people from religion. There are youth who do not have any relation to Muslimhood" (Suat Yalçın, interviewed by the author, June 5, 2017).

Anticapitalist Muslims

The organization Anticapitalist Muslims was formed in 2012 by a group of young activists who were gathered around İnşa Cultural House (İnşa Kültür Evi), a nonprofit cultural center run by İhsan Eliaçık, a central figure in the group's ideological evolution. Mostly youngsters, the organization's members come together each week to read passages from the Qur'an and to discuss how these readings can inform contemporary socioeconomic conditions. Unlike the Labor and Justice Platform, Anticapitalist Muslims has a marked ideology, which weaves a radical, antisystemic critique of neoliberal capitalism with an Islamic worldview. Anticapitalist Muslims claim that their "Muslim" identity is an eternal and universal one, while their antagonism toward capitalism is "a historical [contingent] emphasis" because "capitalism is the name of our epoch's dominant system," and that "each prophetic message opposed the dominant system in its own epoch" (Antikapitalist Müslümanlar 2012).

Accordingly, the group's manifesto (Antikapitalist Müslümanlar 2012) provides a critique of capitalist relations that is grounded in different verses from the Qur'an. For instance, based on the verse "And that human has only that for which he labors [strives for]" (Al-Najm 39), it claims that "value is [created in] the space where God's blessing [*nimet*] interacts with labor." Therefore, "the right to property is seen not as a freedom but as an instrument to create hegemony and authority." Evoking a Marxist analysis of superstructure, the group claims that property owners have been using "unjust laws to perpetuate their wealth and power." This system leads to accumulation of wealth in the hands of few, which contradicts the verse "It [the state] should not become a fortune circulating among the rich among you" (Al-Hashr 7). The group envisions a socialist, classless, and sharing society where the oppressed become equal to the rulers. These claims are justified by the citation of the verse "We want to make those who are oppressed the leaders in this world" (Al-Qasas 5).

The group's strong emphasis on economic and social equality confronts the AKP's neoliberal vision. Although the Anticapitalist Muslims' manifesto does not directly mention the AKP by name, it directly targets the party's practices in the following passage, where it calls on everyone

> to say no to those who perform ablution to capitalism, who do not change the behavior of the state but make their own behavior statist, who do not create an alternative political-economic system but include themselves in the current exploitative financial class, who compete to accumulate wealth through using public privileges, who follow personal desires under the cloak of religiosity and conservatism. (Antikapitalist Müslümanlar 2012)

The passage poses a fundamental critique of the AKP's attempts to merge its constituents' Muslim identities with a statist, neoliberal worldview. In particular, Anticapitalist Muslims highlights the degeneration of Islam's image under AKP rule as patronage politics, corruption, and bribery became more prevalent not only among party members but also among conservative businesspersons and Islamic circles, which advocated for clean politics in the past. Anticapitalist Muslims claims that the profit motive and proximity to power corrupts not only these economic and political figures but also the image of the religion they claim to represent.

Beyond its ideological claims, Anticapitalist Muslims also engages in protest activities to challenge the AKP's hegemonic version of neoliberal Islamic politics. The group's participation in the May Day celebrations in 2012 was a conscious attempt to become visible to the larger society. Close to a thousand supporters participated in an in absentia, symbolic funeral prayer in Fatih mosque for workers who had lost their lives in work accidents, and then they joined other leftist groups in Taksim for the main gathering. After gaining some traction in mainstream circles because of its participation in the May Day celebrations, Anticapitalist Muslims also protested against highway privatization bids by Ulker, one of the most well-known Islamic corporations in Turkey, and supported Kurdish prisoners who went on a hunger strike to protest against prison conditions (Birelma 2013, 64–65).

The group's active participation in the Gezi Park protests of 2013 is also worthy of mention. Anticapitalist Muslims was the Gezi Park protest movement's most visible constituent group with an explicit religious identity.[6] The group protested over the Istanbul municipality's plans to raze the park, raising a banner stating "Property Belongs to God, Capital Get Out" ("Mülk Allahındır, Sermaye Defol"). According to group members, this slogan indicated that Gezi Park belonged to all Istanbul residents, to all God's creatures and animals, to all humanity, and to nature's order and therefore could not be converted to a mall serving the rich (Birelma 2013, 67–68). During the uprising, the group undertook Islamic practices of solidarity, such as distributing savory rolls covered with sesame to other protesters during Lailat Miraj (Miraç Kandili). By raising a banner that read "Holy Nights Are Times of Unification, Equality, and Solidarity for Nations" ("Kandiller Halkların Birlik, Eşitlik, Dayanışma Günleridir"), Anticapitalist Muslims also publicized a message of ethnic peace and socioeconomic solidarity through religious symbolism (Birelma 2013, 70).

Anticapitalist Muslims as a New Social Movement

Anticapitalist Muslims possesses the characteristics of an NSM in its claims and organizational strategies and therefore diverges from mainstream Islamism in Turkey. Similar to the Platform, Anticapitalist Muslims has a horizontal organization, and group members are cognizant of the dangers of organizational hierarchy and leadership cult. Therefore, they embrace the concept of "responsibility consciousness among equals" as an organizational logic and make decisions through *shura*, in which group members participate directly (Antikapitalist Müslümanlar 2013). In addition, the group has adopted a rotating-leadership structure,

6. Although other Islamic groups also participated in or supported the Gezi Park protests, Anticapitalist Muslims' participation was much more persistent and visible compared to that of other groups.

designating four spokespersons, who serve as the representatives of the group and are replaced every six months (Birelma 2013, 75).

Group members are so wary about hierarchy that the group issued an official declaration stating that İhsan Eliaçık is not the group's representative when media outlets cast him as its leader because of his seniority and popularity in certain intellectual circles (Antikapitalist Müslümanlar 2013). Such a response reveals that the group is skeptical of representative, elitist forms of democracy and has adopted as its operative organizational logic a form of participatory democracy, where deliberation and equality are highly valued (Barber 1984; Habermas 1994). The skepticism toward organizational hierarchy and state authority among the predominantly young members of both Anticapitalist Muslims and the Labor and Justice Platform can also be seen as an indication of a more general intergenerational value shift—namely, a movement toward postmaterial values among the youth in postindustrial urban settings (Inglehart 1995, 2006).

Similar to the Platform and other NSMs, Anticapitalist Muslims aims primarily to change informal, societal, or normative practices rather than to engage with formal politics. Anticapitalist Muslims threw simple potluck-type *iftars* called "earth tables" (*yeryüzü sofraları*) during the Gezi Park protests in 2013, fashioning them after the *iftar* dinners first organized by the Labor and Justice Platform. Earth tables were attended by more than ten thousand people (Doğan 2013, 311–12) and were continued in subsequent years. In these potluck-type *iftars*, attendees sat on the ground cross-legged and shared the food they brought from home with each other, utilizing used newspapers as tablecloths. These simple, egalitarian dinners posed a stark contrast to the formal fast-breaking dinners AKP officials and Islamic bourgeoisie threw during Ramadan. As Sedat Doğan, one of the group members, wrote:

> If you tell a government or a CEO that 10,000 people will break fast in Taksim and ask how we can do this, the first thing that would come to their mind is to find a sponsor. They would line up people, pacify them, and make them look dependent to a sovereign. In earth tables in Taksim, none of these happened. Everyone set up a pluralistic table with no sponsor, no flag, and no protocol and shared their food. People

from different faiths and cultures, those who fast and those who don't, contributed to that table and became the table's subjects. Isn't it this type of brotherhood that we search for on earth? If 10,000 people can share with each other their livelihoods, and if no one stays hungry, then these people can also govern their localities together and can produce and share together in their workplaces. (2013, 311–12)

This type of democratic praxis, to which participants actively contribute and in which their status is equal, contrasts with elitist, capitalistic constellations that reduce participants to passive objects. One activist claimed that the practice of sitting cross-legged, eating on the ground, and sharing food from the same pot is part of Anatolian cultural mores and that the earth tables thus revive local Anatolian practices in a highly urbanized setting (Anticapitalist Muslims group member, quoted in İplikçi 2013, 336).

Anticapitalist Muslims has organized these potluck dinners every Ramadan since 2013, on different days and in multiple locations. They take place on streets and public spaces, showing that "streets, as spaces of flow and movements, are not only where people express grievances, but also where they forge identities, enlarge solidarities, and *extend* their protest beyond their immediate circles to include the unknown, the strangers" (Bayat 2010, 12, emphasis in original). These *iftar*s brought together individuals from secular and religious segments of the society and therefore led each group to learn from each other's habitus (Göle 2013). The softening of boundaries between two segments of Turkish society that have been antagonistic creates a democratizing and reconciliatory effect on the ground, particularly in a Turkish sociopolitical climate that cultivates polarizing and binary categories along a religious-secular divide. Passersby are also invited to attend these communal public events. The street thereby serves as "a medium through which strangers or casual passersby are able to establish latent communication with one another by recognizing their mutual interests and shared sentiments" (Bayat 2010, 12).

Finally, similar to contemporary social movements elsewhere, the discourse of Anticapitalist Muslims emphasizes a crisis of the conventional channels of political participation, such as the Parliament and political parties (Offe 1987). While Anticapitalist Muslims is critical of the AKP and the mainstream Islamists in Turkey, its members do not support any other formal political parties and have a skeptical attitude toward formal political institutions in general. In this regard, Anticapitalist Muslims differs from the Labor and Justice Platform in that the latter group does not categorically reject working with political parties. This approach was particularly visible when the Platform actively worked for the People's Voice Party (Halkın Sesi Partisi) during the electoral campaign of 2011, which many members thought was a genuine political opportunity for carving a space for the Islamic Left in mainstream Turkish politics. One young member of Anticapitalist Muslims explained the group's skepticism toward formal politics:

> CHP [Cumhuriyet Halk Partisi (Republican People's Party), the main opposition], AKP, they are all the same. The parties of the system. I don't believe in the legitimacy of the government, whomever it belongs to. In the last twenty years, the relationship between state and capital is very clear. The national [secular] segment also fostered its own capital. They represented the conflict between their capitals as the conflict between conservatives and seculars. In this regard, Anticapitalist Muslims have a reading outside of the system. They have a reading that is outside what is represented to us. (quoted in İplikçi 2013, 241)

In line with this statement, Anticapitalist Muslims refrain from supporting parties or candidates in local and national elections but rather engage in social activities, such as supporting worker strikes or demanding better rights for seasonal workers through awareness raising.

Conclusion

Three general observations can be made from the discussion of these two Islamic youth grassroots movements on the left. First, these groups represent a potential sociological rift within Islamism in Turkey. From a sociological perspective, the demands made by the Labor and Justice Platform and Anticapitalist Muslims expose a rift in the cross-class alliance the AKP has forged between the urban poor and the Muslim middle classes. Both of these grassroots organizations maintain and propagate that the dominance of neoliberal policies during AKP rule has undermined economically underprivileged populations in Turkey, including the urban poor, in favor of the Muslim bourgeoisie. The political success of these grassroots movements depends on their ability to link with this underprivileged constituency, to convince the urban poor of the truth of their messages, and to detach them from the AKP's political orbit. So far the popular appeal of these groups seems to be rather limited. This is particularly the case in the past few years, in which the AKP has been successful in polarizing Turkish society and consolidating its base of support among Muslims by painting all dissent against itself in populist, conspiratorial terms.

Second, both the Labor and Justice Platform and Anticapitalist Muslims' political claims, movement structures, and political praxis are similar to those of new social movements, and thereby these groups distinguish themselves from mainstream Islamist movements. Both of these grassroots groups are composed primarily of urban Muslim youth, organize themselves in horizontal, egalitarian structures, are critical of any hierarchy, engage in democratizing everyday practices, and maintain a distance, albeit to differing degrees, from formal politics and state power. In this regard, they pose a significant contrast with the vertically organized, hierarchical Islamist organizations of the MGH and the AKP, which see electoral politics as the most important legitimizing political arena. In stark contrast to the AKP's emphasis on representative, majoritarian democracy, the Platform and Anticapitalist Muslims embrace participatory and deliberative views of democracy with an emphasis on a radical understanding of equality.

Finally, the new discourse created by these two urban Muslim youth-based movements demonstrates that there are voices in the Islamic public sphere that consciously challenge the AKP's form of neoliberal Islamic authoritarianism, even in the face of the party's apparent hegemony in Islamic politics in Turkey and its success in co-opting many formerly autonomous Islamic civil society organizations for its project. Despite growing pessimism about an increasingly univocal Islamic public sphere in the past years in Turkey, groups that embrace a more egalitarian view of Islamic sociopolitics are emerging. The Platform and Anticapitalist

Muslims not only critique the AKP's form of Islamic identity politics but also create parallel discursive spaces where group members engage in new interpretations of religious texts and translate them into praxis and resistance. The creation of these alternative religiopolitical interpretations is not limited to the two movements discussed here. The Right Initiative (Hak İnsiyatifi), a human rights advocacy group that documents the AKP governments' human rights abuses; *Reçel*, an Islamic feminist blog that highlights the struggles of pious women in Turkey; and the Muslim Initiative against Violence against Women (Kadına Karşı Şiddete Karşı Müslümanlar İnsiyatifi), a Muslim women's rights group fighting violence against women within the Islamic community, are all groups that act together with the Labor and Justice Platform and Anticapitalist Muslims as part of a counterpublic, where independent, oppositional, feminist, and liberatory interpretations of Islam are created. These organizations' work shows that the Islamic public sphere cannot be reduced to the claims made by dominant religious actors.

References

Akdoğan, Yalçın. 2006. "The Meaning of Conservative Democratic Identity." In *The Emergence of a New Turkey Democracy and the AK Parti*, edited by Hakan Yavuz, 49–65. Salt Lake City: Univ. of Utah Press.

Altıntaş, Ali. 2014. "Madencilik kader olamaz" [Mining Cannot Be Fate]. In Emek ve Adalet Platformu, *Başucu yazıları* [Bedside Writings]. Istanbul: Emek ve Adalet Platformu. At http://www.emekveadalet.org/wp-content /uploads/bas-ucu-yazilari.pdf.

Antikapitalist Müslümanlar. 2012. "Antikapitalist Müslümanlar manifestosu" [Manifesto of Anticapitalist Muslims]. At http://www.antikapitalistmus lumanlar.org/manifesto.htm.

———. 2013. "Antikapitalist Müslümanlardan basına ve kamuoyuna duyurudur" [Announcement to the Press and the Public by Anticapitalist Muslims]. June 28. At https://tr-tr.facebook.com/notes/kapitalizmle-m%C3%BCcadele-derne %C4%9Fi/anti-kapitalist-m%C3%BCsl%C3%BCmanlardan-basina-ve-kam uoyuna-duyurudur/382942998477592.

Bağımsız Gazetecilik Platformu (Platform for Independent Journalism). 2017. "Olağanüstü hâl'de gazeteciler—115" [Journalists under the State

of Emergency—115], Nov. 3. At http://platform24.org/medya-izleme/2526
/olaganustu-h-l-de-gazeteciler—115.

Bayat, Asef. 2010. *Life as Politics: How Ordinary People Change the Middle East.*
Stanford, CA: Stanford Univ. Press.

———, ed. 2013. *Post-Islamism: The Many Faces of Political Islam.* Oxford:
Oxford Univ. Press.

Barber, Benjamin. 1984. *Strong Democracy: Participatory Politics for a New Age.*
Berkeley: Univ. of California Press.

Birelma, Alpkan. 2013. "Antikapitalist Müslümanlar grubu üyeleriyle söyleşi:
'Bizim yapmak istediğimiz, mahalleler arasında geçişkenliği sağlamak'"
[Interview with Members of the Group Anticapitalist Muslims: "What We
Try to Do Is to Enable the Penetration between Neighborhoods"]. *Birikim*
293:61–76.

Bulaç, Ali. 2014. "Kamudan cemaatlere bağış" [Donation from the State to Religious Communities]. *Zaman,* Jan. 27.

Castells, Manuel. 2012. *Networks of Outrage and Hope: Social Movements in the
Internet Age.* New York: Wiley.

Cizreli, Delil. 2012. Interview on *Güvercin Günlükleri,* IMCTV. At http://
www.emekveadalet.org/faaliyetler/imc-tv-guvercin-gunlukleri-emek-ve
-adalet-platformu/.

Dagi, Ihsan. 2006. "The Justice and Development Party: Identity, Politics, and
Human Rights Discourse in the Search for Security and Legitimacy." In *The
Emergence of a New Turkey Democracy and the AK Parti,* edited by Hakan
Yavuz, 88–106. Salt Lake City: Univ. of Utah Press.

———. 2013. "Post-Islamism à la Turca." In *Post-Islamism: The Many Faces of
Political Islam,* edited by Asef Bayat, 71–108. Oxford: Oxford Univ. Press.

Dede, Alper. 2011. "The Arab Uprisings: Debating 'The Turkish Model.'" *Insight
Turkey* 13, no. 2: 23–32.

Della Porta, Donatella, and Mario Diani. 2006. *Social Movements: An Introduction.* Oxford: Blackwell.

Doğan, Sedat. 2013. "Mülk Allahındır sermaye defol" [Property Belongs to God:
Capital Get Out]. In *Sıcak Haziran sonraki direnişe mektup* [Hot June Let-
ter to Next Resistance], edited by Nuray Sencer, 309–12. Istanbul: Evrensel
Basım Yayın.

Emek ve Adalet Platformu (Labor and Justice Platform). 2011. "Emek ve Adalet
Platformu ilkeleri" [Principles of Justice and Labor Platform]. At http://
www.emekveadalet.org/bizkimiz/.

————. 2012a. *Emek ve Adalet Platformu 2011 yılı değerlendirmesi* [Justice and Labor Platform 2011 Yearly Evaluation]. At http://www.emekveadalet.org /wp-content/uploads/EmekveAdaletPlatformu2011YiliDegerlendirmesi.pdf.

————. 2012b. "Kardeşlik İftarları'na dair mütevazı bir muhasebe" [A Humble Evaluation on Brotherhood Iftars]. At http://www.emekveadalet.org /faaliyetler/kardeslik-iftarlarina-dair-mutevazi-bir-muhasebe/.

————. 2014a. "Ardarda gelen iş kazası haberleri tesadüf eseri mi?" [Are Recurring Work Accidents a Matter of Coincidence?]. At http://www.emekve adalet.org/haberyorum/ardarda-gelen-is-kazasi-haberleri-tesaduf-eseri-mi/.

————. 2014b. "Emek ve Adalet Platformu ilkeleri" [Principles of Justice and Labor Platform]. At http://www.emekveadalet.org/duyurular/emek-ve-adalet -platformu-ilkeleri-2/.

Fraser, Nancy. 1990. "Rethinking the Public Sphere: A Contribution to the Critique of Actually Existing Democracy." *Social Text* 25–26:56–80.

Freedom House. 2015. "Turkey: Five Year Decline in Press Freedom." At https:// freedomhouse.org/report/freedom-press/2015/turkey.

Göle, Nilüfer. 2013. "Yer sofrası ve sınır ihlalleri" [Earth Table and Border Infringements]. *T24 Bağımsız İnternet Gazetesi*, July 15. At http://t24.com .tr/yazarlar/nilufer-gole/yer-sofrasi-ve-sinir-ihlalleri,7056.

Habermas, Jürgen. 1994. "Three Normative Models of Democracy." *Constellations* 1, no. 1: 1–10.

Hale, William, and Ergun Özbudun. 2011. *Islamism, Democracy, and Liberalism in Turkey: The Case of AKP.* London: Routledge.

Hirschkind, Charles. 2001. "Civic Virtue and Religious Reason: An Islamic Counterpublic." *Cultural Anthropology* 16, no. 1: 3–34.

Inglehart, Ronald. 1995. "Changing Values, Economic Development, and Political Change." *International Social Science Journal* 145:379–403.

————. 2006. "Mapping Global Values." *Comparative Sociology* 5, nos. 2–3: 115–36.

İnsan Hakları Ortak Platformu (Human Rights Joint Platform). 2017. *Olağanüstü hal tedbir ve düzenlemeleri* [State of Emergency Measures and Regulations]. Ankara: İnsan Hakları Ortak Platformu, Sept. 12.

İplikçi, Müge. 2013. *Biz orada mutluyduk: Gezi Parkı direnişindeki gençler anlatıyor* [We Were Happy There: Youngsters in Gezi Park Resistance Tell]. Istanbul: Doğan Kitap.

Johnston, Hank, Enrique Larana, and Joseph R. Gusfield. 1994. "Identities, Grievances, and New Social Movements." In *New Social Movements: From*

Ideology to Identity, edited by Enrique Larana and Hank Johnston, 3–35. Philadelphia: Temple Univ. Press.

Kızılkaya, Sinan. 2014. "Kişisel bir not: İslamcılık ve Kürtçülük" [A Personal Note: Islamism and Kurdism]. Emek ve Adalet Platformu (Labor and Justice Platform), Nov. 1. At http://www.emekveadalet.org/alinti/kisisel-bir -not-islamcilik-ve-kurtluk/.

Melucci, Alberto. 1996. *Challenging Codes: Collective Action in the Information Age.* Cambridge: Cambridge Univ. Press.

Offe, Claus. 1987. "Challenging the Boundaries of Institutional Politics: Social Movements since the 1960s." In *Changing Boundaries of the Political*, edited by Charles Maier, 63–106. Cambridge: Cambridge Univ. Press.

Palczewski, Catherine Helen. 2001. "Cyber-Movements, New Social Movements, and Counterpublics." In *Counterpublics and the State*, edited by Robert Asen and Daniel Brouwer, 161–86. Albany: State Univ. of New York Press.

Saim [*sic*]. 2012. "Lüks otel önü iftarlarına dair . . ." [On *Iftars* in Front of Luxury Hotels . . .]. In *Emek ve Adalet Platformu 2011 yılı değerlendirmesi* [Justice and Labor Platform 2011 Yearly Evaluation], edited by Emek ve Adalet Platformu, 15–19. At http://www.emekveadalet.org/wp-content/uploads/Emekve AdaletPlatformu2011YiliDegerlendirmesi.pdf.

Sarfati, Yusuf. 2015. "Dynamics of Mobilization during Gezi Park Protests in Turkey." In *The Whole World Is Texting*, edited by Irving Epstein, 25–43. Rotterdam: Sense.

———. 2017. "How Turkey's Slide to Authoritarianism Defies Modernization Theory." *Turkish Studies* 18, no. 3: 395–415.

T24 Bağımsız İnternet Gazetesi. 2013. "Dindar aydınlar: Eskiden mazlum olmak zalimin yanında olmamızı gerektirmez" [Religious Intellectuals: To Be Victims of the Past Does Not Necessitate Standing Next to the Oppressor]. June 14.

Wiktorowicz, Quintan. 2004. "Introduction: Islamic Activism and Social Movement Theory." In *Islamic Activism: A Social Movement Theory*, edited by Quintan Wiktorowicz, 1–36. Bloomington: Indiana Univ. Press.

Yalçın, Suat. 2015. "Bir hâl olarak halkçılık" [Populism as a Condition]. In *Başucu yazıları* [Bedside Writings], edited by Emek ve Adalet Platformu (Labor and Justice Platform). Istanbul: Emek ve Adalet Platformu. At http://www.emekve adalet.org/wp-content/uploads/bas-ucu-yazilari.pdf.

Yildirim, A. Kadir. 2015. "Clientelism 2.0 vs. Democracy in Erdogan's 'New Turkey.'" *Washington Post*, Mar. 13.

7 The Pashtun Woman Blogger

Marginality, Empowerment,
and the Struggle for Recognition

SHEHNAZ HAQQANI

Many studies have shown that the Internet provides an excellent medium for various kinds of exchanges, including social and political ones. Women's engagement with patriarchy through blogging, for instance, is well known. What remains understudied, however, is the use of the Internet by young Muslims to mobilize change in their communities in an effort to eradicate religious extremism. Afghan women's blogging activities capture their efforts against both patriarchy and religious extremism. The objective is to shift the conversation from generalized and monolithic assumptions about Pashtun women to consider the ways that Pashtun women (re)present themselves in the digital world. The implications of such a consideration extend beyond Pashtun women—the study of which has the potential to offer readers insights into alternative discourses created and dominated by women through their use of digital media. In this chapter, I analyze the role that blogging plays in empowering young women by encouraging them to reshape their religious and gender identities. I focus solely on female bloggers in response to popular perceptions of Pashtun women because they are often portrayed as voiceless victims of their cultures and religion and in need of saving by outsiders. Contrary to such perceptions in the media, there are many active voices from within Pashtun culture who deserve acknowledgment and attention. It must be noted that most of the bloggers surveyed here are also young people living in the West (mainly the United States and western Europe), which requires an understanding of how the diaspora communities maintain their traditional practices and beliefs. For the diasporic Pashtuns in this study, the uniting factor is their ethnic identity as Pashtuns, whose homeland or memory of a homeland is the Pashtun part of Afghanistan or Pakistan. They also maintain close ties with their homeland and have relatives still living there.

In the spaces created by Afghan bloggers, numerous political and social issues speak to the concerns of a society (Pashtun/Afghan) marred and devastated by religious extremism and radicalization. With an audience restricted to English-speaking Afghans and Pashtuns, the bloggers I describe here represent voices typically ignored and marginalized in all other forms of media. They address, reflect and comment on, and critique existing political, social, and religious structures that facilitate the production of violence in their societies. The blogosphere, then, illustrates the role of political, religious, and social contexts in acknowledging these online spaces as worthy of analysis and discussion because of their ability to serve as tools for their communities. Of particular importance, however, is the role of Pashtun or Afghan bloggers as potential enablers of positive change in their communities with respect to marginalization on multiple fronts, including as minorities within a broader Muslim minority community in the West, where Desi (South Asian) and Arab Muslims are often privileged as the real faces of Islam. As Nabil Echchaibi points out in his discussion of the power and roles of different types of blogs, "Less-known blogs not only incarnate better the potential of Internet users to challenge elite control of news production, but they also show us on a smaller scale how individuals and communities use network technologies to sustain new forms of social, cultural, and economic solidarity" (2009, 12). These blogs are thus viable sites that, according to Echchaibi, "critically engage the shifting boundaries of communication and political power" in the modern world (12). Framing the blogosphere as well as other online fora as spaces that facilitate, enable, and mediate particular kinds of marginalized conversations as well engagements with wider surroundings helps to recognize the youth's role in countering religious extremism. Through such engagements, they not only form and transform their identities (religious, political, social, and otherwise) but also, as future leaders of their communities, shape and guide the future of their communities.

This chapter highlights the sorts of conversations and perspectives that blogs by Pashtun women promote and the bloggers' role, as they understand it, in guiding the dialogue in response to religious extremism in their societies. I approach empowerment as a process that mobilizes an individual intellectually, mentally, and physically in such a way that she realizes her worth as a participant in her society and community and thus contributes to that community by engaging in activities she finds purposeful and productive. These activities instill in her a sense of personal significance; through this process, she recognizes, appreciates, and exercises her power as a significant community member.

Understanding Empowerment

When I first decided to write on the topic of Pashtun women's empowerment through social networking and specifically through blogging, I was searching for the blogs of Pashtun women engaged in "intellectual" discussions, writing on "serious" topics, such as politics, society, and religion. I was not looking for blogs replete with "gossip" or "everyday things." I wanted to find signs of heterodoxy, explicit discussions of taboo subjects, and disagreement with the status quo and with the roles typically assigned to Pashtun and other Muslim women (primarily a domestic and private role as opposed to a public role). I eventually realized that I was excluding an important circle of Pashtun women bloggers who might be engaging with patriarchy in different ways. Hence, I had to ask: What *does* it mean to be empowered? What does an empowered woman do or talk about, and how does she display her empowerment? Is she in fact obligated to exhibit visible signs of her empowerment? This mode of questioning resembles Saba Mahmood's discussion on agency and resistance to feminist thought:

> Even in instances when an explicit feminist agency is difficult to locate, there is tendency among scholars to look for expressions and moments of resistance that may suggest a challenge to male domination. When women's actions seem to reinscribe what appear to be "instruments of their own oppression," the social analysis can point to moments of disruption of, and articulation of points of opposition to, male authority. . . .

> Agency, in this form of analysis, is understood as the capacity to realize
> one's own interests against the weight of custom, tradition, transcen-
> dental will, or other obstacles (whether individual or collective). Thus,
> the humanist desire for autonomy and self-expression constitutes the
> substrate, the slumbering ember that can spark to flame in the form of
> an act of resistance when conditions permit. (2005, 8)

In other words, the Pashtun blogger I was initially interested in was one
who had realized her agency as an empowered woman and who was
explicitly vocal against male domination. Through such a position, I was
essentializing empowerment as necessarily resistance to some system of
power, often expressed in "unlikely" ways that Western researchers do not
expect from women of Muslim backgrounds. My expectation to find "serious" bloggers is reinforced by much of the literature on women's sense
of empowerment. Fereshteh Nouraie-Simone, who writes on Iranian
women bloggers, states that for "educated young Iranian women, cyberspace is a liberating territory of one's own—a place to resist a traditionally imposed subordinate identity while providing a break from pervasive
Islamic restrictions in public physical space" (2014, 124). Her study examines the various identities that Iranian women assume on the Internet,
most of them as anonymous writers whose frustrations with not being
able to speak and think freely in the physical spaces of Iranian society have
reached a level that compels them to turn to another medium to express
their feelings, desires, beliefs, and identities. These bloggers write primarily on issues of sex and sexuality, and Nouraie-Simone reads this choice of
subject as empowerment—rightly so, given the context in which this select
group of bloggers operates.

The highly acclaimed book *I Want to Get Married!* (2010) by Ghada
Abdel Aal, an Egyptian woman who started the book as a blog in 2006, is
identified as another case of empowerment. Abdel Aal received immense
support from her readers, including the Egyptian ones, and was encouraged to publish the blog as a book, which is the story of a well-educated
Egyptian female pharmacist who is unable to find a suitable partner for
marriage for reasons she does not directly state but leaves it to the readers
to understand through the anecdotes she shares. Readers gain a strong

understanding not only of how the process of marriage works in contemporary Egyptian society but also of how social and religious ideas as well as economic conditions contribute to the understanding of marriage there. The book is a critique of the society in which Abdel Aal's search takes place. Nora Eltahawy, the translator, writes, "In a culture that likes to use the saying 'Homes are made of secrets,' Abdel Aal has opened the door to hers, challenging the pressure traditionally placed on women to keep silent about such issues within the Middle East, and defying Western onlookers' expectations of the exclusive performance of that traditionalism" (Eltahawy 2010, xi).

Such readings of the blogosphere suggest that for a female blogger to be empowered or to express her empowerment, she must engage in public discussions of "taboo" subjects such as sex or, in the Egyptian case, expose the "secrets" of her home or society. Without denying the empowerment of these women, I suggest, however, that engagement with such topics is merely one form of empowerment. What about empowered women who do not feel comfortable writing about taboo subjects or simply do not wish to write about them or are not interested in such subjects? Is it possible for a woman to operate and live inside a social, political, and religious system that limits her but still to feel empowered? Must she express disagreements with and challenge to her society and surroundings in order to show that she is an empowered being? Or can she be an empowered critic of her society but still choose to express her empowerment through other means? This reading of women's empowerment excludes those women who prefer to express their empowerment by writing about subjects such as sex, love, and marriage. After all, in cyberspace "[no] tale is unworthy of narration, and no other medium can carry the stories of everyday life as easily, quickly, and widely as blogs" (Nouraie-Simone 2014, 126). Most Pashtun women bloggers do not have the luxury to blog about taboo issues, such as romance and sex, because their political, religious, and social contexts—riddled with war and conflict, religious extremism, and diasporic issues of identity and change—do not enable such conversations.

Almost all of the Pashtun female bloggers mentioned here and many others write using their real names and share their photos. Given the patriarchal-influenced social and religious contexts to which these women are responding through blogs, I read their choice to speak with their real names as a response to extremist forms of religion that require women to be anonymous and faceless. This decision makes sense most in the Taliban and post-Taliban era of Afghanistan, which has also affected neighboring Pashtun regions in Pakistan. Restrictions that the Taliban and other religious extremist groups continue to place on women are well documented.[1] Through their blogging activities, these women not only challenge traditional understandings of Pashtunwali—the unwritten code of ethics that theoretically guides Pashtun behavior and life—that women embody the private and must remain as invisible as possible, as sheltered from the public view as possible, but also embody the ideals to which they hope future generations of Pashtuns will aspire. Self-expression is an important part of empowerment, and in the Pashtun context specifically the fact that these women willfully choose to risk such exposure speaks significantly to their demand for recognition as themselves. These efforts to reclaim their identities, to put a face and a name to their online activism, must be appreciated as a struggle to navigate and defy the marginality that limits them. The relationships between marginality and identity as well as between empowerment and marginality are interwoven: understanding one's marginal place in society, in the mainstream, can be a source of empowerment and a source of celebration of one's identity.

Blogging as a Tool of Empowerment

Blogging especially serves as a necessary tool of political and social change in societies struggling with religious extremism. With few exceptions, Pashtun women's blogs are informed by the bloggers' experiences with extremism, particularly with respect to their status as women. They constantly write about issues of war, religion, and gender, with emphasis on restrictions against women living under religious extremism.[2]

1. For a list of these restrictions, see the Revolutionary Association of the Women of Afghanistan's website at http://www.rawa.org/rules.htm.

2. For examples of such conversations, please see the following blogs: *Afghan Watch* by Malali Bashir (n.d.), whose blog is inundated with postings on politics, Afghanistan, society,

Why Blog?

Blogging is a relatively new phenomenon. Jill Walker Rettberg points out that blogs are "part of the history of communication and literacy, and emblematic of a shift from uni-directional mass media to participatory media, where viewers and readers become creators of media. Blogs are also part of the history of literature and writing" (2008, 1). Hence, blogging is a form of media, a form of literature, a subcategory of history, a response to globalization supported and enhanced by modern technology. When people blog, they are therefore contributing to all of these genres, participating as citizens of the world, responding to global changes and historical (technological) developments.

Why would someone choose to blog?[3] A Pashtun female reader of my blog, who asked to be identified as "Durrani," tells me in an email exchange that although she has not started blogging yet but intends to do so soon, she imagines that the mere thought of being read by readers from anywhere in the world, people one may never encounter in real life, is empowering in itself. Sabina Khan-Ibarra, a California-based Pashtun woman, started her blog after the death of her infant son, Ibrahim, in solidarity with other Muslim parents who have suffered the same loss, to let them know that they are not alone: "After losing [Ibrahim], I wished there was an online resource where I could turn to. I felt I needed to read about other Muslim mothers and/or fathers who had been through the same. I wanted to know how they survived and kept their Imaan [faith in God] intact" (Khan-Ibarra n.d.). Aneela, of Pakistan, writes that her son had a febrile seizure:

> If this blogger turned soul sister had not blogged about her experience with her boy's seizure a while ago, I am pretty sure I might not have

---

economy, gender; the blog by Sara Basharmal (n.d.), who writes on politics and gender issues; *Orzala's Blog* by Orzala (n.d.), whose blog is oriented mostly toward gender and Afghanistan; and *Coffee Shop Diplomat* by Sabina Khan (n.d.), who blogs on foreign-policy issues, war, and conflict, with an emphasis on Federally Administered Tribal Areas and terrorism.

3. In January 2011, the *Muslim Feminists* blog posed its readers the question "Why do you blog?" (Muslim Feminists 2011).

recognized it for what it was and perhaps made things worse. . . . None of my "real people" [i.e., people in real life] shared their children's horror stories regards seizures with me. . . . So yes I will be forever grateful for what this blog has brought to my life. For frankly it kept me sane during that scary minute. (*Roots in Air* n.d.)

Blogging, therefore, connects these women with others, and they are able to share and communicate their fears and joys and other experiences with each other and in the process learn with and from each other in a way they might not be able to do so in the "real" world.

Another Pashtun blogger, Zara Khan,[4] who is based in London, tells me that she turned to blogging because "many years ago," when she was in her twenties, she wanted to address the limitations that Pashtun women faced by not having any platforms where they could speak up. She started her own blog after coming across other bloggers:

The online community was growing and there were always topics I desperately wanted to talk about but there were limitations for women (especially Pukhtanay[5]) and a lack of platforms to speak. Although [online discussion] forums had male and female members, the male members dominated with their opinions (even on forums where more female members were active in comparison to male members!). I then came across a friend's blog and loved the idea, and it rolled on from there. I started off with my daily ramblings but as I got more comfortable I slowly started to talk about deeper issues.

Zara's sense of empowerment can be easily detected in this response. In answering a question about what blogging means to her and whether she finds it empowering, she explains that blogging is certainly an empowering act for her and has taught her to express her opinions and be taken seriously:

---

4. All quotations from Zara Khan come from her personal communications with me.

5. *Pukhtanay* is another word for Pashtun females, a variant of *Pashtaney*. The terms *Pashtun* and *Pukhtun* are interchangeable, depending on the dialect.

I absolutely do find it empowering but I have to give credit for that to the men out there who are supportive of my opinions and my blog. Even now if I get the odd person who disregards my opinion I do feel belittled for being spoken to in a bad manner purely for being a woman, but that feeling is easily overcome because I realise it's my blog, it's my world, and my rules apply! It means a lot for women to have that space, especially women like me who have little or no option to be open about their views amongst family and friends, so my blog is where I can talk about anything and everything and not risk a family riot in return.

In this response, Zara begins by acknowledging her empowerment through blogging and attributes it to men who are supportive of her opinions and her blog. On the one hand, she may be acknowledging men's authority, men's power over the decisions a woman makes, a sort of validation through men's support. Otherwise, why would she also not attribute her empowerment to the females who support her? On the other hand, this statement—especially when read in the context of her complete response, including the reference to being a Pashtun—can be understood to mean that she does not or would not expect (Pashtun) males to be supportive of her blog or of her speaking up and making her identity and her existence public, things that women are generally discouraged from doing in the Pashtun society. Thus, Zara is acknowledging and appreciating the support that men give her; she might *expect* women to be supportive of her, so this support would not be a surprise or need an acknowledgment.

Recognizing the support of male Pashtun readers is common among Pashtun women bloggers. Peymana Assad,[6] a British Pashtun, also states when discussing the negative consequences of her blogging activities, with their deep interest in politics and gender, that although she faces criticism for blogging, she also has a large group of Pashtun male supporters:

Alhamdulillah [praise be to God] as many of [the] negative consequences, I have had more positive ones. And I think that should be noted because nobody would be able to succeed if there weren't people

6. All quotations from Peymana Assad come from Assad n.d.

out there encouraging and supporting your role online and blogging. Many of my supporters have been male Afghan men and Pashtun men. They have sent me not only words of encouragement but have enjoyed reading my blogs and my columns. They ask me to write more and cover more topics. The amount of support I saw at the BBC Afghan service has been unprecedented. They gave me a platform to express my opinions to such a wide audience! For that anyone could be grateful. The exposure on BBC has led others to take my opinion seriously and invite me onto talk shows. So the positive consequences of writing and blogging have been endless.

Zara, quoted earlier, mentions that through blogging she avoids the risk of creating a riot among her own family. Clearly for her, then, blogging is not risky—at least so long as her family members do not discover her blog—possibly because she writes from a country where freedom of expression is not censored to the extent that it is in many others. In his book *The Blogging Revolution* (2008), Antony Loewenstein discusses censorship and the risks many bloggers take by blogging about their hopes, dreams, and daily lives in countries where battles for freedom of expression are being fought. Bloggers have faced harassment and even imprisonment for blogging about police-led torture in Egypt. The risks that bloggers take are manifest in multiple forms, from incurring the disapproval of their parents and other family members to receiving death and other threats (often from anonymous readers and viewers) to being imprisoned. For Salma Jafar, a blogger from Baluchistan who often writes on politics (see, e.g., Jafar 2016), Pashtun issues, and Baluchistan, the consequences of blogging have included receiving warnings from the government of Pakistan:

> I resigned from a very lucrative consultancy I was doing with UN and government of Pakistan when the govt asked me to stop blogging about Balochistan. I resigned . . . it was against my integrity to compromise. . . . I owe more to the land I belong to. They really got it from me and I thought it happened only cause I was a Pashtun woman who could do it . . . non compromising . . . but then I saw other Pashtun woman too very compromising—so I am not sure. It depends how you are raised I have been consistently raised with Pashtun values. . . . It was hammered into

our heads all the time that we are Pashtuns and what we can do or not do for being so. (personal communication to Shehnaz Haqqani, n.d.)

The threats that these bloggers receive are usually from readers who may or may not know the blogger or her family personally but who do not want to see the blogger exercising her freedom of speech and thought, particularly when those thoughts might go against the status quo. Such threats tend to be made when Pashtun women in the West speak up in Pashtun male-dominated spaces,[7] such as conferences or public demonstrations, and appear in Western clothing rather than in traditional Afghan/Pakistani clothing with a *hijab*, or head covering. The argument is often made that these women have no right to speak on Pashtun issues and especially about Pashtun women's rights because of their sartorial choices: they do not dress according to traditional standards of Pashtun women's modesty, which thus diminishes their authority on the subject—and their right to identify themselves as Pashtun.

Peymana has been one of the bloggers attacked for not living up to the standards set for her by other Pashtuns. She speaks about patriarchal responses from Pashtun men to her online activism:

As a Muslim Afghan Pashtun woman, it is VERY difficult to be active on the internet [*sic*], whether it is blogging, YouTube videos or social media and not see difficulties. I have done all these three. . . . Sometimes I believe that by way of blogging, the readers read what you write but are more interested in the person writing than the topics being discussed. That happens especially if it is a woman in my opinion, people need to know what she looks like, is she pretty, how does she dress, what kind of family is she from (many times I have [seen] searches on Google to get to my blog as "Peymana Assad family") so that if she ever expresses or writes something that goes against all norms and their idea of how a woman should be, they attack her character in order for her to lose credibility or be disheartened and not write anymore. The issue with video

7. See, for example, "Pashtun Women's Blogs" n.d. See also the subsequent long quotation from Peymana Assad.

blogs, I made a video blog for a peace organisation on international women's day. The first comment on my YouTube channel was from a male Afghan, "get a real job, nobody will marry you if you keep showing your face on television." That did not shake me, I just learnt to block all the comments from the video. But because someone mentioned that I was making "YouTube videos of myself" to my grandmother here in London, I had to take the video offline for a while, in order to let the gossip of the few die down. I have since, not made any other video blogs. But I believe Video blogs and interactive things like that engage people more, it's just very difficult to do that if you are an Afghan Pashtun woman. I have faced negative consequences from people talking about me, gossiping and making up rumours or trying to tell me how I should behave online.

That Peymana was pressured to take down her video because of the reaction from Pashtun men who sought to police her online behavior and engagement demonstrates the kinds of criticisms Pashtun women receive for speaking up and for asserting their presence in the public. In fact, Peymana temporarily stopped blogging because of the policing she experienced when she first opened her blog. She started blogging in order "to give [herself] a platform to get [her] views out."

I knew that if I was to write for another website then most of my views or what I would write would be edited, whereas with my own blog I could control the content and how it was presented to readers. I only started blogging in 2011. The reason was because I had joined twitter [sic] for the first time then and the views I was expressing on there interested certain people and they suggested I get a blog. When I started following others who were students (like myself at the time) I saw that they also had blogs and had written about many issues.

That others encouraged her to start a blog indicates that they appreciated and acknowledged that she had a voice and needed to be heard more broadly. However, although she had support in the beginning, support that made her feel empowered when she blogged, she began to feel disempowered over time and took a break from blogging:

At first blogging was something very powerful to me. As a woman, British Muslim and Afghan, it was a place for me to finally share my views on all sorts of controversial topics that may not be discussed enough in academia or even personally. As an Afghan, it gave me an opportunity to get rid of this idea that Afghan women are uneducated, illiterate and locked up. Within my identity as an Afghan it gave me the opportunity to show that Pashtun women are not all oppressed and remove the misconceptions about them. . . . [Because of the criticism I received, though,] I didn't find blogging empowering [anymore]. I was limited; as a woman, I found it harder for people to accept my writing and to read it with an open mind. For a while I left blogging and did not really update much. I was then offered to write columns for the BBC Afghan service in Pashto on issues to do with the British Afghan community. . . . I did not want to limit my readers to just Pashto readers, so I translated my columns into English for my blog and uploaded them there, so that I could engage with people of all backgrounds not just Afghans. [This] was received well and many people like the fact that I am one of the few (or only one I think) that translates my columns from the BBC into English for a wider audience. In this sense a new, renewed feeling of empowerment has returned but I still feel limited in many areas, because I can't discuss issues at a very detailed or personal level to me due to the impact they would have those closest to me personally. I always believe that writing is more powerful when it is personal and you can explore the issue more. But writing about personal changes or struggles, as an Afghan woman, would get your character attacked . . . whereas men tend not to get character assassination attempts.

It is important to highlight Peymana's point that she believes empowerment has much to do with not feeling limited, not fearing censorship, and not being a potential victim of character assassination simply because one is expressing one's view openly. All of these fears are heightened when one—especially if one is a Pashtun woman, as Peymana notes—writes about personal issues. One can therefore feel disempowered by not being able to discuss the topics and issues one wants to. Empowerment, therefore, is in one's mind: blogging can empower one if one can confidently and openly write what is on one's mind without feeling threatened or without facing censorship.

Zara offers a different insight into the negative consequences that Pashtun women bloggers face:

> Negative consequences are not felt in my personal life as much, because I keep my online life and personal life miles apart, but definitely online I feel people form an image of me and my character and this causes them to generalise their views of me and any other online female blogger, and attach that view to every western female Pukhtana [a Pashtun female]. People already don't think high of western Pukhtanay and have negative ideas (a different discussion altogether!) so if I have even the slightest difference of opinion from theirs, that would put a stamp on those ideas. This makes it hard because I can't help but feel like I'm responsible/or an example of western Pukhtanay, even though I cannot ever speak for the majority of us, I feel such a responsibility is thrown on us by default. It's quite daft, a bit like a girl in hijab is always expected to be the perfect Muslim because she's thought of being the "representative" of Muslim women! In my initial blogging days I was [conscious] of that, but now as I've matured I really don't care much about it because there are a lot more Pashtun female bloggers and I have seen many good people supportive of us bloggers.

To avoid risk, separating her personal life from her cyber presence is essential for Zara. But the consequences of blogging or speaking up are not limited to threats, hate, and lack of support. Another negative consequence is when readers take the blogger's perspectives and apply them to all those who can be placed in similar categories, gender, geography, ethnicity, and so on, so that unfair and sometimes psychologically harmful generalizations are made about anyone who shares an identity with the blogger. For instance, if a Western Pashtun blogger expresses her views on divorce in a way that appears to be less traditional or is not expected of the "average" Pashtun woman, it is likely that some Pashtun readers might take her personal views to be representative of all Western Pashtun women's views, whether that is the case or not. This harmful overgeneralization is indeed an unintended and unfortunate consequence of blogging.

These bloggers believe that blogging, besides being useful to them-selves, can be of benefit to other Pashtuns, especially those in the diaspora. Zara, for example, believes that blogging

> can help the new generation of western Pashtuns build a different view of Pashtunwali or Pashtuns in general. From when I started to blog, the only Pashtun blogs/websites I saw were talking of Pashtun History, or had praise-full articles, and I formed the idea that we're the best thing since sliced bread. Nowadays the discussions are forcing people into reality checks which I find healthy for the new generation. However the reality checks are causing the community to fight, though it's mostly online I am sure it does impact the youth in their everyday lives too. There are people who believe everything is great in Pashtunwali, and people who believe everything is bad, and then there are people who accept the middle ground. Frustrations are high nowadays on such forums but with every good there comes bad, and vice versa. Hopefully when the initial shock of reality is over with, the generation after this one would stop the fighting and just mingle!

Blogging therefore offers different, more individualized approaches to understanding Pashtunwali, its impact, and its relevance in the lives of contemporary Pashtuns, specifically in the West. For the Pashtuns in Pak-istan and Afghanistan, opines Peymana, blogging "is really a chance to highlight their plight and their issues, sometimes it is an escape from the torments of everyday life. But those with access to the Internet in the first place are at a different class of society and so would be engaging in conver-sation about different topics."

These bloggers also continue to write in order to correct the reductive portrayals of Pashtuns, especially Pashtun women, in the media. For Zara, blogging "can help the new generation of western Pashtuns build a differ-ent view of Pashtunwali or Pashtuns in general," contrary to the images, history, and reputation applied to them in the media. Peymana similarly explains that of the things that motivates her to blog is

> this desire inside me to remove the misconceptions that people have about Afghans and to also help open the debate for Afghans and

Pashtuns about things that affect them. If we don't talk or discuss the problems we will not find solutions for them. . . . It is also the idea that, as an Afghan living in the West I want to stand in opposition against the insight offered by (mostly) white privileged men who class Afghans and Pashtuns as barbaric. . . . What makes me continue is the fact that I want to change this perception and make the white privileged to take the opinion of an Afghan, and a Pashtun, as serious, academic and intellectual. I had this idea that during my MA, I would finally engage with white people who understood Afghans and Afghanistan, and the problems facing it. What I found was that most of famous academia on Afghanistan and its people is clouded with opinions and writing that is colonialist and racist. Whilst slowly there are blogs going up by expats in the country trying to show that non-Afghan people can understand it, I still find it a bit difficult because they will still make comments that are either patronising or with the whole notion that "well they can't stick up for themselves so I will do it for them." What makes me continue is that I want people to understand that Afghan and Pashtun women can defend themselves and in a manner where we would not and should not lose credibility in the eyes of anyone.

The notions that Pashtuns, whether men or women, can stand up for themselves, that they know how to run their own country, and that they do not need the services of any outsiders appear in the various themes that Pashtuns generally blog about, which range from politics to religion to society.

Pashtuns from Afghanistan usually center their blog postings on Afghanistan (whereas the Pashtuns from Pakistan do not necessarily center their blogs on either Pakistan or Afghanistan), and they generally lean toward political discussions more so than Pashtuns from Pakistan. There are, however, exceptions. One Afghan blogger, for example, who blogs under the pen name "Afghan Wife," frequently writes about social issues such as marriage, pregnancy, and education among Afghans in the United States and Afghanistan.[8] Another blogger, a native of South Waziristan,

8. See, for example, her blog post titled "Marriage: Marry Someone in the US or Afghanistan?" (Afghan Wife 2011).

Pakistan, who writes using her real name, Sabina Khan, blogs about political issues and conflict (Khan n.d.). It nonetheless makes sense that Afghan bloggers typically concentrate on political issues because of the impacts of war on their nation and its people. Arzo Wardak's blog (Wardak n.d.), too, highlights political issues faced by not only Afghans inside Afghanistan but also those in the diaspora. She also works actively toward the political, social, and professional empowerment of Afghan Americans, as seen through her media interviews as well as through her activism in the Afghan American community. The blog form is one of the most widely used ways in which diasporic Afghan women work toward the eradication of extremism in diasporic communities and in which the youth are empowered to work toward activism for the improvement of their communities. Malali Bashir (n.d.), Sara Basharmal (n.d.), Mona Naseer (n.d.), and Orzala (n.d.) are among the Afghan women who are leading political and religious conversations in their societies by means of their blogs as well as occasionally in other media, as in Bashir's case. The three most common themes in their writings are women's rights, religious extremism, and the wars in Afghanistan and Pakistan's Federally Administered Tribal Areas.

Discussion

Several issues have surfaced in the picture painted in the previous material, including the notion of the ideal Pashtun woman according to expectations expressed on the Internet, primarily by the critics of the bloggers studied here; the question of identity and of being and doing Pashto; and the struggle of the diasporic Pashtun. Because religious extremism thrives on patriarchal assumptions and expectations that, it insists, must guide society, it is no surprise that patriarchy is a popular theme in the blogs of the women discussed in this study. In challenging the patriarchal expectations they must embody, these women establish a sense of identity in their online personas that push their audiences to reflect. Their awareness and recognition of their role as shapers of mindsets can be gleaned through their ardent blogging activities. If they did not believe in themselves and their ability to promote positive change, they would not be writing and raising the issues they highlight.

The question of identity, of what it means to be Pashtun, is an essential part of the conversation about what constitutes a "proper" Pashtun woman. Pashtuns are keen to note that one does not simply speak Pashto; one actually "does" Pashto as well. Pashto is performed and embodied, not simply spoken, by the Pashtun (Grima 1992, 4). The notion of honor in Pashtunwali is strictly linked to the idea that honor and Pashto are the same as well. Piper O'Sullivan describes this connection: "To act contrary to Pashtunwali or Pashto is to be dishonorable, and with that stigma, it becomes virtually impossible to function in tribal society especially in rural areas" (2012, 9). These ideas help contextualize some of the negative comments that Pashtun women bloggers receive. Their detractors' understanding is that the ideal Pashtun, in particular the Pashtun woman, embodies Pashto in a way that distinguishes her from non-Pashtuns and from other women—particularly from the women whom Pashtun women must not emulate. For a Pashtun woman to blog about issues that the Pashtun woman is traditionally and socially not expected to speak about is ultimately to dishonor herself, to transgress against Pashto—her identity. Her choice to accept willingly the consequences of blogging, particularly about issues that she is least expected to be versed in and discuss, is a form of her resistance to the extremism that her society has fallen prey to. It also demonstrates her role in redressing the problems of the religious extremism that denies her a sense of identity and empowerment.

Another issue to address is that of the diaspora. The diaspora is often burdened with the responsibility of representing and passing on their "authentic," traditional cultures, even as those in their homeland progress and reform. This holds true for Pashtuns as well: as Pashtuns in the West adopt, however gradually, to the Western cultures in which they live, claims about their having abandoned their culture are spread among the Pashtuns in their hometowns in Pakistan or Afghanistan. Yet many Pashtun parents are so resistant to adapting to American culture or to any other Western culture that they often do not realize how much their native Pashtun culture is evolving in Pakistan and Afghanistan. These problems are familiar to diasporic communities everywhere, and scholars have addressed the issue of intergenerational conflicts, immigrant communities' fear of change, and other similar concerns.[9] Pashtun women bloggers' writings display their acknowledgment of their diasporic identity as the mediators of a new, "third" culture. As mediators of this new culture, they are also aware that their cultural identities, shaped by their diasporic concerns as well as by the problems of religious extremism many of their parents fled, are a major force of change.

Conclusion

Academics have recently started relying on the blogosphere to understand the role that the Internet, in particular blogs and online social networks, plays in the lives of those people whose means of expression are limited in their society. Fascinating research is also available on the role of blogging in the lives of Egyptian, Iranian, and other Muslim women living in societies where their freedoms of expression and thought are highly limited, or at least strictly monitored. As such, the blogosphere offers a nuanced but powerful representations of how bloggers—and often their readers—express their individuality and creativity as blogging provides them the space in which they can share thoughts and ideas that they are often unable to share in physical spaces. Integral to the conversation on blogging and its roles in and impacts on Muslim women's lives is the issue of empowerment in that blogging can be approached as a tool of empowerment for Muslim women who blog. This empowerment becomes of particular significance for women in societies that uphold the practice of gender segregation and notably those that limit women's roles to practices inside the home. Through blogging, their identities and roles are extended well beyond those of daughters, wives, and mothers, and the bloggers establish their individual selves as equal and active participants in their societies. They become thinkers, teachers, writers, artists, activists, leaders, critics, and they prove, with their diverse skills and intersectional identities, that empowerment comes in multiple forms, essentially affirming their empowerment as female participants in and members of their societies.

9. See, for example, Nayar 2004 and Singh 2013.

This study has examined how young Pashtun women bloggers from Afghanistan and Pakistan challenge both common Western perceptions of their identities, cultures, and native countries as well as patriarchal, extremist expectations of Pashtun woman. Most blog to address tiring, unfair, and politically motivated opinions about Pashtuns, reclaiming their voices and opinions and refusing to accept others' appropriation of their identities and roles. Responding to social, political, and religious issues exacerbated by the religious extremism from which their societies continue to suffer, these women contribute to the changing identity of their generation as well as to the changing identities of future generations as they challenge extremist approaches, especially to questions of religion and women. Debunking the idea of the political and focusing on these women's online participation, this study has relied extensively on Pashtun women's blogs and their experiences as active bloggers to demonstrate what empowerment means for Pashtun women as performers in and creators of a third culture in which they are not only valuable members but also primary mediators. In contrast to the popular media portrayal of Pashtun women as victims of their own culture, this chapter presents them as empowered individuals who have forged for themselves a space in a world that they themselves monitor.

References

Abdel Aal, Ghada. 2010. *I Want to Get Married! One Wannabe Bride's Misadventures with Handsome Houdinis, Technicolor Grooms, Morality Police, and Other Mr. Not-Quite-Rights*. Translated by Nora Eltahawy. Austin: Center for Middle Eastern Studies, Univ. of Texas.

Afghan Wife. 2011. "Marriage: Marry Someone in the US or Afghanistan?" *Afghan Wife*, blog, July. At http://afghanwife.blogspot.com/2011/07/marriage-marry-someone-in-us-or.html.

Assad, Peymana. n.d. *Peymana Assad—Afghanistan*. Blog. At http://peymanaassad.wordpress.com/. Last accessed Sept. 20, 2013.

Basharmal, Sara. n.d. Blog. At http://sarabasharmal.wordpress.com/.

Bashir, Malali. n.d. *Afghan Watch*. Blog. At http://afghanwatch.blogspot.com/. Last accessed Sept. 20, 2015.

Echchaibi, Nabil. 2009. "From the Margins to the Center: New Media and the Case of *Bondy Blog* in France." In *International Blogging: Identity, Politics, and Networked Publics*, edited by Adrienne Russell and Nabil Echchaibi, 11–28. New York: Peter Lang.

Eltahawy, Nora. 2010. "Translator's Note." In *I Want to Get Married! One Wannabe Bride's Misadventures with Handsome Houdinis, Technicolor Grooms, Morality Police, and Other Mr. Not-Quite-Rights*, Ghada Abdel Aal, translated by Nora Eltahawy, xi–xiv. Austin: Center for Middle Eastern Studies, Univ. of Texas.

Grima, Benedicte. 1992. *The Performance of Emotion among Paxtun Women: "The Misfortunes Which Have Befallen Me."* Austin: Univ. of Texas Press.

Jafar, Salma. 2016. "Karachi Politics: Make Space for the Pashtuns." *Express Tribune* blog entry, July 16. At http://blogs.tribune.com.pk/author/623/salma-jafar/.

Khan, Sabina. n.d. *Coffee Shop Diplomat*. Blog. At http://coffeeshopdiplomat.wordpress.com/. Last accessed Sept. 20, 2013.

Khan-Ibarra, Sabina. n.d. *Ibrahim's Tree*. Blog. At http://www.ibrahimstree.com. Last accessed Sept. 2, 2013.

Loewenstein, Antony. 2008. *The Blogging Revolution*. Carlton, Australia: Melbourne Univ. Press.

Mahmood, Saba. 2005. *Politics of Piety: The Islamic Revival and the Feminist Subject*. Princeton, NJ: Princeton Univ. Press.

Muslim Feminists. 2011. "Why Do You Blog?" *Muslim Feminists*, blog, Jan. 3. At http://musfem.wordpress.com/2011/01/03/why-do-you-blog/#comments.

Naseer, Mona. n.d. *Mona Writes*. Blog. At https://monanaseer.wordpress.com/. Last accessed Sept. 20, 2013.

Nayar, Kamala. 2004. *The Sikh Diaspora in Vancouver: Three Generations amid Tradition, Modernity, and Multiculturalism*. Toronto: Univ. of Toronto Press.

Nouraie-Simone, Fereshteh. 2014. "Wings of Freedom: Iranian Women, Identity, and Cyberspace." In *On Shifting Ground: Muslim Women in the Global Era*, edited by Fereshteh Nouraie-Simone, 124–43. New York: Feminist Press at the City Univ. of New York.

Orzala. n.d. *Orzala's Blog*. At http://orzala.wordpress.com/. Last accessed Sept. 20, 2013.

O'Sullivan, Piper. 2012. "Pride and Propaganda: Analyses of Modern Pashto Poetry in Translation: Mid-20th Century to Present." Master's thesis, University of Indiana.

"Pashtun Women's Blogs." n.d. Blog entry. At https://orbala.wordpress.com /pashtun-blogs/. Last accessed Aug. 20, 2015.

Rettberg, Jill Walker. 2008. *Blogging*. Cambridge: Polity.

Roots in Air. n.d. Blog. At http://golkamra.blogspot.com. Last accessed Sept. 1, 2013.

Singh, Amarjit. 2013. *Indian Diaspora: Voices of Grandparents and Grandparenting*. Rotterdam: Sense.

Wardak, Arzo. n.d. *My Two Cents*. Blog. At https://arzowardak.wordpress.com/. Last accessed Sept. 20, 2013.

8 Changing the Tune?

Pakistani Music, Politics, and Social Reform

CHLOE GILL-KHAN

> It is an illusion that youth is happy, an illusion of those who have lost
> it; but the young know they are wretched for they are full of truth-
> less ideals which have been instilled into them, and each time they
> come in contact with the real, they are bruised and wounded.
> —Somerset Maugham, *Of Human Bondage*

The state of popular music in Pakistan is inseparable from the nation's
tense politicoreligious landscape. Since the 1970s, pop musicians have
navigated the political agendas of multiple governments and state censorship, suspended between contesting secular and Islamic visions of
the nation (Toor 2011). Indeed, Pakistani music is another battlefront on
which political, religious, and national ideologies continue to be exer-
cised. In an autobiographical account, Salman Ahmad, former member
of the pioneering Sufi rock band Junoon, reveals the impact of censorship
on music across the decades in Pakistan. He writes how during the 1980s
Zia ul-Haq's promotion of Wahabbism in a predominantly Sufi nation
began to seize control of the state media, madrassas, and college campuses, transforming universities into "virtual war zones" that resulted in
shootings and violence (2010, 69). A medical student with a passion for
music in Lahore in 1982, Ahmad describes an incident at a college talent
show when he played his Les Paul guitar. As Ahmad dazzled his fellow
students with sounds they had never heard before, violence erupted when
some students stormed the event, calling his music *haram* and smashing
his guitar (2010, 12).

Ahmad describes his subsequent musical career as emanating from this moment when he decided that he would wage a "rock and roll jihad" against politicians' distortion of the role of music and poetry in Pakistan. Ahmad's success with Vital Signs inspired him to see the band's popular appeal as a platform for social change, but when this view conflicted with his bandmates' vision of the band's purpose, he left Vital Signs and formed his own band, Junoon. Salman took his inspiration from the *qawwali* music and *ghazal* poetic forms and imbued them with local Sufi traditions, creating a new musical form, Sufi rock. His song "Ehtesaab," which calls for accountancy and transparency in politics, influenced the organization of a march in Lahore and of a free concert in Karachi, but the concert was banned on state television, and Prime Minister Nawaz Sharif later banned Junoon. General Pervez Musharraf would eventually lift the ban in 1999 following his military coup, attending the band's performance at Muhammad Ali Jinnah's mausoleum in Karachi (Ahmad 2010, 184). But religious criticisms of Junoon's music continued. Ahmad also received threats and protests from politicians and teachers, who objected to his use of Sufi poetry and his setting of national poet Muhammad Iqbal's work to the distinct Junoon sound. Even though the name "Junoon" is still active, the band members have spilt, and Ahmad dedicates himself to charity work, acting as a United Nations ambassador for HIV/AIDS awareness and teaching music in the United States to promote cross-cultural knowledge.

In her nostalgic memoir "Pop Idols" (2010), Kamila Shamsie explores the impact of contesting religious ideologies on musicians and their careers. The future paths of the members of the first homegrown pop group, Vital Signs, who stormed to success in 1987 with "Dil Dil Pakistan," demonstrate the deep schisms of Pakistan's politicoreligious landscape. The lead singer of Vital Signs, Junaid Jamshed, retired from pop music, declaring it *haram*; joined the missionary Tablighi Jama'at movement, through which he has dedicated himself to singing *hamd*s (praises of God) and *naat*s (praises of the Prophet Muhammad); ran a successful fashion business; provided religious instruction; and did philanthropic work. He died in an airplane crash in Pakistan in December 2016. Salman Ahmad, who quit Vital Signs to form the famous Sufi rock band Junoon, vacillates between his Sufi faith and corporate marketing (Shamsie 2010, 209). Ahmad's bandmate Ali Azmat promotes the popular "security analyst" Zaid Hamid and denounces Zionists, even though when asked he fails to explain his understanding of Zionism (Shamsie 2010, 213). How these famous pop stars—trailblazers in Pakistani music—have ended up is not what Pakistanis want, however: "in Pakistan, as all around the world, what we most crave from our musicians is music" (Shamsie 2010, 214). But what is artistic expression without its connections and dialogic relationships to the prevailing social, political, cultural, and aesthetic contexts of the time?

This opening section brings to attention how the artistic and biographical trajectories of young musicians in Pakistan since the 1970s have been intertwined with the shifting place of religion in public life. The disparate paths taken by the Vital Signs band members are part and parcel of ongoing questions of state censorship, religion, contestations over engagements with the "West," and the role of the artist in a postcolonial nation, a role that has shaped the aesthetic, political, cultural, and moral perceptions of music in Pakistan. If earlier attempts to introduce innovation and cross-cultural influences (for example, Sufi music and rock) into popular music were met with disappointment, this chapter examines the emergence of a new wave of musicians and sociopolitical concerns that emerged following the rise of media industries. In the mid-2000s, under General Pervez Musharraf's rule, the relaxation of media laws witnessed the spectacular growth of the media—and the middle class—in Pakistan (Lodhi 2011, 50). From 2000 to 2007, Pakistan was one of the fastest-growing South Asian economies (Lodhi 2011, 67). The proliferation of television and satellite channels opened up cultural production and consumption to mass audiences, in particular the youth, who make up almost 60 percent of the nation. In 1999, there was one state-owned television network; by 2010, there were about one hundred (Lodhi 2011, 67). Writing during this time, Mohsin Hamid expressed the euphoric "cultural revolution" that was taking place across Pakistani cities: "Pakistan is witnessing an explosion" in music that was part of a revolution in art and media, fueling "a new culture—one not limited to a 'narrow Westernized elite.'" Hamid concluded that "even if overshadowed in the news by the explosions of bombs,

Pakistan's other explosions—of music, media and mass culture—are powerful and growing sources of hope" (2004, 80, 94).

Although Hamid's optimism regarding the nation's economic and structural development proved to be short-lived, mass media (television, Internet, satellite, mobile telecommunication) have grown from strength to strength. However, one must proceed with caution in articulating this "freedom"—and the possibilities of mass media. Pakistan has the one of highest rates of murdered national and foreign journalists (Junaidi 2012). Yet, despite censorship remaining entrenched across media outlets and precarious sociopolitical conditions in which rock and pop concerts remain a privilege of the elite, musicians have appropriated media platforms such as television, the Internet, and mobile phone technologies as popular channels of political engagement, critique, and activism in forms that were not seen earlier. Mark LeVine travels the rock and metal scene among affluent circles in Islamabad, Peshawar, Lahore, and Karachi. Commenting on a gathering in Islamabad, he writes that the consumption of alcohol and drugs and the general atmosphere were clearly worlds apart from the armed guards present at such private parties. And just a few kilometers away, "in Islamabad's downtown, 6,000 male and female students from the Jamia Hafsa religious seminary gathered to burn—literally—CDs, video recorders, and even televisions worth tens of thousands of dollars as part of a conference on 'the enforcement of *sharia* and glory of jihad'" (2008, 222).

In particular, the satirical political protest song has proved to be a popular genre over the past decade. Such songs satirize and critique Pakistani and international politics, the establishment, civic structures, and popular attitudes toward the state of Pakistan. In this chapter, I examine how young musicians are turning to civic matters, rather than to the question of religion and music, to voice discontent and envision sociopolitical reform. This shift from religious to civic matters in popular Pakistani music provides a crucial intervention into dominant narratives of the processes of identity making in young Muslims. Rejecting both religious "extremism" and liberalism as an antidote to the current malaise, this genre of music takes issue with the urgent need to make sense of postcolonial politics. In the process, alternative frameworks for conceptualizing the processes of Muslim youth identities are envisioned that pose serious questions regarding the prevailing narratives of Muslim "radicalization," fundamentalism, and conservatism. The music of the Communist band Laal (Red), the band Beygairat (Shameless) Brigade, and the artist Shehzad Roy offer diverse and contesting perspectives of Pakistan's political problems. Whereas some artists endorse resistance to neocolonial mentalities and foreign occupation that are continuing to exercise their power over the nation, others criticize domestic political and the military establishment. If some appeal to the language of ethics and morals and individual responsibilities toward one another as an antidote to political exploitation, violence, and foreign intervention, others satirize the perpetual status quo in Pakistan. However, what unites these musicians is their commitment to sociopolitical reform outside the parameters of the religious that defined the previous generation of socially conscious musicians.

The following section reflects on the growth of the media in a nation with gross uneven development and asks to what extent young urban middle-class cultural artists who are carving spaces for themselves as social agents can translate dissent into cultural, political, and social change. Scholars have pointed out that the rise of the mass media in developing countries is no indicator of democratic forms of expression and participation. In relation to the Internet, Massimo Ragnedda and Glenn Muschert (2013) examine the "digital divide" across developed and developing societies, probing the perpetuation of old forms of social inequality and the emergence of new forms. Indeed, Pakistan ranks as one of the least-connected countries in the world. Just 10 percent of an estimated 180 million people have access to the Internet. Writing about the Arab world, Maha Taki states, however, that such deterministic indicators, "framed in terms of access and development," do not tell us what happens after access has been achieved (2009, 185). The historical, political, and cultural contexts are crucial when examining new technologies in developing countries. Taki argues, "The digital divide is a political outcome rooted in these historical systems of power and privilege and not simply a gap in access to and use of the Internet and computers" (190).

Rather than dismissing the mass-media industries as new sites of contesting power relations, this chapter examines theories of media content and effect. Focusing on Shehzad Roy's song "Apney ulloo" (Our Fools, 2011) and its related docudrama *Wasu or mein* (Wasu and Me), I argue that musicians' access to places, spaces, and peoples enabled via communication technologies demonstrates the multiple and creative potential of the mass media in the Pakistani context. In a context of the crumbling infrastructure and precarious conditions for travel in Pakistan, young musicians are appropriating media platforms to transcend physical restrictions and to explore the nation's rich geographies, peoples, and cultures. In the process, a collective citizenship is imagined, which attempts to challenge an entrenched clientelism and politics of self-perpetuation (Lodhi 2011, 54).

"Qismat Apney Haath Mein" (Destiny Is in Our Hands): "Paranoidistan" and the Satirical Protest Song

Following the start of the global "war on terror" in 2001, Pakistan's official alliance with the United States in the invasion of Afghanistan belied deep divisions in the nation's response to Pakistan's role in that invasion. Discontent over that involvement became apparent in strong anti-US sentiments, giving rise to conspiracy theories that attributed all of Pakistan's ills to US stratagems (Jalal 2011, 8). Terrorist attacks carried out by the Pakistani Taliban were "blamed on American private security agencies such as Blackwater and DynCorp as strategic revenge for Pakistan's refusal to break off ties with the Afghan Taliban and deliver the ever-elusive Osama bin Laden" (Jalal 2011, 8). Even "liberal-minded Pakistanis . . . for patriotic reasons . . . join[ed] the national chorus condemning American-led conspiracies to destabilise Pakistan" (Jalal 2011, 9). A top columnist for the *Washington Times* described Pakistan as "Paranoidistan"—"a state that suspects every U.S. move as designed to weaken Pakistan for the benefit of a secret U.S. alliance with India" (Jalal 2011, 7). But it was not just concerning anxieties over a secret alliance with India that "Paranoidistan's" anti-US sentiments were dissected in American journalism. In 2009 Adam B. Ellick interrogated anti-US sentiments in Pakistani pop music, questioning why such artists were not singing against the Taliban and claiming that the lyrics reflected widespread views among the educated classes that the United States, not the Taliban, was Pakistan's main problem.

It was in this charged political context, with anti-US sentiments running high, that Shehzad Roy's hit song "Laga reh" (Keep at It/Carry On) climbed to the top of the charts in 2008 (the song was later banned). Rather than staging a debate between music and religion or causing direct offense, the song is laced with satire and humor that critiques people's apathetic attitudes toward the stagnant state of the Pakistani political establishment. The music video is shot as a fiction film that requires an understanding of Pakistani politics to pick up the biting political satire. The song is set in the hustle, bustle, and chaos of central Karachi, where both people from diverse walks of life and contemporaneous political events are treated with humor and satire. "Laga reh" opens around a political address, satirizing the corruption and cronyism of the status quo. Roy asks one political worker why is he supporting a politician when he knows that there is no hope, and the worker replies, "What shall I do? Admit defeat?" Roy states, "No, carry on." Next, Roy speaks to a *buzurg* (wise man) on a bus. The man implores Roy to tell him how the nation will continue to function, and after observing the bus driver's dangerous maneuvers, which result in a crash with a rickshaw, Roy replies, "I am not worried about how it will carry on. I am worried that it does not carry on like this."

After Roy and the *buzurg* get off the bus, the two witness violent clashes between civilians and the police as well as people robbing the helpless people injured in the crash. The *buzurg* assures Roy to leave it all to God. He asks Roy whether any pious people are left, to which Roy replies that the pious ones are those who have not had the chance (to fill their pockets). The final refrain takes on a sinister tone when Roy sees an American official lurking around while people are fighting with and looting one another. Roy follows the official and finds an ordinary man sleeping in the open air, unaware of the fate that awaits him. Roy warns the man, who is about to become a victim of US political stratagems, but to no effect.

In "Laga reh," the reconstruction of social reform, national belonging, and citizenship are depicted as inseparable from ethical and moral duties toward one another, which also have the power to resist political stagnation, chaos, and foreign intervention. In the space of Karachi, which becomes a microcosm of the nation, Pakistanis from all walks of life are positioned. Media personalities, politicians, lawyers, earnest religious elders, bystanders, poor workers, criminals, and the police forces are represented; no one is spared, and each person and class are held accountable for the nation's stagnation. The song views internal discord as the principal factor of political and, in particular, foreign exploitation. Rather than moralizing, it understands the conditions that have led people to lose their sense of reason, which is evident in the poor laborer's openness to guile and manipulation by external forces intent on capitalizing on the nation's civil discord, which has left people like him vulnerable. But the song also treats people with power as conscious agents who have the choice to make decisions rather than engage in the cycle of destruction. "Laga reh" envisions a citizenship based on common morals, ethics, and duties we owe to one another beyond political interests or class and ethnic divisions (Muhajir, Sindhi, Punjabi, Baluchi, Pathan, etc.). It views individual social reform as essential to resist foreign players waiting in the wings.

This perspective regarding citizens reforming their attitudes to one another and the nation is reflected in Roy's social project djuice, a mobile phone package provided by Telenor that is popular with the youth. Djuice launched a nationwide campaign, "Khamoshi ka Boycott" (Boycott Silence), aimed at Pakistan's young people to take a stand against social injustice through making small changes and taking stands in their lives to engender changes at the lowest level, which, it is hoped, will lead to collective reform. This approach is reflected in Roy's song "Kya derta hai?" (What Are You Afraid Of?), recorded for the Telenor commercial for djuice. The song appeals to young people to take a stand in their own lives and is complemented by a video that represents young people from all walks of life, such as female students on public buses encountering harassment by groups of young men with no respect for traffic signals. In a scene at the end of the song, when the young people have decided to take a stand and march for justice, collective individual screams of euphoria are heard, and the final sound is the *adhaan*, the call to worship. The suggestion is that Pakistan's plural cultural expressions can coexist without threatening each culture's influence and social standing.

If "Laga reh" views internal discord as enabling foreign intervention, the Communist band Laal's song "Deshatgardi murdabad" (Death to

Terrorism, 2011) condemns how Pakistan has come to be perceived as a nation of terrorists or a people who support terrorism. At the same time, it presents a kaleidoscope of US-Pakistani political stratagems that interrogate the "roots" of terrorism in Pakistan. The song opens with a statement from Hillary Clinton, "The people [Taliban] we are fighting today, we funded twenty years ago." The song begins with the Afghan Revolution in 1978, the US operation in 1979, and the collusion between the US Central Intelligence Agency (CIA) and the Pakistan Inter-Services Intelligence agency (ISI), whose agents are shown photographed together. It calls the enemies in the struggle against the Taliban in this period "America's stooges." It unpacks how these figures have come to be seen in certain national media narratives as Pakistan's "friends." Laal's website (www .lubpak.com) explicates further this issue of the war of images in Pakistan relating to the Taliban. Laal argues that the dominant narratives in Pakistan perpetuate right-wing agendas to marginalize the collusion of the ISI and the CIA in supporting figures in the Taliban. This erasure from public discourse, according to Laal, has meant that histories of the rise of religious fundamentalism remain without critique. Certain narratives have come to articulate the notion that the Taliban is safeguarding Islam from US imperialism, which exonerates the state's involvement in the Taliban's creation in collusion with the United States.

"Deshatgardi murdabad" attempts to empower people to make sense of the terrain that is Pakistani politics. In the process, it creates a sense of belonging by appealing to the notion of unlearning specific historical narratives that transcend ethnic, class, and religious divides. Laal has also examined the plight of peasants and caste structures, bonded child labor, Sufi histories of the region, and land rights. The song "Utho meri duniya" (Rise Up, My People, 2010) includes Allama Iqbal's poem "Farman-e-Khuda," and the music video captures Laal and Anjuman Muzareen's campaign for land rights in March 2010. Notwithstanding the controversies surrounding the band and its politics, the powerful appeal for social change in Laal's music and political activism reflects how cultural artists are embedded in their political and social contexts.

Beygairat Brigade's song "Aalu anday" (Potatoes and Eggs, 2011) critiques the status quo of Pakistani politics, sparing no one in its satirical commentary. The song satirizes political parties and prominent politicians, from Prime Minister Nawaz Sharif to Imran Khan and the Pakistan Movement for Justice, the Pakistan People's Party, and the former army chief of staff General Ashfaq Kayani. It also critiques the media's glorification of terrorists, the now forgotten Pakistani scientist Abdus Salam, and events such as how a Taliban mullah, Maulana Abdul Aziz, tried to escape during the government's siege of the Lal Masjid (Red Mosque) in 2007 by wearing a burqa. The forgotten tale of Nobel Prize winner Abdus Salam critiques his erasure from the public sphere because he is Ahmadi, a persecuted religious minority in Pakistan. In contrast to Laal's focus on external political forces in "Deshatgardi murdabad," in "Aalu anday" Beygairat Brigade satirizes the trend toward attributing all of Pakistan's ills to international political machinations. They sing,

> Why take Blackwater's tension
> This is where from within attacks happen.

The video ends with a placard, "This video is sponsored by Zionists," which further satirizes popular conspiracy theories promulgated in media circles.

Beygairat Brigade's second song, "Dhinak dhinak" (2013, its title using untranslatable terms for musical tones), grapples with what few have dared to: the military. The lyrics critique "the coup, the throne, with such ease":

> Proxy are the wars they fight to appease
> In them it's our men who are dead and deceased.

The song emphasizes the "generals'" unbridled power over civic and political establishments: "Budget, policy, and aid, they regulate." The song also critiques the generals' influence on the media: "News reports give them support / When a free car is a gift, an analyst's tone shifts." Beygairat Brigade's upfront satirical portraits of off-limits topics have resulted in a ban on their music as well as a prohibition on social networking sites where the band releases its music.

Roy's, Laal's, and Beygairat Brigade's political-protest music reflects the multiple perspectives from which cultural artists are making sense of and expressing the nation's turmoil. The diverse viewpoints have opened up a discourse about making sense of the nation's politics, attracting national and international attention, controversies, and censorship. But to what extent can change be engendered through their music? The final section turns to this question.

"Mock Revolutions?"

Is this trend in Pakistani pop music just an armchair hope for revolution? The *Dawn* critic Nadeem F. Paracha describes Pakistani pop music as staging "mock revolutions." Paracha writes that until the late 1970s "songs parodying or satirising political personalities or social issues were not all that common in Pakistan." Those that dared were, like in the West, "left/liberal in leaning." The consequence of this, according to Paracha, was that "when the children who had belonged to educated urban middle-classes under the reactionary Zia regime reached their teens in the mid-1990s, their ideological orientation began to naturally tilt towards the rightist sides of the conventional ideological divide. This generation became a magnet for a number of modern Islamic evangelical groups and organisations" (2012). Paracha includes Junoon and Roy in this new wave of post-1996 bourgeois musicians, who, he argues, critique politicians and the illiterate masses but remain silent about the armed forces. Paracha writes that just two songs have challenged the "right-wing swing of the urban middle-classes and the media": "Aalu anday" by Beygairat Brigade and "Waderey ka beta" (2012) by Ali Gul Pir. "Waderey ka beta" satirizes the son of a Sindhi feudal landlord (*waderey ka beta*), whose main aim in life is to drive four-wheel-drive Pajeros, "chill," and wear gold Rolex watches and starched black suits. This son trades on his unrefined characteristics in comparison to the urban "burger boys," who fail to attract women. His exam results are fake, and he has ten guards ready to develop a false case against anyone. In his songwriting, Pir has turned his back on the "burning/breaking news 'issues' with which the media is obsessed" and is "more interested on commenting on everyday people than on sensational political abstractions and imaginary demons" (Paracha 2012).

Indeed, although the growth of the mass media in Pakistan has strengthened the middle classes and the promulgation of certain political perspectives, it has also offered platforms for challenging the idea that media-enabled music is just another site of expression. Another way to examine the intersections between sociopolitical change, mass media, and music in Pakistan would be to explore their effect on social behavior (Sakr 2009). Writing about television during the 1980s, Joshua Meyrowitz argued that "it was not the power of any particular television message that accounted for change, but the way the whole medium of television physically reorganised the social settings within which people interact" (quoted in Sakr 2009, 10). Naomi Sakr explains,

> The logic of this analysis is not that leaders will be forced to act more democratically if their actions are exposed to public view. On the contrary, violence against demonstrators on camera in Cairo, Damascus and elsewhere proves that to be untrue. It is simply that people gain a different sense of their own potential when they can use electronic media to overcome restrictions on social interaction that are imposed by physical space. (2009, 10–11)

In a similar fashion, the existence of mass-media platforms or even satirical political protest songs in Pakistan do not guarantee more democratic forms of expression, participation, and representation but does present opportunities for reorganizing "social settings within which people interact." In opening up to mass audiences, the rich and diverse musical traditions of Pakistan—as seen and heard in the television series *Coke Studio*, for example—challenge singular visions of Pakistani culture and heritage (Azmat 2011). *Coke Studio* went on air in 2007 based on a novel formula that has been imitated even in India, pointing to the power of one of Pakistan's best exports to reimagine the nation. The series showcases diverse musicians, ranging from pop to traditional Sufi, introduces new acts, pushes musical boundaries, and reignites interest in old classics as well as experiments with them. *Coke Studio* "has pushed gender, social class and ethnic divides, and delivered a product with mass and wide-ranging appeal," (Azmat 2011, 106). The show has seen musical fusions that have gone viral on the Internet, such as Meesha Shafi and Arif Lohar's duet "Jugni" (based on the Sufi *kalam* "Alif Allah chambey di booti" [My Master Has Planted the Fragrant Seed]). The show has also "pushed the boundaries of what can be mainstream in Pakistan" and has taken risks in "incorporating the culture and languages of ethnic minorities in Pakistan," such as Marvari, Brahui, Seraiki, and Poorvi (Azmat 2011, 107).

Although it is clear that power relations are renewed and maintained through various strategies in the mass media, dismissing such technologies as perpetuating unequal power relations overlooks the question of content and audience response. A people who have been the subject of decades of propaganda and singular (or specific) visions of national identities, in a country where the multiple ethnicities, languages, cultures, and geographies remain on the fringes, media technologies present creative opportunities for discovering the nation. Shehzad Roy's song "Apney ulloo" (Our Fools, 2011) is an example of one such opportunity for making connections and for bringing into the cultural sphere marginalized sections of the nation.

"Apney ulloo" narrates Pakistan's political history from 1947 to the present in a tour de force song lasting six minutes. The video to the song is set in a corrupt office, where Roy plays the role of a bureaucrat at the lower rungs and Wasu (the same person as in "Wasu and Me") is the feudal worker in the modern "official" setting. The song opens by taking Quaid-e-Azam as the nation's liberator from the English colonizers, but "after Quaid-e-Azam, whoever came to power was interested in serving only his own interests." Muhammad Ali Jinnah is more commonly known as Quaid-e-Azam (the Great Leader) in Pakistan. The song makes an explicit reference to the Americans and the US dollar:

> We are still serving someone else's interest [foreign elements]
> They are still controlling us.

This expression of rebellion is offset by images of the bureaucrat anxious to please his superiors in a colonial fashion that sustains inequalities between classes and ethnicities. The song then runs through the history of Pakistan's political leaders and their vested interests. News flashes that are dismissed as "barking news" reflect how the contest for ratings thrives on sensation. Roy sings,

> Politicians have stolen everything from us.
> But we do not learn a lesson and will bring them into power again.
> And they will continue to steal and hoard.

The song ends with,

> Shehzad Roy produced a song, which no one understood.
> Angelina Jolie came over and everyone understood!

"Apney ulloo" hints at frustration with "corporate feudalism," which is also satirized in Beygairat Brigade's song "Dhinak dhinak" (Pintak 2009, 122–25). The audience becomes a market not just for parties who fund private channels but also for ratings. The story behind the song points to the possibilities that the media can bring together different peoples and perceive the audience as a public rather than a market. The song's background narrative was televised in a serialized program titled *Wasu aur mein* (Wasu and Me). The first show begins with Roy expressing his fear that future generations may forget Quaid-e-Azam's dreams altogether. Roy discovers a mobile video uploaded on YouTube by Wasu, the Baluchi man who sings the political narrative in "Apney ulloo." At a time when Internet connections were more reliable, Roy comments that "maybe only the Internet can bridge the gap between the rich and the poor." Roy is intrigued by the man who sang Pakistan's sixty-year history in four and a half minutes in a Baluchi village, a history that Roy could not understand, having taken three years to memorize it from his Pakistani studies textbook. His efforts to find Wasu demonstrate the realities of Pakistan—armed guards travel with Roy to Jaffrabad, the place in Baluchistan that Wasu comes from. Expecting Wasu to be employed in a senior post, Roy finds that Wasu makes *naan* (flatbread) for a living. He takes Wasu to Karachi to record the song. The program is also a story of two very different people coming together and seeing Pakistan from one another's perspective. When Roy asks Wasu about the inspiration for his song, Wasu replies, "I didn't make

a tune. . . . I saw it in a dream at night and I recited it in the morning."
Wasu is then reluctant to sing the song Roy is interested in and prefers to
sing a Baluchi song. At an exclusive debut of "Apney ulloo," Wasu states
that he doesn't like the song because "people will think that everything is
bad in Pakistan."

Following their travels across Karachi to Bangladesh, Wasu tells Roy
that the conditions of the poor will never change, and the two go back to
their own lives. Roy then decides to visit Wasu in Baluchistan to convince
him that things can change. His efforts at engendering change are cap-
tured in the three closing episodes of *Wasu aur mein*. Roy spends time
in Wasu's village, discovering how people have no choice but to survive
without jobs, electricity and gas, clean water, health services, and political will to aid the poor. Roy meets various politicians in Baluchistan in
an attempt to understand the province's problems. Roy meets with a
cross-section of people and stakeholders, including the chief minister of
Baluchistan in Quetta and students at Baluchistan University. A strong
sentiment expressed among the students is that the Pakistani state has
treated Baluchistan like an occupied province and that there is no will
for development and change. When Roy brings up the question of foreign intervention, one student states that they also see Pakistan as a foreign force. Young Baluchis are depressed about the state of affairs; most
of Pakistan's gas comes from Baluchistan, yet the locals do not have gas
in their homes, and it is almost impossible to open dialogue about these
issues with the authorities. Furthermore, the media has failed to highlight
frequent kidnappings of Baluchis. To gain another perspective, Roy meets
with Hamid Mir, the prominent journalist. Mir states that the ongoing
problem of Baluchistan is not due to foreign intervention or local land-
lords, as is often expressed in the media. Since 1947, Baluchistan has been
under the control of the armed forces and was the object of major military
operations in 1948, 1958, 1962, 1974, and 2006. Mir argues the same constitutional rights need to be extended to Baluchis as citizens.

Having embarked on a personal mission to help Wasu, Roy realizes
the limitations of his power, of his perspective on Pakistani nationhood
and citizenship, and of his perceived solution to Pakistan's deep-seated
problems. If the idea of Pakistan represents freedom for some, it signifies

oppression for others—a Baluchi perspective opens up singular stories of governance and nationhood. Toward the end of the series, Wasu is thinking of immigrating to Oman. When Roy tries to convince him to stay, Wasu replies that when rich people leave, no one points a finger at them, but when a poor man leaves, people say that he does not love his country.

The issues raised in Roy's project and in the rise of middle-class artists in general challenge the perpetuation of dynastic politics and clientelism built around a "political elite that was feudal and tribal in origin and has remained so in outlook" (Lodhi 2011, 54). Political parties "are extensions of *biraderies* [familial networks] and influential families" (Lodhi 2011, 55). This means that politics remain focused on narrow issues and that such politics operate "in the Pakistani case in a manner that is antithetical to the notion of citizenship" (Lodhi 2011, 55). The politics of patronage resist reform in areas such as land reform and taxation. The coming together of an urban popular musician from Karachi and a poor man from Baluchistan who makes *naan* for a living transcends their political allegiances as they learn one another's stories and attempt to find a common language of citizenship and belonging for the betterment of their land and its people.

Conclusions

It is no exaggeration to state that young Muslims have come to be associated with religious "extremism," "radicalization," violence, and a whole web of hostile images that pit them in a cosmic ideological war against the West. In bringing to attention a particular genre of music in Pakistan, this chapter has attempted to disrupt this prevailing narrative about how young Muslims are fashioning their identities in a postcolonial world. Since the 1970s, the tense pop-music scene in Pakistan has been inextricably tied to state-sanctioned religious conservatism and the US-Afghan-Russian-Pakistan political matrix in the region. With the gradual decline of musical experimentation and other modes of artistic expression, artists emerging in the new media age have brought attention to how young Muslims have written themselves into alternative narratives that grapple with intellectual and civic decline. Given the shrinking parameters of public discussion and the disintegration of public space, services, and infrastructure that erodes movement and exchange, the musicians discussed in this chapter open up singular narratives to multiple perspectives, people, and geographies. This turn from religious to civic matters in part reflects the dangerous terrain of music and religion, but it also provides crucial reflection on the scale of decline faced by the Pakistani people.

Ayesha Jalal argues that it is the absence of a sound historical consciousness that has made the Pakistani people susceptible to selective narratives and has "stunted the development of a critical intellectual tradition" (2011, 10). She suggests "Pakistanis will be better served if they are taught how to delve into the depths of their own history" (20). This outcome is far on the horizon given the fact that school textbooks have remained unchanged for decades and political self-interest has weakened the ambition of even conceptualizing a Pakistan for all. Perhaps the cultural sphere can envision the bridging of geographical, political, and ethnic divides. Roy and Wasu's project and *Coke Studio* demonstrate the creative possibilities that media platforms offer to explore the lands that constitute the nation of Pakistan. It is no accident that South Asia is home to rich poetic traditions that attempt to break divides between its peoples, giving rise to strong pluralizing impulses as an antidote to repressive and stagnant politicoreligious sentiments and establishments. One can see this movement in contemporaneous musical attempts to construct a collective citizenship. Young musicians' efforts continue the long tradition of holding authorities to account with an attempt to articulate a common language of rights and responsibilities rooted in ethical obligations toward the disenfranchised—a vision shared by all religious teachings.

References

Ahmad, Salman. 2010. *Rock & Roll Jihad: A Muslim Rock Star's Revolution*. New York: Free Press.

Azmat, Hira. 2011. "Bridging Cultural Divides." *Libas* 24, no. 3: 106–14.

Ellick, Adam B. 2009. "Tuning Out the Taliban." *New York Times*, Nov. 11.

Hamid, Mohsin. 2004. "Reinventing Pakistan." *Smithsonian* 35, no. 4: 80–95.

Jalal, Ayesha. 2011. "The Past as Present." In *Pakistan: Beyond the "Crisis State,"* edited by Maleeha Lodhi, 7–21. New York: Columbia Univ. Press.

Junaidi, Ikram. 2012. "'Over 90 Journalists Killed in Pakistan since 2000.'" *Dawn*, Nov. 20.

LeVine, Mark. 2008. *Heavy Metal Islam: Rock, Resistance, and the Struggle for the Soul of Islam*. New York: Three Rivers Press.

Lodhi, Maleeha. 2011. "Beyond the Crisis State." In *Pakistan: Beyond the "Crisis State,"* edited by Maleeha Lodhi, 45–79. New York: Columbia Univ. Press.

Maugham, William Somerset. 1915. *Of Human Bondage*. New York: George H. Doran.

Paracha, Nadeem F. 2012. "Mock Revolutions." *Dawn*, June 28.

Pintak, Lawrence. 2009. "Journalist as Change Agent—Government Repression, Corporate Feudalism, and the Evolving Mission of Arab Journalism." In *The Middle East in the Media: Conflicts, Censorship, and Public Opinion*, edited by Arnim Heinemann, Olfa Lamloum, and Anne Françoise Weber, 116–31. London: Saqi.

Ragnedda, Massimo, and Glenn W. Muschert. 2013. *The Digital Divide: The Internet and Social Inequality in International Perspective*. London: Routledge.

Sakr, Naomi. 2009. "Approaches to Exploring Media-Politics Connections in the Arab World." In *Arab Media and Political Renewal: Community Legitimacy and Public Life*, edited by Naomi Sakr, 1–12. London: I. B. Tauris.

Shamsie, Kamila. 2010. "Pop Idols." *Granta* 112:197–215.

Taki, Maha. 2009. "Beyond Utopias and Dystopias: Internet in the Arab World." In *The Middle East in the Media: Conflicts, Censorship, and Public Opinion*, edited by Arnim Heinemann, Olfa Lamloum, and Anne Françoise Weber, 184–95. London: Saqi.

Toor, Sadia. 2011. *The State of Islam: Culture and Cold War Politics in Pakistan*. London: Pluto Press.

9

Contribution of the Critical Thinking Forum in the Deradicalization of Pakistani Youth

A Case Study

MUNAZZA YAQOOB

In security terms, Pakistan is considered a frontline state—first in the war against the Russian invasion of Afghanistan in the 1980s and then in the war on terror led by the United States after the attacks on September 11, 2001 (9/11). These two wars have had a devastating impact on the socio-political environment of Pakistan. For more than two decades, Pakistan has been suffering from militancy, violence, and terrorism, which have impaired the country's social fabric and economic growth. As such, the state has not been able to focus its attention on devising policies for social stability and economic growth. Socioeconomic and political policies are directed toward antiterrorism, so education, health, social welfare, and the society's sociocultural cohesion are ignored as a policy priority. The situation has resulted in poor governance, economic instability, and political uncertainty, which have further aggravated the issue of intolerance and extremism in society. It has also affected youth in the same way as these other segments of society because they are one of the most significant demographics in Pakistan's population. According to the Pakistan Economic Survey of 2013–14, Pakistan is one of the largest youth-bulge countries in the world, with 48 percent of its population between the ages of fifteen and forty-nine. This should be a sign of a prosperous future for the country, but the Pakistani youth, bereft of opportunities to excel, are perceived to be radical, intolerant, violent, and thus vulnerable to extremist groups.

Pakistani Youth and the Issue of Radicalization

A significant volume of research shows that the absence of opportunities for education and cultural participation is a leading factor in motivating disillusioned youth to join violent and radical groups and networks in their struggle for social justice and in the raising of their political voice. Pakistan's socioeconomic policies and conditions are considered the main factors leading Pakistani youth toward radicalization and extremism. Natasha Underhill explains that as a result of a limited national policy to cater to the needs of a growing young population, the youth remain deprived of opportunities and social participation. They feel discriminated against and racially marginalized in local contexts as well as at a global level and subsequently become vulnerable to radical groups. She also regards the lack of educational opportunities as the primary factor in creating frustration among youth, which leads them to radical activities (2014, 103). Similarly, Marc Sageman (2004) argues that the lack of social opportunities and cultural participation is the primary cause of disillusionment among the younger population and leads them to terrorism. A survey report by the Pakistan Institute for Peace Studies (2010) presents a similar conclusion. According to the report, young people are dissatisfied both with state policies and with efforts directed at effecting positive social change and building peace in Pakistan. They want a more active role in society (9). The report recommends that Pakistan pay greater attention to the factors that cause nonviolent radicalization among young people. In particular, it refers to frustrated youth engaged in resistance against ethnic and religious diversity as a result of the absence of social cohesion and educational opportunities. Similarly, according to a Jinnah Institute Research (2013) report, opinion polls highlight that young Pakistanis are dissatisfied with the political institutions and political leaders of Pakistan and are frustrated with not getting the opportunity to participate in politics. As the youth seek political participation as empowerment to change social structures, they are frustrated because their input on socio-political policies is not considered. They want to be involved and to partic-ipate in the political process and the political system of Pakistan (Jinnah Institute 2013, 6).

The war on terror and the post-9/11 political scenario and policies have further complicated the state of affairs. Young and educated Paki-stanis seem to be aware of the potential danger to the country but can-not find any way to set things right. Leti Volpp (2002), Mustafa Bayoumi (2006), Junaid Rana (2007, 2011), Tomas Precht (2007), and Mehdi Semati (2010) suggest that as a result of Islamophobia after 9/11, Muslim youth experienced an identity crises. After 9/11, there has been an avalanche of discourses on Islam that construct Muslims as a single "race," ignoring their cultural and social diversity and reducing them to a single category. This reductionist religious identity constructed by the Orientalist logic of binaries presents Muslims as a primitive peoples and a potential threat to the liberal West, especially America. According to these theorists, this marginalization of Muslims has served as the main factor driving Muslim youth toward the adoption of a religious identity that serves as a resis-tance strategy in response to Western exclusionary politics (Sirin and Fine 2007; Maira 2009). Erin Steuter and Deborah Wills (2009) and Peter Morey and Amina Yaqin (2011) highlight the role of ideological discourses constructed by media and other cultural texts such as fiction and film in portraying Muslims as terrorists and the "other" as well as reducing Islam to a race and ignoring its cultural diversity and history. Sohail Abbas's study *Civil Society Initiatives: Probing the Jihadi Mindset* (2007), Moeed Yusuf's report *Prospects of Youth Radicalization in Pakistan* (2008), and Saba Noor's case study *Radicalization among Educated Pakistani Youth* (2009) present similar discussions on the factors leading to radicalization among Pakistani youth.

The Pakistani government seems seriously concerned about the increasing disintegration of society, the failing economy, and in particu-lar the anxieties of youth, who are the country's best human resource. Some of the critical steps taken by the government in this regard include establishment of the Youth Parliament in August 2005 and many other programs, such as the Prime Minister's Youth Program, the Youth Business Loan Scheme, the Young Development Fellows Program, and the Youth Welfare Organization to provide frustrated youth with alternative opportunities to channel their potential for positive and constructive activity. During the campaign for the election in 2013, almost all of the political parties included education and employment for youth in their political agendas and manifestos (Jinnah Institute 2013, 5).

However, despite these efforts there can be no substantial change to the current sociopolitical environment without including the broader civil society. This civil society, with its access to people at the grass roots, has the potential to enhance peace building in Pakistan. Awareness-raising activities such as conferences, seminars, dialogues, public demonstrations, and media campaigns organized by various civil society groups are effective means to eradicate violence (Mirahmadi, Farooq, and Ziad 2012, 5–6). The civil society of Pakistan is conscious of its responsibility to engage in mitigating extremism and actively promoting peace in society. A report by the Centre for Peace and Development (2012) appreciates the roles and efforts of Pakistani civil society to curtail radicalization through the promotion of intracultural understanding. The report emphasizes the expanded and meaningful role of women and youth in making civil society efforts effective in having a deeper impact on society. In this regard, the report refers to commonwealth associations and efforts to promote peace in Pakistan. Civil society groups, which include women's organizations, lawyers, doctors, and journalists, have been participating in social activities. Both the government of Pakistan and civil society have realized that alternate pathways are necessary for the young population to use their skills and their potential to help others refrain from extremism.

Youth-Led Civil Organizations in Pakistan

It is claimed that the rate of participation of youth in youth-led civil society organizations in Pakistan has been "unprecedented" for the past five years (Mirahmadi, Farooq, and Ziad 2012, 9). A significant number of young

Pakistani students and professionals have come forward in recent years to engage the youth in positive and productive activities to make them more tolerant, peaceful, and productive citizens of the country. Some of the youth organizations and networks have engaged in peace-building measures, the eradication of violence and extremism, and the raising of awareness and consciousness for a peaceful Pakistan. They include the Pakistan Youth Forum, Pakistani Youth Organization, Pakistani Youth Council, Organization for Youth and Development, Youth Welfare Organization, and the Pakistan Youth Alliance.[1] They are formed and run by young students and professionals from different walks of life. These groups and networks independently engage young people in various social, political, and academic activities to cultivate a democratic mind. They demonstrate the degree of seriousness and concern among common, educated Pakistanis for the establishment of a nonviolent, harmonious, and tolerant society. The collected data on these organizations provide insight into the measures being taken by Pakistani youth to promote peace and tolerance in society and indicate how effective these efforts are in dismantling radical and extremist discourses that have seeped into the society and among its young population.

Some of these groups, such as the Pakistan Youth Forum, the Pakistani Youth Organization, and the Organization for Youth and Development, have engaged youth in social welfare activities, education, economic development, disaster management, and entrepreneurship. The Pakistan Youth Forum provides a platform for young people to express themselves. It trains them to be responsive to the situations that call for help, and it enables them to participate in various campaigns and activities of social welfare. The Pakistani Youth Organization focuses on child education and promotes peace and solidarity through media campaigns and dramas. It provides a platform to young people to interact with each other through volunteer activities. The Organization for Youth and Development works to make Pakistan a progressive and tolerant country by empowering its

1. These organizations' websites are listed at the end of this chapter.

youth, educating communities, and promoting the concept of entrepreneurship. Its aim is to promote the country's socioeconomic uplift by providing quality education and health facilities to underprivileged citizens of rural communities and the necessary skills to make semieducated youth useful citizens.

The Pakistani Youth Council's main objectives are to train young workers within political parties to conduct fair elections, to strengthen political parties, to enhance the role of young women in the political process, and to make the youth aware of the responsibilities of political representatives and government institutions. The Pakistan Youth Alliance, a youth activist organization, is working in the fields of counterextremism, peace building, and social welfare for underprivileged groups. The organization engages youth in activities that promote democratic values and proactive activism. It uses visual art, street theater, workshops, seminars, discussions, social media, and digital sources to create awareness about sociopolitical issues. It mobilizes youth for peaceful protests and involves them in social welfare activities, such as relief and rehabilitation. Other youth organizations, such as the Pakistani Youth Council, work for political participation and consciousness raising regarding democracy and leadership. Other organizations, such as the Youth Welfare Organization and the Bargad Organization for Youth Development, are engaged in social activism, like all of the other organizations and forums discussed earlier, but they are distinct in that they involve broader civil society and academia in the discussion of various aspects of radicalization in Pakistani society.

The Youth Welfare Organization works to spread awareness among youth regarding various academic, social, and national issues. The organization consists of a team of young students who organize on- and off-campus activities and conduct seminars, conferences, and workshops to guide youth on issues such as education, health, and social networking. Similarly, the Bargad Organization for Youth Development is a student-led grassroots organization.[2] Bargad has actively played a role in formulating

2. Bargad's website is listed at the end of this chapter.

the Punjab Youth Policy and is providing similar assistance to the provincial governments of Sindh, Balochistan, Khyber Pakhtunkhwa, and the state government of Azad Jammu and Kashmir to develop their youth policies. Bargad initiated the youth peace diplomacy track in South Asia, involving youth from Pakistan, India, and Afghanistan. It collaborates with universities and organizes conferences on themes such as youth extremism and leadership among women using social research methodology. It also has a volunteer network that organizes different events and activities to promote peace and harmony in society.

Critical Thinking Forum

One of the main factors responsible for engendering violence among Pakistani youth is their marginalized position. The lack of opportunities to voice their opinions and viewpoints on sociopolitical issues has built frustration among them. In the absence of authentic pathways and platforms to raise their voices, some are driven to radical movements. Therefore, groups and networks such as the university-based Critical Thinking Forum (CTF) are essential academic spaces in societies such as Pakistan because they provide a platform for young men and women to get together to share their narratives, to critique sociocultural oppressive structures, and to think about the possibilities of change and praxis in nonviolent ways.

All the organizations discussed in the previous section share a similar trait: involvement of youth in the organizations' respective efforts to eradicate violence and to better society. They focus on practical participation and social welfare awareness campaigns based on issues of social and national import. The distinctive feature of CTF, however, is that it engages its members in serious intellectual activities, fostering in them scholarship, critical thinking, and a spirit of intercultural harmony.[3] All of the other groups mentioned engage with academia, but their primary project remains social activism. The CTF is distinctive for being rooted in

---

3. The CTF's website is listed at the end of this chapter.

academia because its members are young university researchers. Its activities focus on critical reading, are research based, and are directed toward academic activism instead of social activism. Thus, the CTF, by setting up reading sessions and engaging its members in theoretical debates, provides a deeper understanding of the sociopolitical issues and dismantles "distinction between academy and activism" (Yaqoob 2015, 4). Most of its members are women researchers at the different universities in Pakistan. The core committee members are from the International Islamic University–Islamabad, and other members are from both that university and other universities. The core founding members are in different academic fields, such as humanities and cultural studies, Islamic studies, sharia and legal studies, political science and international relations, and management sciences, and they all come from different parts of Pakistan and have diverse linguistic and ethnic backgrounds: northern and southern Punjab, Khyber Pakhtunkhwa, Azad Jammu and Kashmir, Baluchistan, and Gilgit-Baltistan. The original vision for the CTF was that it would serve as a hub where young researchers could share their ideas and work together. As such, the CTF provides a platform to its young members to engage in dialogue on pressing issues of sociopolitical, cultural, and religious concern and to be informed about the latest theories and research in their fields of interest. By providing them space to discuss, debate, and engage in dialogue on issues of conflict in a conducive environment, the CTF inculcates in them the spirit and value of peaceful coexistence and tolerance. Members are encouraged to expand their visions, analyze them critically, and think outside the box to dismantle and unlearn their prejudices and biases. Those young women and men who can disseminate this message to larger communities within their institutions as well as carry it to their families and local communities are given preferential membership.

The CTF was established in 2011 by a small group of motivated young research scholars at the International Islamic University–Islamabad. The forum's central aim since its inception has to been to offer such a platform to emerging researchers from different academic disciplines and ethnic backgrounds and to engage them in discussions on significant contemporary sociopolitical and academic issues. Individuals, as Jon Elster (2005) observes, often construct their identity around their commitment to particular political, religious, or ideological group. Therefore, group ideology becomes a personal identity and serves as a lens through which individuals perform their social, cultural, and political roles. This group bonding and commitment to group ideology has the potential to breed inflexibility and to develop an extremist worldview in individuals, who then become intolerant toward the political and social existence of other groups. This tendency can be observed in their inflexible behavior, dislike of diversity, and lack of resilience for intercultural dialogue. The CTF therefore considers education and the development of critical-thinking skills as essential to transforming rigid mindsets. Members of the CTF read, discuss, debate, participate in panels, and interact with a wide range of scholars and civil society representatives to enable them to grapple with the issues and to communicate with those at risk. The forum provides support to women researchers in particular, and it encourages them to develop a special frame of reference based on social harmony, equality, and intercultural understanding. In Pakistan, as in other South Asian societies, women are confined largely to the ideal standards of their cultural roles, position in society, and femininity (Yaqoob 2015, 12). The typical roles highlight the virtues of obedience and submissiveness to patriarchy, domesticity, and filial or familial responsibilities. In these patriarchal societies, "discrimination between men and women is generally marked, definite, and largely non-negotiable" (Jia 2003, 370). Through critical reading, exposure to international forums and organizations, participation on panels, and cultural visits, these women discover their potential and voices. They gain confidence and the necessary knowledge to view themselves and their society through a nuanced lens, which, it is hoped, will contribute to bringing about a sustainable and peaceful social change. They endeavor to become active citizens, rejecting their role as the "invisible half" of the country (Nazaria-e-Pakistan Trust 2015).

The upsurge in extremist tendencies seen in Pakistani youth during the past two decades, as discussed earlier, is owing largely to the absence and denial of legitimate and peaceful ways to protest, participate, and vent grievances. In this regard, Margarita Bizina and David Gray (2014) recommend a counterterrorism policy that emphasizes youth engagement in consciousness-raising activities. They also suggest that young people's understanding of materialistic trends, competitive economic and social spaces in contemporary societies, and the resultant individualism that can drive youth to disillusionment, alienation, and estrangement should be strengthened. The societies in which young people from different ethnic and linguistic groups are not duly integrated into the social fabric and processes and in which young people from disadvantaged areas are not encouraged to participate meaningfully in mainstream society experience more dissenting movements. Therefore, these factors should be adequately addressed, and through community engagement young people should be motivated to adopt "peaceful means of protest" (Bizina and Gray 2014, 77). In this regard, teachers, coaches, and parents can play a significant role in the deradicalization of youth because they can meaningfully engage youth in community and social activities at the grassroots level. The situation makes it urgent that state and civil society introduce common forums that offer and serve as alternative pathways for youth to become engaged citizens. Among such alternative pathways, especially for educated youth, are meaningful academic activities that build a connection between classrooms and society at large. Ayesha Siddiqa writes that along with encouraging youth to read books, there is a strong need to promote activities among youth that encourage intercultural dialogue and foster critical thinking. For her, activities such as "inter-faith dialogue . . . youth conferences, festivals, seminars and conferences to explain the 'other' and build confidence amongst various civilizations" are essential to counter radical tendencies and "latent" or passive extremism in youth (2010, 90). The CTF, one such alternative pathway, provides a space for young students and researchers from different parts of Pakistan to examine the socioeconomic, political, and cultural complexities of Pakistan from multiple perspectives and to think about practical and concrete solutions to these problems. Young scholars are trained to become self-aware, well-informed, and confident individuals with effective critical-reflective and communication skills to help combat the challenges posed by the negative and ideological discourses shaping the present socioreligious identity of Muslim and Pakistani youth.

As a consciousness-raising group, the CTF engages its members in academic activities that can have a deep sociocultural impact. The academic discussions and activities are designed to keep the sociocultural context of Pakistani society in view. In all of these activities, members are motivated to develop personal friendships and professional collaborations and to engage in friendly interaction to nourish solidarity among themselves. Critical reading and discussion sessions, conferences, seminars, and roundtables are organized and keep in view the research on developing thinking skills and creative problem solving, "by which a new mental representation is formed through the transformation of information by a complex interaction of mental attributes of judging transformation, reasoning, imagining and problem-solving" (Solso 2004, 417). Similarly, creative problem solving is a whole-brain process that involves gathering and sharing information, analyzing this information critically to develop a better understanding of it, and arriving at some workable solution (Lumsdaine and Lumsdaine 1995, 17–18; Halpern 1996, 370; King 2003, 2). In all of the CTF's activities, participants are encouraged to share, interact with, reflect on, and evaluate the information presented to them as well as their personal experiences. They are also encouraged to integrate their personal stories with academic reading and discussions. After critically evaluating all aspects of an issue, they attempt to develop strategies for changing their lives and society at large. For instance, in close reading sessions that are organized fortnightly, participants discuss works of classical and contemporary thinkers and theorists in the disciplines of sociology, politics and internal relations, history, law, literary, critical and cultural studies, journalism, and media studies. Some of the thinkers whose works have been discussed in these sessions are Ibn Khaldun, Shah Wali Allah, Michel Foucault, Antonio Gramsci, Paulo Freire, Frantz Fanon, Fredric Jameson, Hayden White, Edward Said, Immanuel Kant, René Descartes, Edmund Husserl, Martin Heidegger, Jürgen Habermas, Colectivo Situaciones, Allama Mohammad Iqbal, Sir Syed Ahmad Khan, Hamid Dabashi, Talal Asad, Fatima Mernisi, and Saba Mahmood. The CTF trains its members to become informed and responsible citizens whose analytical thinking and comments become even more knowledgeable, diverse, and rational. These readings are aimed to familiarize CTF members on issues of sociopolitical, cultural, and religious significance by going over the classical debates as well as the developing current debates. Members are motivated to critically review the content they are reading and to reflect upon it. Furthermore, critical reading and discussion help them determine the adaptability and efficacy of a particular theory within its sociocultural setting. Thus, a part of their training includes filtering the influx of information presented to them.

These sessions are designed on an experiential learning model (Kolb 1984) in that the participants' lived personal experiences are integrated into academic discussions. Participants are encouraged to draw comparisons from their experiences and share their observations in the larger sociocultural and political context. This process develops a collective understanding of the sociocultural structure of Pakistani society and its position in an international context. Members also learn to think strategically about changing oppressive structures and to find new ways to negotiate with and work within these structures for positive change. The young scholars are also trained in these friendly sessions to be flexible in their thinking and to understand the significance of tolerance, harmony, and peaceful mutual coexistence. They are motivated to respect divergent and conflicting viewpoints and opinions rather than to be harsh or aggressive in response to them.

As an academic platform, the CTF supports young researchers' efforts to engage in discussion with international scholars and civil society actors on various sociocultural and political issues. These interactions play a significant role in dismantling a reductionist religious identity associated with Pakistani youth. For instance, CTF invited the renowned US filmmaker Jennifer Lee to screen her documentary on the women's movement in the 1960s and 1970s and to discuss the role of that movement in the United States and its relevance in the Pakistani context. Through interaction with Lee, female CTF members successfully presented a positive image of educated and dynamic women on the international scene, as Lee wrote on her piece in the *Broad Side*: "Before visiting Pakistan I thought of Pakistani women as all the same—veiled and oppressed. Screening my film in Islamabad changed my opinion" (2013). The documentary generated a series of discussions on the position and prospects of women in Pakistani culture. The debates during these sessions analyzed the roles of Pakistani women in different spheres, the constraints they experienced, and the possible solutions to their existing problems. An array of diverse perspectives related to women in Pakistan—such as women's domestic responsibilities and patriarchal, oppressive structures that confine women to cultural standards of femininity and hinder their professional growth and intellectual pursuits—were presented in these debates. The issues of women rights and their marginalization in contemporary Pakistani society were explored and evaluated from several different perspectives to enhance the participants' awareness of the topic, to critique varied and complex social structures, and to discover ways and means to gradually liberate and empower women within their sociocultural settings. The postdocumentary session also considered the value of integrating women's voices and roles in the development of sociopolitical policies. It was concluded that an increase in women's sociopolitical participation could pave the way for positive social change.

The CTF has developed useful academic linkages with Pakistani universities and institutions, such as the National University of Modern Languages, Iqra University, Fatimah Jinnah Women University, Punjab University, the Da'wa Center for Women, the International Islamic University–Islamabad, Allama Iqbal Open University, and the Pakistan Academy of Letters. These local linkages have served to build the local academic networks of young teachers and students as they work together, share their experiences, and agree to strengthen their collaboration to achieve goals of mutual interest. Apart from local linkages, the CTF has also established useful collaborations with reputed international organizations, such as the United States Educational Foundation Pakistan in Islamabad, the Association for the Study of Literature and Environment, and the Comparative Literature Association of India. Because of its serious efforts to increase intercultural harmony in Pakistan, the CTF has been invited to attend international conferences, including "The Role of the Grassroots/ Community Leaders in Building Peace" (2013) and "Interreligious Consortium Grassroots & Community Initiatives towards Rebuilding the US-Pakistan Relationship" (2014), to engage in discussion on interfaith and intercultural issues in Pakistani society. In 2014, the CTF also won an international grant in an open competition under the Women Empowerment Program offered by the US State Department through the US embassy in

Pakistan. The grant enabled the two-year project Consciousness-Raising of Pakistani Women on Contemporary Academic and Social Issues (2015–17), which aimed to enhance the awareness of youth, in particular young women, on contemporary issues of sociopolitical and religious relevance. Similarly, some selected members of the CTF participated in academic and cultural exchange visits to Los Angeles in 2016 and London in 2017 to develop intercultural literacy. These collaborative linkages with international institutions were the opportunities for members to be involved in discussions on interfaith and intercultural harmony. These discussions, according to the members, stimulated them to review their misconceptions and specific frames of reference relating to other faiths and cultures. Information and ideas generated in multiple forms through multiple sources serve to develop pluralistic mindsets (Irum 2015–17).

"Meet the Writer" is one of the important activities arranged by the CTF. Invited authors and poets share with CTF members their writings, the objectives of their work, their creative experiences, and the sociocultural and political context of their ideas. Qaisera Shahraz, Muhammad Hanif, Bilal Tanweer, Akbar S. Ahmad, Kristiane Backer, Masood Raja, Fateh Muhammad Malik, Hameed Shahid, and Shahid Siddiqui are just a few of the many prominent writers who have been invited to speak.

Conclusion

Nadeem F. Paracha, a famous Pakistani journalist and writer, writes in one of his columns in the newspaper *Dawn*, "Islamic fundamentalism has had an active presence in the milieu of youth and student movements and politics in Pakistan" (2012). For Paracha, it was during Zia's military dictatorial rule that students' political unions were banned and that the "presence and influence of fundamentalist student groups" became strong on campuses under the project of "Islamisation" (2012). A second equally strong wave of extremism and radicalization spread across the country after 9/11, when Pakistan under General Pervez Musharraf's military rule decided to engage in the US-led war on terror. Ayesha Siddiqa states that student wings of politicoreligious parties still actively operate on the campuses, and she also confirms that Pakistani youth in universities show their strong commitment to Islam and follow Islamic practices in their daily life (2010). Similarly, Saba Noor's study in 2009 confirms this tendency among the youth in Pakistan. As regards CTF members, religion plays a pivotal role in their life, and they are committed to Islamic faith and practices, but they reject radicalism and consider religious and ethnic diversity an enriching element of Pakistani society. The CTF's distinctive contribution lies in the fact that students and academics do not join this forum to assert their political or religious/political affiliation or to voice their political or religious identity. They take part in it mainly because it promotes academic debate and peace through intellectual dialogue. Members do not seek any political opportunities or work to achieve any political office. They instead have a passion for working as young academics to help revive a culture of reading and dialogue in Pakistan while holding informed discussions based on a theoretical reading of the multidimensional issues confronting contemporary Pakistani society. The forum dismantles the general assumption that young people who keep their religious commitment are conservative and exclusionary and oppose critical thinking and inter-civilizational and intercultural dialogue (Siddiqa 2010, 4). Through their active participation in democratic conversation with the guest speakers from various religious, ethnic, and racial backgrounds as well as in the sessions and panels addressing Western audiences in Los Angeles, London, and various universities in Pakistan, the members demonstrate that their thinking is not restrictive and that their vision is inclusive. The fact that they are deeply religious does not mean they are extremist, violent, and intolerant of other civilizations. They have the capacity and ability to communicate with different groups and to develop meaningful human connections with them. The CTF works under this broader definition of education. The discussion here illustrates that the CTF has contributed positively to achieving this broadened vision of education to combat the challenges posed by the radicalization of youth in Pakistani society.

References

Abbas, Sohail. 2007. *Civil Society Initiatives: Probing the Jihadi Mindset.* Islamabad: National Book Foundation.

Bayoumi, Mustafa. 2006. "'Racing Religion.'" *CR: The New Centennial Review* 6, no. 2: 267–93.

Bizina, Margarita, and David H. Gray. 2014. "Radicalization of Youth as a Growing Concern for Counter-Terrorism Policy." *Global Security Studies* 5, no. 1: 72–79.

Elster, Jon. 2005. "Motivations and Beliefs in Suicide Missions." In *Making Sense of Suicide Missions*, edited by Diego Gambetta, 233–58. Oxford: Oxford Univ. Press.

Halpern, Diane F. 1996. *Thought and Knowledge: An Introduction to Critical Thinking.* 3rd ed. Mahwah, NJ: Lawrence Erlbaum.

Irum, Sonia, comp. *Consciousness-Raising of Pakistani Women.* Edited by Sofia Hussain. Final project report. Islamabad: CTF, 2015–17.

Jia, Lisa Lau Ee. 2003. "Equating Womanhood with Victimhood: The Positionality of Women Protagonists in the Contemporary Writings of South Asian Women." *Women's Studies International Forum* 26, no. 4: 369–78.

Jinnah Institute. 2013. *Apolitical or Depoliticised? Pakistan's Youth and Politics: A Historical Analysis of Youth Participation in Pakistan Politics.* Research report. Edited by Raza Rumi and Qasim Nauman. Islamabad: Jinnah Institute.

King, Lloyd. 2003. *Test Your Creative Thinking: Enhance Your Lateral Thinking; Learn to Think Outside the Box.* London: Kogan Page.

Kolb, David, A. 1984. *Experiential Learning.* Englewood Cliffs, NJ: Prentice-Hall.

Lee, Jennifer Hall. 2013. "An American Feminist Visits Islamabad." *Broad Side*, n.d. At http://www.the-broad-side.com/an-american-feminist-visits -islamabad.

Lumsdaine, Edward, and Monika Lumsdaine. 1995. *Creative Problem Solving: Thinking Skill for a Changing World.* New York: McGraw-Hill.

Maira, Sunaina. 2009. *Missing: Youth, Citizenship and Empire after 9/11.* Durham, NC: Duke Univ. Press.

Mirahmadi, Hedieh, Mehreen Farooq, and Waleed Ziad. 2012. *Pakistan's Civil Society: Alternative Channels to Countering Violent Extremism.* Washington, DC: World Organization for Resource Development and Education.

Morey, Peter, and Amina Yaqin. 2011. *Framing Muslims: Stereotyping and Representation after 9/11.* Cambridge, MA: Harvard Univ. Press.

Nazaria-e-Pakistan Trust. 2015. "Women in Pakistan." At http://www.nazariapak .info/Women-Pakistan/National-Policy.php. Last modified Apr. 25, 2015.

Noor, Saba. 2009. *Radicalization among Educated Pakistani Youth*. Islamabad: Pak Institute for Peace Studies.

Pak Institute for Peace Studies. 2010. *Radicalization: Perceptions of Educated Youth in Pakistan*. Islamabad: Pak Institute for Peace Studies.

Paracha, Nadeem F. 2012. "Islamic Fundamentalism and Youth in Pakistan." *Dawn*, May 31.

Precht, Tomas. 2007. *Home Grown Terrorism and Islamist Radicalization in Europe*. Copenhagen: Danish Ministry of Justice.

Rana, Junaid. 2007. "The Story of Islamophobia." *Souls: A Critical Journal of Black Politics, Culture, and Society* 9, no. 2: 148–61.

———. 2011. *Terrifying Muslims: Race and Labor in the South Asian Diaspora*. Durham, NC: Duke Univ. Press.

Sageman, Marc. 2004. *Understanding Terror Networks*. Philadelphia: Univ. of Pennsylvania Press.

Semati, Mehdi. 2010. "Islamophobia, Culture, and Race in the Age of Empire." *Cultural Studies* 24, no. 2: 256–75.

Siddiqa, Ayesha. 2010. *Red Hot Chili Peppers Islam—Is the Youth in Elite Universities in Pakistan Radical?* Berlin: Heinrich Boll Stiftung.

Sirin, Selcuk R., and Michelle Fine. 2007. "Hyphenated Selves: Muslim American Youth Negotiating Identities on the Faultlines of Global Conflict." *Applied Development Science* 11, no. 3: 151–63.

Solso, Robert L. 2004. *Cognitive Psychology*. 6th ed. Delhi: Pearson Education.

Steuter, Erin, and Deborah Wills. 2009. "Discourses of Dehumanization: Enemy Construction and Canadian Media Complicity in the Framing of the War on Terror." *Global Media Journal Canadian Edition* 2, no. 2: 7–24.

Underhill, Natasha. 2014. *Countering Global Terrorism and Insurgency: Calculating the Risk of State Failure in Afghanistan, Pakistan, and Iraq*. Basingstoke, UK: Palgrave Macmillan.

Volpp, Leti. 2002. "The Citizen and the Terrorist." *UCLA Law Review* 49, no. 5: 1575–1600.

Yaqoob, Munazza. 2015. "Consciousness-Raising in South Asian Women's Fiction in English: A Feminist Critique." *Pakistan Journal of Women Studies: Alam-e-Niswan* 22, no. 1: 1–14.

Yusuf, Moeed. 2008. *Prospects of Youth Radicalization in Pakistan: Implications for US Policy*. Washington, DC: Saban Center for Middle East Policy, Brookings Institution.

Websites

Bargad Organization for Youth Development. At http://bargad.org.pk/page
/1122-bargad-organisation-for-youth-development.
Critical Thinking Forum. At http://www.iiu.edu.pk/?page_id=16372.
Pakistan Youth Alliance. At http://www.pya.org.pk/.
Pakistan Youth Council. At http://www.pakistanyouthcouncil.org/.
Pakistan Youth Forum. At http://pyfpakistan.org/.
Pakistan Youth Organization. At http://www.pyo.org.pk.

10 Kashmir's Children of War

Religion, Politics, and Nonviolent Mobilization

IDRISA PANDIT

In the current atmosphere of global politics, Muslim youth, regardless of the circumstances and context, are generalized as unique in their discontent. Under the looming shadow of the terrorist attacks on the United States on September 11, 2001 (9/11), and the language of the war on terror, most Muslim youth are discontent, and resistance is framed in the context of terrorism, thus overshadowing varying responses of resistance to hegemony and occupation. The popularized monolithic image of Muslim youth as an angry radicalized population completely disregards the complexity of Muslim youth around the world, who, despite their faith and culture and the time and place they live in, share similar hopes and aspirations, just like any ordinary youth, something they have in common with their counterparts around the world (Bayat and Herrera 2010). A widespread narrative of youth discontent in Muslim countries attributes this discontent to a lack of economic opportunities and the rise of religious fanaticism. But both conclusions are challenged by the results of the largest research study polling Muslims around the world, which found only a tenuous link between poverty, unemployment, and radicalism (Esposito and Mogahed 2008). Hence, there is greater need to understand what drives Muslim youth activism around the world and how the youth themselves situate their lives in the arena of global politics. This study is an attempt to describe the activist youth of Kashmir Valley in their context, devoid of external projected labels such as *terrorism* and *religious fanaticism*.

In Kashmir, a place that has been plagued with political discontent ever since the partition of the subcontinent into India and Pakistan in 1947, youth have historically played a central role in the struggle for *azadi* (freedom). For the people of Kashmir, it is a struggle for their right to express their will, their right to self-determination, and the basic human right to exercise a choice regarding their political future, which was promised to them nearly sixty years ago and upheld by numerous United Nations resolutions. The people of Kashmir continue to be held hostage to what Kamal Chenoy calls the "bitterly contending nationalisms" of India and Pakistan (2006, 24). It is estimated that there are more than seven hundred thousand Indian soldiers in Jammu and Kashmir, making it the world's most militarized zone (Mishra 2010). The number of armed forces has not changed even with the dramatic decrease in and near dissolution of militant groups. According to the reports of the Indian police and army, the total number of militants in 2012 was estimated to be only around 300 to 350 (Pandit 2012). Militancy in Kashmir has waned in the past twenty-five years, since the beginning of mass popular insurrection and violent resistance in the early 1990s. Either most of the former militant groups have completely dissolved, or members of these groups have formally become part of a nonviolent political movement for the reunification of Pakistani and Indian Kahsmir (*BBC News* 2012). The Indian army, however, continues to claim that highly educated and wealthy Kahsmiri youth are joining militant ranks (Masood 2015).

In the past twenty-five years, draconian laws have been implemented in Kashmir. In contravention of international humanitarian laws, numerous national laws grant absolute impunity to Indian armed forces: the Armed Forces Special Powers Act (enacted in Kashmir in 1990), which allows Indian forces to search houses without warrant, arrest Kashmiris without warrant, destroy property, and shoot at unarmed civilians, all with absolute impunity from prosecution; the Terrorist and Disruptive Activities Act of 1987, which treats every Kashmiri as a combatant and terrorist; and the Jammu and Kashmir Public Safety Act of 1978, which allows the state to arrest anyone for expressing his or her views on Kashmir's disputed nature or for publishing any documents related to the dispute. The report published by the International People's Tribunal on Human Rights and Justice in Indian Administered Kashmir in 2009 states:

> Kashmir's militarization has resulted in crimes against humanity and the fabrication of a culture of grief through extrajudicial or "fake encounter" executions, custodial brutality and deaths (70,000+ between 1990–2005), enforced disappearances (as many as 8000+), unknown, unmarked, mass graves, landmines used as weapons, and bodily disablement by the military, with 60,000+ tortured, 100,000 orphaned, and a very high rate of people with suicidal behavior. (23)

So why do people continue to resist oppression and hegemony? This question is perhaps best answered in the words of an Indian soldier who became a victim of violence while on active duty in Kashmir:

> As a soldier you have to believe that terrorism is bad for your country. But when you see it close up, you realize there is a reason for resistance—usually a result of some failing by the State. . . . Kashmir remains the most militarized places on earth. It is often said that ethnicity creates violence; but I think violence creates ethnicity—people who have lived in amity for centuries are moved by injustice, and the divisiveness of that injustice focuses on ethnicity or religion. (quoted in Seabrook 2010)

These words of a former Indian army major, Gopal Mitra, who lost both his eyes in an encounter while serving in Kashmir and had to undergo facial reconstruction, touch upon the key issues of the Kashmir conflict, issues this study tries to investigate from the perspective of the youth activists of Kashmir: How do young people born into and raised during the recent Kashmiri struggle for independence choose to respond to years of violence and oppression, and what factors shape their resistance? Is it fair to brand the Kashmiri resistance, especially the nonviolent youth resistance of 2008 and 2010, as "terrorism"? In what way has the violent state response to nonviolent youth movements changed the nature of youth resistance?

Kashmir's children of war have grown up under the shadow of the gun, enduring tremendous trauma and pain. Since the early years of the militant uprising in 1990s, youth have played a crucial role in resistance to Indian occupation. They have been advocates for change as well as targets of state-sponsored violence.

Of all the conflict zones on earth, Kashmir is perhaps one of the regions of the world where the impact of persistent violence on the youth and children has not really been well studied. Very little data are available to assess the impact of violence on Kashmiris in general and on Kashmiri youth in particular. In fact, the literature on torture and incarceration is scant, as Javaid Rashid acknowledges in his study, because researchers are not allowed easy access to incarcerated youth (2012, 634). First, difficulties with documenting such cases entail great risks for the participants as well as for the researchers (634). Second, members of the local academy have been silenced or compromised. Although there is a plethora of writings on the history of the Kashmir conflict, there are hardly any studies, especially studies from local universities, documenting the reality of the situation on the ground. Academics at local universities are silenced under severe threat of reprisal for researching and writing on the realities of Kashmir. Barring a few controlled sociological studies, no literature documents the human rights aspects of the Kashmir conflict. Young scholars face the threat of being barred from the academy for working on issues deemed "antinational" or "seditious," a threat that thereby completely suppresses intellectual inquiry. Scholars who venture into local issues that may portray the Indian state establishment negatively are censored. I met a scholar whose thesis investigating the history of one of the pro-freedom groups was rejected at the last stage because it was considered "antigovernment." He was forced to change the premise of his thesis, ignore the data, and change the language before being granted approval to move forward with his work. Lack of academic freedom has also resulted in the clampdown of academic streams, such as the Human Rights Program in the Faculty of Law at the University of Kashmir. There is also a distrust of local academics, resulting in the importation of Indian academics to teach at the local universities as well as the hiring of Indian educators as chief administrators. With ongoing surveillance of local academics and threats to their job security, intellectual freedom has been severely curtailed, and most of the scholarship on local issues is conducted mostly by scholars from outside Kashmir, always without disclosing the real purpose of their visit. When the Indian government does recognize the work of those who highlight such realities, they bar them from entering Kashmir. Among the scholars and writers who have been punished for their human rights work in Kashmir are David Barsamian and Richard Shapiro, who were deported; Gautam Navlakha, a key member of the Human Rights Tribunal who was denied entry to Kashmir; and local human rights activists and writers who have been threatened and assaulted (Vij 2011). The government has even charged Arundhati Roy, a famous Indian writer and a vocal advocate of social justice and human rights, with sedition (Chamberlain 2010).

Who Are the Children of War?

The best way to understand the children of war is to see them through their own lens. As one participant in my study (which I describe in the next section) put it,

> We are children of the conflict. It is in our blood; it is part of our subconscious to resist. Our views are completely different than the global political scenarios because we see things that happen through the prisoners' door, things that are happening right in front of us. This will not be an issue for a child in Boston, London, or Sydney, but kids born here are politically mature.

There has been a generational shift in the resistance movement in Kashmir, with the lion's share of the freedom movement taken on by the young, those who were either born during or came of age in the recent years of militarization of Kashmir. Through the narratives of Kashmiri youth, this study examines the impact of the violent response to the nonviolent youth resistance between 2008 and 2010 and how it reshaped the current worldview of these children of war. From 2008 to 2010, these children of war confounded the state machinery by leading mass nonviolent resistance marches and protests. Documenting the uprising in 2010, Dil-naz Boga states that

> growing up in Indian-controlled Kashmir, the most highly militarized region in the world, hits children hard. Kashmiri youth view Indian soldiers as an occupational force. Some assert their dissent by throwing stones, chasing soldiers down streets, or driving them out of the territory as they chant slogans of freedom. They sometimes end up being arrested, shot or maimed by armed Indian security personnel. (2010)

Kashmiri youth also became the prime victims of state violence when in 2010, called "the year of the killing of the youth," more than a hundred young people were killed and several thousand were detained under draconian laws such as the Armed Forces Special Powers Act, the Disturbed Areas Act of 1976, and the Public Safety Act, all allowing absolute impunity to arrest, torture, and kill on the pretext of threat to national security. According to a report by the Asian Centre for Human Rights, the Public Safety Act is used for preventive detention of minors for up to two years (Child Rights International Network 2011). It was also in 2010 that the military forces adapted the "bullet for a stone" policy in response to youth resistance in street protests, where they were seen as perpetrating what the state classified as "agitational terrorism," an infraction punishable by death or life imprisonment (Hoffman and Duchinski 2013). Teenagers who were incarcerated under the Public Safety Act ended up in jail cells with hardened criminals, many enduring grave sexual violence. As a fourteen-year-old boy recounted, "The treatment meted out to us was worse than Abu Ghraib . . . we were not in a position to walk" (quoted in Boga 2010). It is these incarcerated youth who, according to psychiatrists, turn to activism, often violent activism. For many, the transformation from being a stone thrower to a militant occurs after the torture they suffer during their incarceration. Their response is to pick up the gun, a reality that is affirmed by the growing trend in youth who were harassed in 2008 and subsequently considered joining militant groups (Dar 2013). The trauma and pain that youth undergo during torture leave deep scars. A group of senior doctors report that conflict in the valley is the main cause of mental illness and that there is an alarming increase in mental illnesses such as post-traumatic stress syndrome, trauma, and clinical depression:

> Due to continuing conflict in Kashmir during the last 18 years there has been a phenomenal increase in psychiatric morbidity. The results reveal that the prevalence of depression is 55.72%. The prevalence is highest (66.67%) in the 15 to 25 years age group, followed by 65.33% in the 26 to 35 years age group. The difference in the prevalence of depression among males and females is significant. Depression is much higher in rural areas (84.73%) as compared to urban areas (15.26%). In rural areas the prevalence of depression among females is higher (93.10 %) as compared to males (6.8%). (Amin and Khan 2009, 213)

Depression has been determined to be a factor affecting various aspects of the everyday life of most Kashmiris, especially young women, for whom mental illness is also taking a toll on their reproductive health (Yousuf 2014). These youth are vulnerable to the wish to end their lives as a result of mental stress and the pressures of their life experiences, evidenced by a dramatic increase in the rate of suicides in the Kashmir Valley. In one year, there were 836 documented suicides, almost all of them youth, especially young girls trying to end their lives by consuming poison (Yaqoob 2013).

The definitions of youth within a globalized world are ever changing—from the brave and bold to the irresponsible and troubled. As recent events such as the massive popular uprisings in the Middle East and North Africa in 2011 have shown, Muslim youth are not passive and distant observers or recipients of change. After the revolutionary movements in the Arab world, the superimposed negative image of irresponsible and careless youth was changed to an image of active, caring, and passionate people, deeply involved in shaping the world around them. The youth of Kashmir, whose portraits we encounter in this chapter, are part of the larger paradigm of global youth, who are indeed shaping the politics of the lands in which they are growing up. In this chapter, I move away from fitting the Kashmiri youth activists to a generalized theoretical model of Muslim youth behavior. These decontextualized models are often misrepresentative of the reality and diversity of global Muslim youth experience.

I also do not use any preconceived notions of a conflict zone. The themes that emerge from the data gathered and the thick descriptions used provide the reader with a sense and feel for the youth of Kashmir, who see themselves as active resisters; these themes allow the reader to understand the youth as human beings who struggle to maintain self-worth and dignity and defy the labels *jihadi* and *terrorist*. This study is merely a glimpse, not the total picture, of Kashmiri youth resistance. However, this portrait of the youth, even though incomplete in some ways, is not an artificial construction of defining the "other"; rather, it is an attempt at humanizing the face of Kashmiri youth so as to allow others to hear them speak about themselves, their circumstances, their elders, their political leaders, and their worldviews.

Operating in a Conflict Zone

Conducting research in conflict zones poses its own unique challenges for the researcher and any participants in a study (Wood 2006). As Jonathan Goodhand (2000) argues, there is indeed a need for creating a framework for conducting ethical research in conflict zones. At the same time, each situation is contextual, and, besides observing basic ethical principles, a researcher must have the ability to adapt to the circumstances while upholding the main principle of "do no harm." It is important to situate myself as a researcher in this case. I am a native of the land, aware of Kashmir's history as well as of its political, social, and security challenges. Therefore, the youth I spoke with did not have the added burden of explaining the context or the history of the conflict to me. Given my ability to speak all three languages in which the interviewees responded, there was no chance of losing any data in translation. However, in spite of the fact that I was an insider in many ways, building trust among the youth did not always come easy. Mistrust is pervasive because of the prevalence of counterinsurgency measures, including the use of informants employed by the armed forces to implicate the populace. Being constantly aware of surveillance by Indian intelligence agencies and role of informants in the struggle, I had to invest in trust building, and my contacts in the civil society as well as among former students and colleagues were crucial in getting access to key informants and providing assurances on my behalf. Almost everyone who participated in the study expressed to me that if others had not vouchsafed for my credibility, they would not trust me or speak to me. Not knowing what all these youth had endured in their lives, I had also to be constantly aware of trauma, both the trauma that these young people relived in relating their stories as well as my own vicarious trauma. As a member of Kashmir society, albeit more a visitor for two months out of twelve every year, I have been witness to some of the pain over the years. I lived through the mass nonviolent protests of the summers of 2008 and 2010 and lived under the curfews and restrictions imposed in response. I was also involved in documenting some of the human rights abuses in the early years of the struggle. As is the case with almost all Kashmiri families, my friends, neighbors, family, and I have been affected by the conflict and its aftermath.

My primary data-gathering tools were an online survey and semistructured in-depth interviews with the youth of the Kashmir Valley, the heart of the conflict zone. The youth ranged in age from eighteen to thirty years, mostly college and university students actively engaged in the youth resistance movement of Kashmir. My aim was to allow these youth to describe in their own words how they were shaping the resistance movement in Kashmir. These children of war, born and raised during the two and half decades of the latest Kashmiri struggle, have been both witnesses to *and* victims of the conflict. Although several of the youth I interviewed had formerly been detained, incarcerated, and tortured for their activism, I did not have access to youth who were languishing in jails for their involvement in the nonviolent struggle in 2008 and 2010. All the interviews were carried out in various spaces to guarantee the participants' safety and were conducted in a mix of English, Urdu, and Kashmiri, with constant reassurances of confidentiality. Interestingly, because some had been punished for their online activities and nonviolent social media resistance, not everyone participated in the online survey. There was always an element of surveillance present in the interviews, and I had to take extra precaution with regard to place and time of meetings so as not to endanger these youths' lives. Although I recognized the ethical challenges of conducting research in Kashmir, I followed the principle of "do no harm." It was because of their desire to have their voices heard that some did volunteer to speak with me and often facilitated my meeting with other youth activists.

Understanding Kashmir's Youth Resistance

Kashmiri youth classify themselves as politically more mature than their elders, aware of global politics as well as grounded realities. These children of war have witnessed oppression and confrontation in their own community and are very well aware of the history of conflicts in other Muslim countries—Afghanistan, Iraq, Syria, and Palestine. They recognize the political nature of the Kashmir conflict and all of the United Nations resolutions related to the issue, yet, unlike their parents and grandparents, they strongly express a lack of faith in any of the international players, be it powerful nation-states such as the United States and Russia or international organizations such as the United Nations. They believe in indigenous, novel ways of finding a solution. They distrust various separatist leaders of the freedom movement, pointing out these leaders' incapacity to make any difference on the ground for years, other than rallying people around empty slogans. The youth acknowledge that there was an ever-present desire for freedom among those of their parents' generation, but they consider that generation to have failed in transforming that desire into active resistance. Therefore, the youth characterize their resistance as distinct because it is not dictated by any powerful figures. Learning about and from other resistance movements around the world has made them aware of the games that world powers play, which has helped them to understand the nature of India's and Pakistan's interests in Kashmir and how those interests ignore the wishes of the Kashmiri people. For the youth, the leaders of various separatist groups do not share their sentiments. The youth feel that political leaders have used them for their personal gain, often coloring a political struggle with a religious agenda. As prime victims of draconian laws such as the Armed Forces Special Powers Act and the Public Safety Act, they find such leaders incapable of changing even a single injunction that has caused such pain and misery for the youth of Kashmir: "We have no faith in leaders; we do not believe in rhetoric. We know our history, and we have to find a new path to solve our problems."

So What Do the Young Want?

Every single participant in my study clearly defined the Kashmir conflict as an illegal occupation of Kashmir by India. Although part of the territory of Kashmir is under Pakistani and Chinese control, the word *occupation* was never used in reference to either of these countries. Its use was confined to India's hold over 65 percent of the territory in Jammu and Kashmir, with the main focus on the valley. Although the Kashmir conflict dates back to 1947, all of the participants in my study were born and raised in the past twenty-three years of conflict. They all were keenly aware of the occupation and resistance during this period. The oft-repeated reasons for choosing resistance against occupation were the basic right to life; an end to oppression and exploitation; the protection of integrity, dignity, and honor; and, above all, the right to choose their own political fate—the right to self-determination. In defining the nature of the conflict, every single participant understood it as a political and territorial conflict but not a religious one.

Although there was clarity on the issue being solely political, not religious, everyone acknowledged that religion is a prime motivator for many to resist the occupation. Multiple religious ideologies and interpretations of Islam exist among the youth. Those who favor a religious interpretation of the conflict use the language of pan-Islamism, as in the struggle to bind the *ummah*, a view that in this case is interpreted as favoring a merger of Kashmir with Pakistan. Others categorically state that the fight for freedom has no religious roots. Unlike in the past and distinct from their parents' generation, a very small minority, less than 2 percent of the youth interviewed, showed an affinity for the Pakistani perspective. Those who did have such an affinity expressed it as such: "The love for Pakistan is embedded in Kashmiris. . . . Let's not mix faith and politics. It is just the love and support for another Muslim brother or country. It is respecting the fact that they always supported us, morally, politically, in every way.

They have sacrificed themselves for us. We hope this love will pave the way for freedom of Kashmir."

If not religion, culture seems to be a driving force for resistance. It is an issue of preserving the Kashmiri identity, something the youth see eroding under the cultural influences of the Indian media and entertainment industry: "The innumerable crimes being committed against people of Kashmir, the bloodshed, the disappearances, the half-widows, half-orphans, rape victims, all forms of impetus . . . I don't think faith plays any part here; yes, culture does. It is about our cultural identity, fighting to preserve our Kashmiri identity" (ellipses indicate a pause).

For others, religion is the unifying rallying cry that binds everyone to seek freedom by invoking the principle of the oneness of God: "Religion plays an important role in determining the nature of reaction toward any incident. The rallying cry is the declaration of divinity of Allah. It has always been 'Azaadi ka matlab kya. La ilah illa lah' [What does freedom mean? There is only one God]. The people of Kashmir are united on the religious front."

Others see mixing religion with politics as dangerous and detrimental to the Kashmiri cause. They are wary of youth using religion as an opiate and easily becoming victims of antisocial elements interested in creating hate in the community, especially the growing trend of sectarianism, both among various Sunni groups and between Shias and Sunnis. Such divisions are alienating most Kashmiri Muslims as well as members of the minority communities, who are threatened by conflating religion with politics:

Sectarianism is growing. Many young people find refuge in religion. They think by praying they are doing their duty, so they do not need to do anything else. When youth were tortured and beaten in 2008 and 2010, they turned to religion for comfort, and some of them were brainwashed, so you have some highly educated youth becoming militants when even their families do not even know. . . . Religion is abused here. We have minorities such as Sikhs and others supporting our cause. What about them and our common freedom struggle? I believe if religion had been kept out of the Kashmir issue, this problem would have been solved.

When asked to define the term *jihad* and whether they consider Kashmir's struggle for independence as jihad, all the youths interviewed agreed that *jihad* means to struggle to end all forms of oppression but not to pick up arms against the enemy. The slogan of "jihad," which was used as a rallying cry in the early years of the struggle, when foreign fighters came to offer assistance, holds no appeal for these youth. They instead emphasize fully understanding the reason for their decision to fight rather than blindly following the orders of any group or a leader:

> Jihad is to struggle against oppression. "Jihad bil nafs" [struggle of the soul] is the highest form of jihad, and the one after that is to stand up for those who are being oppressed. Jihad is to stand up for justice. In Kashmir, we are victims of oppression, so anyone who fights this oppression is a *mujahid*. . . . *Violent resistance* is a Western term; it does not fit us. As Muslims, we have to fight for anyone who is oppressed.
>
> . . . The picture of jihad has changed in Kashmir. The youth are studying and understanding *fiqh* [Islamic jurisprudence] for themselves. In the '90s, it was en masse taking up arms without checking capacities. In sharia, not everyone can go for jihad. Turns out many people were infiltrating the struggle, but now the filtration process has occurred. Those few who take up arms now do so knowingly. In the past, thousands would go for arms training across the border; now there are very few locally but really committed ones. They are not exploited; they are self-motivated.

Even the most respected of Muslim leaders, Syed Ali Shah Geelani, historically a supporter of the Party of Mujahideen (Hizbul Mujahideen), a Kashmiri militant group, and other leaders associated with various political and religious groups consider the linking of the Kashmiri movement with the international calls for jihad as a way to sabotage Kashmiris' genuine resistance. Geelani insists that the Kashmir struggle has a political, not a religious, agenda and that the Taliban have no place in Kashmir (Qadri 2013). Mirwaiz Umar Farooq, another prominent separatist leader of the group Freedom (Hurriyat), believes that the media are trying to deny the indigenous roots of the Kashmiri struggle and to link "the

genuine Kashmir struggle with the international terrorist movement"
(quoted in Wani 2006).

A similar sentiment was present in the youth I interviewed, who
made the case that the resistance movement has dramatically shifted. They
acknowledged that in the early years of the struggle there were foreign fighters who came from Pakistan, Afghanistan, and other countries to participate in jihad in Kashmir. At present, however, the Kashmiri struggle, they
insist, is carried out not by any foreign fighters but by indigenous Kashmiris, few in number yet fully committed to driving India out of Kashmir.

Why Resist?

One quote best captures the sentiments of all the youth I spoke with. Their
sole desires are to taste freedom and to live with dignity and without fear
and oppression:

> Since I was born, I have seen Kashmir simmering, Kashmiris dying.
> This has made me bitter; I tend to see everything in a negative light.
> What has occupation brought us—insecurity, bloodshed, rapes, disap-
> pearances. When I was young, I did not know what was going on, and
> I would proudly sing the Indian national anthem. When I grew up and
> understood the cause of suffering around me, my mind was changed for
> a lifetime. Every Kashmiri, every household in Kashmir has borne the
> brunt of this occupation. The crimes committed against us are the main
> reason I want to resist. I do not want my children to see this occupation.
> I don't want them to be afraid of men in uniform. I don't want my son to
> be frisked every step of the way by an outsider. All my wants and dreams
> form the factors for me to resist this occupation.

In the early years of the Kashmiri uprising, while documenting gross
human rights violations such as murder, rape, and torture, I often won-
dered how these children who were witnesses to incessant violence would
respond to the excesses committed against them, their parents, their relatives, and their neighbors. It seemed normal that these children would one
day want to avenge rape and torture especially. Instead, the youth defied
their leaders and elders during the nonviolent demonstrations of 2008 and

2010. The events of 2008 gave rise to the pent-up emotions of the young, an excuse to finally let lose all the anger and pain, not by resisting with arms but by challenging and mocking their oppressor in the streets of the valley through spontaneous dancing, an approach that won them the title *"ragda* generation," the generation that developed a rhythmic dance of protest, deriding the occupation, while Indian armed forces struggled to figure out how to respond with their guns (Lepeska 2008).

The violent response to this mass nonviolent insurrection included the killing of youth as young as nine. This response changed the nature of youth resistance, hardening the youth who were incarcerated and tortured for participating in protests and for breaking the months' long curfew by taking to the streets and resorting to social media. The idealism of their nonviolent approach to the struggle was shattered as they paid dearly with their lives. Many of the youth arrested under unjustifiable preemptive detention laws are still languishing in jails in places unknown to their families. Yet, instead of breaking the will of the youth, the heavy-handed Indian response seems to have strengthened their resolve to rid Kashmir of its occupation. For many of the youth, the Indian response, rather than serving as a deterrent, infused life blood into the resistance movement, which in their words was beginning to lose momentum prior to 2008:

> The years of 2008 and 2010 are [a] remarkable part of resistance movement. We started with armed resistance in the '90s, and it was crushed in two to four years. Kids born after 1996 did not witness the early atrocities. Then India invested a lot in the younger generation in making them forget the past. In 2005, most youth opposed resistance, but 2008 and 2010 changed all that. In those years, we secured our resistance movement for the next thirty years. India helped us transition to a beautiful phase of resistance. No speeches and sermons would have made any difference that the Indian response to our 2008 and 2010 nonviolent resistance made. They helped us affirm our commitment and educate others who had forgotten.

As acknowledged by the youth, the younger generation turned away from armed resistance and actively engaged in nonviolent forms of resistance, confounding the Indian state, which struggled to find a quick response to this approach. Some youth, however, expressed regret that they had bought into the narrative of nonviolence prior to 2008. They often attributed the agenda of nonviolent struggle to forces interested in mellowing and co-opting the youth. In hindsight, they felt that various Indian civil society groups as well as numerous nongovernmental agencies were promoting the agenda of nonviolent struggle to distract the youth from their independence struggle. After the deaths of more than a hundred youth and the incarceration of thousands of youth in 2010, they were convinced that nonviolence was no longer a proper response to continuous death, torture, and disappearance of their peers and certainly not the way to send a message to the Indian government that the youth will not give up their desire to seek freedom. It is with a sense of hopelessness that some youth are once again resorting to the gun. As one respondent put it, two years of active nonviolent struggle resulted in a very violent response:

A tremendous element of fatigue set in people. They felt their efforts had gone to waste. The years of 2008 to 2010 are seen as years during which the general populace, young and old, were supporting the nonviolent approach. Even opinion makers, various community elders, leaders in darasgahs [religious schools], insisted nonviolence was the way. Even Hizbul Mujahideen [the main separatist group] agreed that [the] gun is no longer an option. Stone pelting as a form of violent resistance never disappeared, and as the state response got more and more disproportionate, the more violent the stone pelting became. There was fear in 2008 and 2010 that the state would use counterinsurgents to commit acts of violence to justify their violent response. However, even those above-ground militants that were co-opted in the past remained steadfast and did not buy into a violent response, something that was unprecedented. Even Geelani [the chairman of Hizbul Mujahideen] insisted throughout the mass protest to not even touch army bunkers; instead, people formed human chains around them. In spite of that, people were arrested under the Public Safety Act on charges of inciting violence and have since been languishing in jails.

I was a witness to the mass nonviolent protests of 2008 and 2010, when a sea of humanity poured out onto the streets and puzzled the security forces as fearless youth danced in front of their military bunkers. In many ways, deciding on a response to stone pelting was much easier: the security forces would just turn their guns on the youth. But they had no mechanism for responding to dancing youth, so they once again resorted to violence. The disenchantment and disillusionment of the youth over the efficacy of nonviolent struggle were palpable as they became convinced that nonviolent struggle was merely a delay tactic that had been imported to pacify the youth of Kashmir. They were convinced that an indigenous, smart, armed struggle was the only way to keep pressure on the Indian administration. On India's part, not engaging the Kashmir youth involved in nonviolent means of resistance was truly a missed opportunity for peace building and nonviolent resolution to the intractable Kashmir conflict.

The violence that unfolded in the Kashmir Valley in the summer of 2016 clearly supports the prediction made by the youth in this study. The extrajudicial killing of Burhan Wani, a young engineering student turned militant, led to protests, with 90 people killed and more than 17,000 injured, many of them youth and children (Ahsan 2017). During the popular protests led by Kashmiri youth, Indian military forces used pellet guns to indiscriminately blind fully or partially thousands of youth and children (Nadimpally 2017). And this violent response continues every day. Such targeted violence against unarmed youth protesting in the streets has further convinced the youth that the Indian government is not interested in a nonviolent resolution of the issue. And reports of youth joining militant groups have been on the rise since Burhan Wani's death. As Umer Farooq, the chairman of the Hurriyet Conference, a moderate separatist faction, states: "Youth feel they have absolutely no space to propagate their views and ideas. They are being hunted down, killed, maimed and blinded. They feel their voices are scuttled and they fear peaceful dialogue will lead nowhere" (quoted in Saha 2016).

Cyber Resistance

In the 2008 and 2010 protests, youth who were not demonstrating on the streets and indoors under curfew channeled their resistance through the Internet. As the voices of the youth grew louder in cyberspace, Internet providers and cellphone services were shut down, as is routinely the case in Kashmir, where denying access to the outside world has always been used a way to punish the local population. In addition to jailing hundreds of youth for street demonstrations, the Indian government arrested thousands of youth for participating in protest by means of social media. Social media proved to be a bigger weapon in the 2008 and 2010 demonstrations because there was no other way of reporting on what was happening in the valley. In spite of all the curbs on their cyber activity, tech-savvy youth managed to keep their online activity alive, in some cases running anonymous Facebook pages documenting the testimonials of youth who were tortured and arrested on charges of participating in antinational activities. Such revelations as well as the stories of the families of disappeared youth and the recent discovery of mass graves were used as tools to embarrass India. The tech-savvy youth Burhan Wani, whose murder by security forces brought Kashmir to a crossroads once again in 2016, used social media effectively to recruit other local youth to join the rebellion, earning his approach the label "new age militancy" (Fahad Shah 2016).

This information campaign is seen as the greatest form of resistance at this point, countering the propaganda of the Indian government and its media control. As a young writer who runs an online alternative journal stated, "I am resisting with my journalism by speaking the truth. . . . When I was young, I used to visit the houses of youth who got killed. I would visit with protestors on the street and even joined the stone throwers. Finally, I picked up the pen. I think different expressions are necessary. A stone thrower is as important as a journalist."

The urgency of creating an awareness about the Kashmir conflict within India as well as throughout the world can be attributed to what Frédéric Grare refers to as the "auto-censorship" of the Indian national press, which prides itself on being open and critical yet is "strangely silent on the issue of Kashmir except when it comes to condemning Pakistani scheming" (2008, 186). None of the work that writers and journalists do in Kashmir comes easy. There are death threats against them, and many of them have been killed in mysterious circumstances. A growing number of alternative media outlets have been set up by young writers. While the creative genius of young Kashmiri writers and poets is being lauded around the world, in Kashmir they suffer from serious threats to their lives as well as from defamation. A special government intelligence branch, the Cyber Cell, is dedicated to putting pressure on writers, especially those who maintain an online presence, to stop reporting facts about Kashmir. The local newspapers are closely monitored, and most mainstream newspapers refrain from publishing anything that may go against the state's narrative on Kashmir. The co-option of the media is linked to government control of newspaper advertisements. Journalists from India are also embedded in local news agencies and in this way monitor publications, and numerous counterpublications are produced and distributed by the army as an attempt to discredit the efforts of local youth who are actively engaged in creating alternative media channels. However, the growing number of very talented young journalists and writers committed to issues of justice seems hard to reverse.

An Intellectual Resistance

As Thomas van der Molen and Ellen Bal (2011) note, the youth of Kashmir have recognized the power of information. Fighting with knowledge, information, and awareness was a common theme in all of my interviews. Recording the history of the recent years of struggle and documenting the stories of the victims of rape and torture, death and destruction seem to be the focus of youth resistance. They recognize the lack of attention paid to the Kashmir struggle all around the world and the silence over all sorts of excesses committed in Kashmir by the Indian armed forces. Therefore, their efforts are geared toward documenting this information on their own and finding ways of letting the world know the reality on the ground while also preserving this knowledge for posterity. A few young academics and activists have created popular youth-engagement programs that provide opportunities for the young to debate issues of local and world history, faith, and culture. Other writers and journalists have begun mentoring younger writers: "What we need most is education. Kashmiris have lost the war; the level of co-option is unparalleled. The way youth are being radicalized is so hopeless. You have extremes of youth—the

'Hollywoodized' and 'Bollywoodized' types that are really far away from faith and the dangerously radicalized Saudi/Qatari sectarian types."

It is the latter youth who fall prey to the dangerous sectarian ideological beliefs that the youth activists and educators are targeting. Religious education that is devoid of hateful sectarian ideology seems to be the most critical need at present because a variety of religious sects formerly unknown in Kashmir are thriving and taking advantage of vulnerable youth. Among other young activists are prominent writers who consider their writing to be the most powerful resistance tool. As a witness to immense violence during his childhood, one of the prominent bloggers and a well-regarded writer found it was only through his writings and filmmaking that he could dispel commonly held misinformation and untruths about Kashmir among Indian citizens as well as in the rest of the world. There are also artists and poets, musicians, and stand-up comedians who use their artistic expression to register their protest against oppression (Syeed 2011).

Activism and the Feminine

Speaking of activism and activists has been a gendered discourse, one that has ignored the reality of women's contributions in the Kashmiri struggle. In my interviews, young women framed their acts of resistance by invoking their writings, poetry, and other art forms as well as their documentation of human rights violations. The female youth narrative, which has been overlooked in most studies, is beginning to get noticed (van der Molen and Bal 2011). In fact, the young men who participated in this study openly acknowledged the role young women are playing in the struggle. Although Islam is often blamed for the lack of participation by women in civil society, it is obvious in Kashmir that some of the key female voices are speaking from within Islam. The greatest factor limiting women's involvement has been the sexual targeting of female civilians by the Indian armed forces (van der Molen and Bal 2011, 95). In a predominantly conservative Muslim society, female activists face an acute challenge. Their parents worry about the risks their daughters take of being harassed and attacked when they go in the field, their inability to find the right kinds of jobs, and their being labeled as troublemakers. Many women give up their activities because of family pressure as well as because of the threat of disappearance and rape by the security forces.

The involvement of women in resistance, as it emerged in my conversations with young activists, is complex and nuanced, defying theoretical definitions of activism in conflict zones. Women's voices have been ever present in the Kashmiri struggle. From the very beginning, women—mothers, wives, and daughters—have paid a heavy price in the current uprising as victims of brutalization and oppression. The number of cases of women with post-traumatic stress syndrome is on the rise, as is women's use of drugs (Hussain 2013). Women are paying the price while juggling their own personal trauma and trying to keep their families together. Besides the mental trauma, the current strife is held responsible for altering Kashmiri women's reproductive cycles. Doctors report that 15.7 percent of women of childbearing age in Kashmir will never have a child without clinical intervention (Farooq Shah 2008).

In a first report of its kind, Kashmiri civil society groups documented various forms of insecurity the women of Kashmir face (Association of the Parents of Disappeared Persons 2011). As noted in this report, Kashmiri women have been long involved in breaking the silence over crimes committed in Kashmir through organizations such as the Association of Parents of Disappeared Persons (2011), founded in 1994. The recent activism of women involves documenting rape in Kashmir. Rape has been used as a weapon of war in Kashmir ever since the beginning of mass insurrection in the early 1990s, and these crimes against women have been absent from the official records of the Indian military and state government. Even in the recently revised rape laws of the Indian Constitution, military forces such as the one operating in Kashmir are still immune from prosecution in what India terms "disturbed areas" (Biswas 2013). The young women I interviewed have broken their silence about the crimes against them and have formed a support group for seeking justice for crimes such as the Kunan Poshpora village mass rape in 1991, when eight hundred soldiers of the Fourth Rajputana Rifles raped between twenty-three and sixty women ages fourteen to seventy in the course of one night. On June 18, 2013, based on a petition filed by the young women activists, the district magistrate of Kashmir's High Court ordered the reopening of the probe into this case—a small victory for these women (Support Group for Justice for the Kunan Poshpora 2013).

Having interviewed the victims of Kunan Poshpora in 1992, I have been a witness to the pain of women struggling to admit the scars of such gruesome violation while balancing family honor and reliving this pain with every new investigation. To add insult to injury, the rapists came back the next day to have the women forcibly sign statements attesting that no incident had occurred. Even the government of India investigation team declared that there was no proof of the soldiers' guilt. The young women activists' success in breaking the state-imposed silence regarding that dark night and in reopening the investigation is an astounding feat (Mohidin and Masood 2013). However, there are continuous attempts to silence the advocates of victims of Kunan Poshpora, even in courts of law (Ghosh 2014). While the Indian judicial system continues to place roadblocks in the process of investigating the case, six victims have since died, as other survivors still await justice (Umar 2017). The young women activists who resurrected the case have not yet won in court, but they have made the world aware of the crime against victims of Kunan Poshpora through their activism and writings. In 2016, five of them published a book, *Do You Remember Kunan Poshpora?*, detailing their journey in exposing the case and the impact of the struggle for justice for women of Kunan Poshpora has had on their lives (Batool et al. 2016).

Women activists of Kashmir also identified information and education as two key aspects of the struggle. Although van der Molen and Bal (2011) attribute the lack of women's engagement in activism to "honor," Kashmir women activists are in fact the most vocal, fully aware of their own agency, and they reject their male peers' image of them as "weak creatures." In my interviews, they never mentioned honor as a concern. Although women have always been present in public demonstrations, vigils, and protests, the new generation of female activists is focusing more on finding alternative ways of protest that have a long-term impact, such as writing:

A pen is mightier than a sword. My activism is nonviolent; it is about going out in the field, documenting and investigating the impact of violence and occupation. My activism is to spread the truth globally. Unless and until we make people around the world aware of our situation and garner support, we will not win. The shackles of silence forced upon us need to be broken off; otherwise, peace will not come, let alone survive.

Kashmiri young women activists have found the documentation of human rights violations as their main tool of resistance and are actively engaged in documenting cases of gender violence as well as enforced disappearances. These women are challenging their own community to ponder internal violence against women as well as state-sponsored gender violence.

The Future of Youth Resistance

Since the spring of 2013, there were indications of a return of the gun to the Kashmir Valley, a cause of concern for the Indian establishment. All of the youth acknowledged in this study attributed the return of the gun to India's disproportionately violent response to the nonviolent protests of 2008 and 2010. During the spring of 2013, there were three separate incidents in which young men attacked the Indian armed forces in North and South Kashmir. The attacks were carried out by local highly educated youth. These young men were well placed in their lives yet made a conscious decision to pick up the gun without the knowledge of their own families. Syed Salahuddin, the Hizbul Mujahideen commander in chief, stated that "a target oriented and well organized resistance movement is a must to achieve the goal of freedom" (quoted in Gul 2013).

Once again, one noticed increased debate in the media and in intellectual circles about Kashmir's new breed of militants—namely, educated young people who knowingly joined militant groups and were willing to sacrifice their lives. The local political parties, such as the National Conference and the People's Democratic Party, all of whom are state actors in the current occupation in Kashmir, started issuing worrisome statements about pockets of militants among the youth of Kashmir and about

254 · Idrisa Pandit

finding ways and means to curb this trend to pick up the gun once again (Bashir 2013).

Indian academics attributed the lure of militancy to the youth's hopelessness and political disillusionment, triggered by the conviction and hanging of Afzal Guru, a Kashmiri young man who was considered a prime suspect in the attack on the Indian Parliament in 2001 (Roy 2013). Happymon Jacob argues that the Indian state has bred hatred in the hearts of Kashmiri youth because of its unjust treatment of them, especially youth who choose to protest nonviolently but are dealt a violent, unjust response. He holds the Indian establishment and its "politically inept and sociologically unwise handling of the situation in Kashmir" responsible for the current rise in militancy (2013).

Conclusion

Among the Kashmiri children of war, there is a sense of urgency in announcing to the world the state of their land and its people—a need to tell their stories through songs, graffiti, memoirs, cartoons, human rights reports, alternative journalism, and cyberactivism. They want to right the wrongs created by misinformation about Kashmiri politics as well as about the reality of their lives. As one youth put it, they want to "embarrass the world's largest democracy" by highlighting the injustices committed by India in Kashmir. They are challenging the false image of a country shaped by Gandhian values of nonviolence by exposing the deadly impact of the violence committed by India in Kashmir. Such efforts are gaining ground with a first ever collection of stories related to youth resistance published in August 2013, *Of Occupation and Resistance: Writing from Kashmir* (Fahad Shah 2013); with underground graffiti artists such as Elhoriah giving cries for *azadi* (freedom) a new form of expression (Qazi 2012); and with Reality of Kashmir (Haqeeqat Kashmir), a group of poets, artists, and actors, celebrating World Peace Day by releasing a CD of revolutionary songs and art in memory of Afzal Guru, a young victim of India's suppression of the Kashmiri struggle for freedom (KT News Service 2013). Diverse forms of artistic expression are proving more powerful than guns and stones as the youth of Kashmir continue to find unique ways of resisting hegemony and defining their fight for dignity and honor through film, poetry, graffiti, photography, and drama. The challenge is growing more difficult, however, as the world overlooks the injustices committed in Kashmir and completely ignores the urgency of solving the Kashmir issue, one of world's longest-running intractable conflicts.

References

Ahsan, Kamil. 2017. "Kashmir's New Uprising." *Dissent*, May 4. At https://www.dissentmagazine.org/online_articles/kashmir-uprising-separatists-burhan-wani-elections.

Amin, Syed, and A. W. Khan. 2009. "Life in Conflict: Characteristics of Depression in Kashmir." *International Journal of Health Sciences (Qassim)* 3, no. 2: 213–23.

Association of the Parents of Disappeared Persons. 2011. *Half Widow, Half Wife: Responding to Gender Violence in Kashmir*. Srinagar, Kashmir: Association for the Parents of Disappeared Persons.

Bashir, Aliya. 2013. "Educated Militants Worry Mainstream Parties." *Kashmir Monitor*, June 8.

Batool, Essar, Ifrah Butt, Samreen Mushtaq, Munaza Rashid, and Natasha Rather. 2016. *Do You Remember Kunan Poshpora?* New Delhi: Zubaan.

Bayat, Asef, and Linda Herrera. 2010. "Introduction: Being Young and Muslim in Neoliberal Times." In *Being Young and Muslim: New Cultural Politics in the Global South and North*, edited by Linda Herrera and Asef Bayat, 3–24. New York: Oxford Univ. Press.

BBC News. 2012. "Who Are the Kashmir Militants?" Aug. 1. At http://www.bbc.com/news/world-asia-18738906.

Biswas, Soutik. 2013. "Explaining India's New Anti-rape Laws." *BBC News*, Mar. 28. At http://www.bbc.com/news/world-asia-india-21950197.

Boga, Dilnaz. 2010. "Minor Offences: India's Brutal Treatment of Kashmiri Youths Is Fueling Conflict." *New Internationalist*, Feb. At http://newint.org/columns/currents/2010/01/01/kashmir/.

Chamberlain, Gethin. 2010. "Arundhati Roy Faces Arrest over Kashmir Remark." *Guardian*, Oct. 26. At http://www.theguardian.com/world/2010/oct/26/arundhati-roy-kashmir-india.

Chenoy, Kamal. 2006. "Contending Nationalism: Kashmir and the Prospects for Peace." *Harvard International Review* 28, no. 3: 24–27.

Child Rights International Network. 2011. "India: Juveniles of Jammu and Kashmir—Unequal before the Law & Denied Justice in Custody." At http://www.crin.org/en/library/publications/india-juveniles-jammu-and-kashmir-unequal-law-denied-justice-custody.

Dar, Showkat. 2013. "26-Hour Shopian Encounter Ends." *Greater Kashmir*, June 1.

Esposito, John, and Dalia Mogahed. 2008. *Who Speaks for Islam? What a Billion Muslims Really Think*. New York: Gallup Press.

Ghosh, Shrimoyee Nandini. 2014. "The Kunan Poshpora Mass Rape Case: Notes from a Hearing." *Warscapes*, Sept. 9. At http://www.warscapes.com/reportage/kunan-poshpora-mass-rape-case-notes-hearing.

Goodhand, Jonathan. 2000. *Research in Conflict Zones: Ethics and Accountability*. Oxford: Refugee Studies Centre, Oxford Univ., in association with the Norwegian Refugee Council/Global IDP Project.

Grare, Frédéric. 2008. "The Armed Forces, Power, and Society." In *Democracies at War against Terrorism: A Comparative Perspective*, edited by Samy Cohen, 173–90. Basingstoke, UK: Palgrave Macmillan.

Gul, Khalid. 2013. "Trail Ambush: Hunt on to Catch Militants Who Slipped Off." *Greater Kashmir*, May 25.

Hoffman, Bruce, and Haley Duchinski. 2013. "Contestation over Law, Power, and Representation in Kashmir Valley." *Interventions: International Journal of Postcolonial Studies*, July, 501–30.

Hussain, Masood. 2013. "Kashmir: Pushed into an Abyss of Trauma with Over Usage of Pleasure Drugs." *Economic Times*, July 27. At http://economictimes.indiatimes.com//articleshow/21388071.cms.

International People's Tribunal on Human Rights and Justice in Indian Administered Kashmir. 2009. *Militarization with Impunity: A Brief on Rape and Murder in Shopian*. Srinagar, Kashmir: International People's Tribunal on Human Rights and Justice in Indian Administered Kashmir.

Jacob, Happymon. 2013. "Kashmir's 'Educated' Militants." *Greater Kashmir*, July 16. At http://www.greaterkashmir.com/news/opinion/kashmir-s-educated-militants/148939.html.

KT News Service. 2013. "Haqeeqat-E-Kashmir Releases a Tribute to Afzal." *Kashmir Times*, Sept. 21. At http://www.kashmirtimes.in/newsdet.aspx?q=22984.

Lepeska, David. 2008. "The Rebirth of Kashmir." *Kashmir Lit*, Fall. At http://www.kashmirlit.org/the-rebirth-of-kashmir/.

Masood, Basharat. 2015. "Guns 'n' Poses: The New Crop of Militants in Kashmir." *Indian Express*, July 26. At http://indianexpress.com/article/india/india
-others/big-picture-guns-n-poses/.

Mishra, Pankaj. 2010. "Why Silence over Kashmir Speaks Volumes." *Guardian*,
Aug. 14. At http://www.theguardian.com/theguardian/2010/aug/14/silence
-over-kashmir-conflict.

Mohidin, Rifat, and Bashaarat Masood. 2013. "Konan Poshpora Mass Rape: The
Silence of a Night." *Indian Express*, July 21. At http://archive.indianexpress
.com/news/konan-poshpora-mass-rape-the-silence-of-a-night/1144455/4.

Nadimpally, Sarojini. 2017. "Use of Pellet Guns Has Caused a Public Health Crisis
in Kashmir." *Wire*, Mar. 3. At https://thewire.in/119579/pellet-guns-kashmir
-public-health/.

Pandit, Saleem. 2012. "Militants May Make a Comeback in Kashmir." *Times of
India*, Mar. 18. At http://articles.timesofindia.indiatimes.com/2012-03-18
/india/31207196_1_militant-outfits-bangroo-kashmir.

Qadri, Haziq. 2013. "The Man Who Opposes Taliban Arrival in Kashmir." *Vox
Kashmir*, June 1. At http://www.thevoxkashmir.com/2013/06/01/the-man
-who-opposes-taliban-arrival-in-kashmir/.

Qazi, Naveed. 2012. "The Art of Graffiti in Kashmir." *Kashmir Walla*, Dec. 2. At
http://www.thekashmirwalla.com/2012/12/the-art-of-graffiti-in-kashmir.

Rashid, Javaid. 2012. "An Analysis of Self Accounts of Children in Conflict with
Law in Kashmir Concerning the Impact of Torture and Detention on Their
Lives." *International Social Work* 55, no. 5: 629–44.

Roy, Arundhati. 2013. "Afzal Guru's Hanging Has Created a Dangerously Radio-
active Political Fallout." *Guardian*, Feb. 18. At http://www.theguardian.com
/commentisfree/2013/feb/18/afzal-guru-dangerous-political-fallout.

Saha, Abhishek. 2016. "At Least 23 South Kashmiri Youth Turned to Militancy
after Burhan Wani's Death." *Hindustan Times*, Nov. 24.

Seabrook, Jeremy. 2010. "A Soldier's Story." *New Internationalist*, Apr. 1.

Shah, Fahad, ed. 2013. *Of Occupation and Resistance: Writing from Kashmir*. New
Delhi: Westland and Tranquebar Press.

———. 2016. "Burhan Wani's Killing Brings Kashmir to a Crossroads." *Diplomat*, July 14. At https://thediplomat.com/2016/07/burhan-wanis-killing-brings
-kashmir-to-a-crossroads/.

Shah, Farooq M. 2008. "15.7% Infertility Prevalence in Kashmir: Study." *Greater
Kashmir*, June 22. At http://wap.greaterkashmir.com/news/news/15-7-infer
tility-prevalence-in-kashmir-study/35953.html.

Support Group for Justice of Kunan Poshpora. 2013. "Kunan Poshpora: The Struggle Must Be Supported." Press release, June 22.

Syeed, Nafeesa. 2011. "Nafeesa Syeed: Kashmiri Youth Take Up Arts amid Conflict." *Guernica: A Magazine of Art and Politics*, Apr. 2. At https://www.guernica mag.com/daily/nafeesa_syeed_kashmiri_youth_t/.

Umar, Mohammad. 2017. "26 Tears after Kunan Poshpora, Army Still Enjoys Immunity for Sexual Violence." *Wire*, Feb. 23. At https://thewire.in/111344 /26-years-after-kunan-poshpora-army-still-enjoys-immunity-for-sexual -violence/.

Van der Molen, Thomas, and Ellen Bal. 2011. "Staging 'Small, Small Incidents': Dissent, Gender, and Militarization among Young People in Kashmir." *Journal of Global and Historical Anthropology* 60:93–107.

Vij, Shivam. 2011. "Gautam Navlakha Detained, Denied Entry into Kashmir: Press Note from IPTK." *Kafila*, May 28. At http://kafila.org/2011/05/28 /gautam-navlakha-detained-entry-into-kashmir-press-note-from-iptk/.

Wani, Riyaz. 2006. "No Role for al Qaeda in Kashmir." *Indian Express*, July 14. At http://archive.indianexpress.com/news/no-role-for-alqaeda-in-kashmir -separatists/8550/.

Wood, Elizabeth Jean. 2006. "The Ethical Challenges of Field Research in Conflict Zones." *Qualitative Sociology* 29, no. 3: 307–41.

Yaqoob, Mudasir. 2013. "Conflict behind Mental Stress, Say Experts." *Greater Kashmir*, Sept. 10. At http://greaterkashmir.com/news/2013/Sep/11/conflict -behind-mental-stress-say-experts-43.asp.

Yousuf, Shazia. 2014. "Depression Casts Cloak of Infertility over Kashmir Valley." InterPress Service, Nov. 19. At http://www.ipsnews.net/2014/11/depression -casts-cloak-of-infertility-over-kashmir-valley/.

11 Renewal, Reactualization, and Reformation

The Trajectory of Muslim Youth Activism in Indonesia

CAROOL KERSTEN

Although the most populous Muslim country in the world, Indonesia and its Islamic tradition remain poorly understood in the fields of academic inquiry that deal with Islam. Scholarly attention tends to focus on the Middle East and—to a lesser extent—on South Asia, while interest in sub-Saharan Africa and Southeast Asia is still marginal. In order to interpret and appreciate the ways in which Islam functions in Indonesia's public sphere and how Muslim youth activism features within that context, some historical background is needed. More specifically, it is necessary to understand how the possibilities and opportunities that are now accorded to Indonesia's politically active Muslims have evolved in the course of the country's seventy-year history as an independent Muslim-majority country that has consistently avoided self-identification as an "Islamic state." Further, it must be noted that, in this chapter at least, "youth" is not taken as a particular age bracket or even as a stage in life. As other scholars working on Muslim youth have suggested, "youth" is understood as a disposition or an aspiration to live an engaging, energetic, and active life (Marsden 2015). Central to the present narrative are successive generations of the young Muslim intelligentsia because what makes Indonesian Muslim assertiveness distinct is not so much its manifestations in "the street" as its intellectual articulations. Other cultural features that circumscribe Islamic youth activism in Indonesia are a deference to age, respect for superior learning, and a tradition of seeking patronage of senior figures, be they teachers, political leaders, or, even better, educated peers. In this chapter, I map out the dynamics of these Indonesian Islamic discourses shaped through mentor-pupil relations, which have more recently also been characterized by a creative tension between custodial care and critique.

The Historical Context of Indonesian Islam

As part of this chapter's historicized approach, it is important to know that Islam began gaining a foothold among the local populations in maritime Southeast Asia relatively late in the history of Islamic expansion. Also relevant is the fact that the religion was initially introduced not through conquest but by peaceful means. Islam was absorbed into heterogeneous cultural settings through a lengthy process of adoption and adaptation. By means of the long-established maritime trade routes crisscrossing the Indian Ocean, Muslim Southeast Asia gradually became more integrated into the wider Islamic world from the seventeenth century on. Finally, it is important to realize that what now constitutes the largest Muslim nation-state in the world is also the product of European colonization: a territorial construct built on nineteenth-century imperialism.

These historical experiences have continued to affect Indonesian culture, society, and politics since Indonesia's inception as an independent republic in 1945. However, although one in every five Muslims in the world calls Indonesia home, there are no references to Islam in the Indonesian Constitution or other founding documents, unlike in Malaysia. As Indonesia developed its own particular way of accommodating and controlling the various religious traditions there, it has kept religion at arm's length from political institutions. This approach continues to determine the ways in which political Muslims (can) operate in Indonesia.

Emergent Indonesian Nationhood and Muslim Civil Society

Successively until the beginning of the new millennium, Dutch colonial authorities, the secular nationalist government of founding president Sukarno, and General Suharto's military-dominated New Order regime all shared a suspicion of political Islam. However, Indonesia's postcolonial regimes continued to follow the Netherlands Indies government in tolerating Islamic organizations that wanted to emancipate Indonesian Muslims by improving Islamic education and advancing religious propagation (da'wa or dakwah in Indonesian). Since the early twentieth century, Muslim mass organizations, locally known as ormas, have been a distinctive feature of Indonesia's public landscape and one of the major platforms and outlets for religiously motivated Muslim youth activism.

As early as 1912, young urban Muslims inspired by the ideas of, among others, Muhammad Abduh united in the Muhammadiyah. A decade later, in 1923, more puritan reformists established Persatuan Islam. In the face of this emergent Islamic modernism, Indonesia's traditionalist Muslims responded with their own mobilization and organization initiatives. Considering themselves People of the Tradition and Community (Ahl al-Sunna wa'l-Jama'a) and "heirs to the Prophet," Islamic religious scholars and teachers, known in Javanese as kyai, banded together in Ulama's Revival (Nahdlatul Ulama, NU) in 1926. Not only do these Indonesian Islamic movements predate Egypt's Muslim Brotherhood and the South Asian Tablighi Jama'at by more than a decade, but the latter two are also dwarfed by the size of their Indonesian counterparts' constituencies, which number in the tens of millions.

In contrast to Islamic mass organizations in many other Muslim countries, in Indonesia these organizations have always been able to operate legally and to exercise uninhibited influence in public life—not least through their sizeable youth wings. During the independence struggle and early postcolonial years, the Muhammadiyah and NU were also openly active in the political domain, initially through the unified Islamic political party Masyumi led by Mohammad Natsir and later in their own right.

Political Islam: From Surveillance to Co-optation

In the wake of restrictions imposed during Sukarno's Guided Democracy (1957–66) and the subsequent New Order regime of General Suharto (1966–98), both Muhammadiyah and NU returned to their original core activities in education and da'wa, grooming young cadres for executive and leadership positions within their own organizations and for employment in the Ministry of Religious Affairs.

Although suspicious of Islamic party politics, successive governments of independent Indonesia supported the development of an Islamic education system as an integral part of exercising control over religion in the public sphere. Here, it is important to note that this system is not administered through the Ministry of Education but through the Ministry of Religious Affairs. Aside from allowing organizations such as the Muhammadiyah and NU to establish and run primary and secondary schools, in 1948 and then in 1960 the government began putting in place an Islamic higher-education system of so-called State Islamic Institutes (Institut Agama Islam Negara, IAIN) (Saeed 1999). Thanks to the financial windfall provided by high oil prices in the 1970s and 1980s, the system expanded into a network of campuses across the country, with a number receiving full university status in 2002. From the 1980s on, the Islamic mass organizations also began deploying initiatives for the establishment of institutions for tertiary education, including private universities. On the back of this expansion of Islamic religious education, the Muhammadiyah and NU organized their youth members into high school and university student unions. Together with the more "ecumenical" Association of Muslim Students (Himpunan Mahasiswa Islam, HMI), these unions function as incubators for Muslim youth activists, politicians, and future *ormas* leaders.

Aside from acting as platforms for Muslim emancipation since late colonial times, these Islamic mass organizations have a darker side. By the mid-1960s, suspicion of political Islam was overtaken by Cold War fears of communism. In the orgy of violence against alleged Communists during the military intervention of 1965, the army was enthusiastically assisted by Muslim youth militias, such as the NU's All-Purpose Forces Front (Barisan Ansor Serba Guna, or Banser). In the absence of any serious in-depth investigation into these pogroms, the concrete effect of this traumatic national experience on shifts in Muslim youth activism remains a matter of speculation. Beginning in the 1970s, although keeping political activities by Muslims under a close watch, Suharto's New Order regime allowed space for Muslim participation in its new economic-development plans. The plans were designed to fix Indonesia's dismal economic situation, and participation in them provided Muslim activists who refrained from pursuing openly political (Islamist) agendas with a chance to help shape their country's future.

From Monitoring to Mentoring the Muslim Youth: The Renewal and Tarbiyah Movements

Since the 1970s, two main strands of Muslim youth activism have continued to shape Indonesia's Islamic discourses: one trend adopted a pragmatic attitude toward the government, whereas the other remained aloof and began shifting toward more reactionary ("puritan," "revivalist") positions. Critics from this other side of the Islamic spectrum characterize the pragmatic attitude as "accommodationist," implying a degree of collaboration and collusion (Hassan 1980, 122, 139). The leading figure among the pragmatic Muslim youth activists was Nurcholish Madjid (also known as "Cak Nur"). A student at Jakarta's State Islamic University (IAIN Syarif Hidayatullah) and chairman of the HMI from 1967 until 1971, Madjid presided over a major recalibration of the HMI's agenda on the basis of a new manifesto: *Nilai-nilai dasar perjuangan* (Basic Values for Struggle), modeled after the political program of Germany's Social Democratic Party (Kersten 2011b, 55). He was initially hailed as a "Natsir *muda*," or "young Natsir," earmarking him as the political heir of the former Masyumi leader.

This view of Madjid changed after two "paradigmatic speeches" in 1970 and 1972, in which he advocated a "renewal of Islamic thinking" (*pembaruan pemikiran Islam*) (Kull 2005, 106). Although an "*anak* Masyumi," or "Masyumi child," by his own admission, to Madjid the New Order's radically different development agenda required an equally drastic change in Islamic thinking, which would come from a new generation of Muslim intellectuals rather than from the former politicians of the now defunct Masyumi Party. A careful reading of Madjid's writings shows that his propositions constitute a coherent and holistic set of ideas dealing with theology, epistemology, political theory, and religious anthropology (see Kersten 2011b, 55–58). However, it was his provocative slogan, "Islam, yes! Islamic Party, no!" that received most attention (Madjid 2003, 315). In addition, Madjid's argument that Islam and secularization are perfectly compatible greatly offended the old Masyumi establishment and their support base among the puritan Muslim youth, not least because it was grounded in the modernization-secularization theses of American sociologists of religion and of theologians such as Robert Bellah, Peter Berger, and Harvey Cox (Kersten 2011b, 62–67).

Notwithstanding these objections, a large segment of the young Muslim intelligentsia embraced Nurcholish Madjid's ideas and formed the Movement for the Renewal of Islamic Thinking (Gerakan Pembaruan Pemikiran Islam). A key characteristic of these young Muslim activists was that they frequently came from mixed traditionalist-modernist Muslim backgrounds; I have argued elsewhere that this cultural hybridity forms a constituent factor in their religious outlook (Kersten 2011b, 50–52). This feature can be traced through at least three generational shifts (Kersten 2011a, 112–14).

The spread of the ideas of the Renewal Movement and their sustained influence were facilitated by support from more senior intellectuals. In the case of the Renewal Movement, this support came in the form of mentoring by (Abdul) Mukti Ali, a professor of comparative religion at the State Islamic Institute of Yogyakarta (IAIN Sunang Kalijaga). A graduate of McGill University and former student of Wilfred Cantwell Smith, Mukti Ali hosted a discussion group for Nurcholish Madjid's fellow activists in Yogyakarta and later set up Indonesia's first interfaith forum. When Mukti Ali was appointed minister of religious affairs in 1973, he initiated and supervised a major overhaul of the Islamic higher-education curriculum, which was executed by his fellow McGill alumnus Harun Nasution, the rector of Jakarta's IAIN Syarif Hidayatullah at the time (for further biographical details on Mukti Ali, see Muzani 1994 and Munhanif 1996). The new curriculum included not only teachings about "heterodox" Islamic sects and schools but also Western scholarship on Islam (Saeed 1999, 185–87).

Although increasing numbers of young Muslim pragmatists found a role as intellectuals or professionals in the New Order's development policies, other youth activists explored a different trajectory. They drew inspiration from the Islamist agenda of the disbanded Masyumi Party and received support from its leadership, including erstwhile leader Mohammad Natsir and Mohammad Rasjidi, a diplomat and politician turned academic. Cut off by the New Order from a return to the political arena and worried by a rise in conversions to Christianity on the part of lapsed Communists and nominal Muslims, these Muslim activists looked to *da'wa* for the mobilization of Indonesia's burgeoning Muslim youth. This shift from politics to proselytization was accompanied by a reactionary turn in formerly open-minded Islamic modernists such as Natsir (Feillard and Madinier 2011, 20). Staying away from party politics, Natsir's "moralizing Islamism" advocated a return to *al-salaf al-salih*, the "pious ancestors," of seventh-century Islam (Feillard and Madinier 2011, 95–96). One of the central concerns of this "moralizing Islamism" was *ghazwul fikri*, the "intellectual invasion" of the Muslim world by Western ideas hostile to religion in general and to Islam in particular, which remains a preoccupation of reactionary Muslim youth activists all over the world today. The rhetorical use of this term can be traced to Indonesia's main Muslim "man of letters" of the twentieth century, Hamka—who used it in a speech at the Muhammadiyah national congress of 1969 (Hamka 1970).

The main outlet for this strand of Islamic *da'wa* is the Indonesian Council of Islamic Propagation (Dewan Dakwah Islamiyah Indonesia, DDII). Because the DDII's aims were sufficiently "nonpolitical," the New Order regime did not object to its establishment. Since its inception in 1967, the DDII has been successful in penetrating and expanding the more puritan segments of Indonesian Muslim society. Thanks to Mohammad Natsir's excellent network of contacts throughout the Muslim world, the DDII became a conduit for international financial support from cash-rich donors in the Persian Gulf.

The DDII also provides a platform for Islamist youth activists. This platform has helped facilitate the establishment of a network of Islamic religious-training initiatives, which became known as the Tarbiyah Movement (Latif 2008, 252, 350). The movement's main targets were initially the campuses of the secular universities rather than the religious universities and other institutes of higher Islamic learning. In the 1970s, two members of the HMI's puritan wing, Imaduddin Abdulrahim and Endang Saefudin

Anshari (one of the key critics of Nurcholish Madjid's Renewal Thinking), began running highly popular three-day training programs for
"preacher combatants" (*latihan mujahid dakwah*) in the Salman Mosque
of the Institute of Technology at Bandung, making it the first epicenter of
"Campus Islam." Owing to the success of these programs, what was initially a loose network transformed into the more centralized Communication Forum of the Indonesian Mosque Youth (Badan Komunikasi Pemuda
Masjid Indonesia), which spread the same formula to campus mosques
across Indonesia (Feillard and Madinier 2011, 118).

Although within the HMI the puritan faction gave way to the Movement for Islamic Renewal Thinking inspired by Nurcholish Madjid, the
Tarbiyah Movement provided the Islamist youth with an infrastructure.
The campus mosques became the nodal points for a new type of networking modeled after the cell-like structure pioneered by Egypt's Muslim
Brotherhood (Feillard and Madinier 2011, 114). This tactical change was
necessitated, however, by a government crackdown on political youth
activism during the mid-1970s, a campaign known as the "normalization
of campus life" (*normalisasi kehidupan kampus*). The more or less open
study circles (*halaqas*) through which Islamic education and training had
been disseminated so far were now turned into more secretive *usroh*, or
family-like minicommunities of dedicated propagandists. Unwittingly,
the government's repressive campaign drove the Islamist activists into a
semiclandestine underground but highly effective network.

Cultural Islam and Its Discontents

In the 1980s, Indonesia underwent a major political reorientation that has
had far-reaching consequences for the place of Islam in public life and for
the opportunities of successive generations of Muslim youth activists until
well into the twenty-first century. After relying for almost two decades on
the military, Suharto fell out with some of his longtime uniformed political associates, who were often from Christian backgrounds. Looking for
an alternative political powerbase, Suharto's eye fell on Indonesia's pious
Muslims as a possible new constituency.

As part of his overtures to the Muslim segment of the population, in 1983 Suharto instructed his new minister of religious affairs, Munawir Sjadzali, to direct a so-called Reactualization Agenda. Implemented in the course of Sjadzali's ten-year tenure in office, this policy advocated what has since then been alternately called "cultural" or "civil" or "cosmopolitan" Islam. Financed with the increased revenues from oil exports, one of the new policy's most important effects was a substantial expansion of the Islamic higher-education sector and the introduction of generous scholarship schemes. These programs enabled large numbers of talented Muslim students to pursue postgraduate degrees abroad, not only in the field of traditional Islamic learning at religious universities in the Middle East but also in the humanities and social sciences faculties at universities in Australia, Canada, Germany, the Netherlands, and the United States (Jabali and Jamhari 2002). Many of these graduates would go on to occupy influential positions in higher education, Muslim mass organizations, Islamic publishing, and—eventually—politics.

In hindsight, the decade of the Reactualization Agenda (1983–93) can be considered a watershed in the recalibration of Islam's role in Indonesian public life and in enhancing the opportunities for young Muslims to be a part of it. The immediate benefactors of this change in Suharto's political course were the Muslim intellectuals who had been associated with the Renewal Movement of the 1970s and the young activists following in their path. These intellectuals have become so influential that what are now the State Islamic Universities (Universitas Islam Negara) of Jakarta and Yogyakarta are also considered distinct Indonesian schools of Islamic thought. IAIN Syarif Hidayatullah in Jakarta and IAIN Sunan Kalijaga in Yogyakarta were transformed into State Islamic Universities in 2002 and 2004, respectively. Named after the urban districts where their campuses are located, they are referred to as Mazhab Ciputat and Mazhab Sapen, respectively. The new IAIN curricula also fostered an intellectual climate that was conducive to a reorientation toward Islam's intellectual legacy that prepared the ground for receiving the ideas of the so-called heritage thinkers from the Arabic-speaking parts of the Muslim world. The work of intellectuals such as the Algerian French historian of Islam Mohammed

Arkoun, the philosopher Hasan Hanafi, the Egyptian literary scholar Nasr Hamid Abu Zayd, and the Moroccan philosopher Muhammad Abid al-Jabri found a welcome reception in Indonesia, generating larger and generally more appreciative audiences among the country's Muslim youth than in their respective homelands.

Within this intellectual climate, a plethora of research institutes, think tanks, and nongovernmental organizations (NGOs) has mushroomed, offering ample opportunity for students, young activists, and researchers to apply newly acquired skills, implement ideas, and live out their ideological ambitions. Activities range from academic publishing to grassroots-level rural-development schemes, but a central and lucrative opportunity is the organization of self-improvement workshops. Pioneered by the Paramadina Foundation, which was established by Nurcholish Madjid after his return from postgraduate studies in Chicago, these study groups first catered to young, upwardly mobile, urban Muslims whose material aspirations were met through the pursuit of lucrative professional careers but whose transfer from small-town or rural Indonesia to a megacity such as Jakarta left many in a spiritual vacuum. Paramadina's programs offered a combination of engaged study of the Islamic tradition and an interpretation of piety grounded in the foundation's own brand of spirituality called "positive Sufism" (*tasawuf positif*) (Kersten 2011b, 91; see also Madjid 2002).

With the convening of exclusive seminars in five-star hotels, the influence of Paramadina's programs gradually percolated through to the New Order elite. This sea change in attitude toward Islam eventually also reached the top echelons of power when Suharto's cabinet and the military top brass began brushing up their religious credentials to match the president's own newly found interest in Islam, epitomized by his pilgrimage to Mecca in 1991. These individuals came to be known as the "Green Generals," and the overall growing Islamization of Indonesian society and politics was called the *penghijauan*, "greening," of Indonesia's public sphere—a reference to the symbolic color of Islam.

One of the generals to take political advantage of this Islamization was Suharto's then son-in-law Prabowo Subianto. However, he took this process in a very different direction by latching on to the ideologies of DDII and even more radical Islamists for whom Paramadina's cultural

Islam and spirituality were anathema. Prabowo established his own think tank, the Center for Policy and Development Studies (the English name and its abbreviation, CPDS, are usually used), led by a young political scientist, Fadli Zon, and a California-educated Muhammadiyah intellectual, Sirajuddin Syamsuddin. After years in voluntary exile in Jordan, Prabowo Subianto reinvented himself as a legitimate politician, running for the presidency in 2014 on behalf of the Great Indonesia Movement Party (Partai Gerakan Indonesia Raya, or Gerindra Party); Fadli Zon became deputy speaker of Parliament; and Sirajuddin Syamsuddin was chairman of the Muhammadiyah (2005–15) and was appointed chairman of the Indonesian Ulama Council (Majelis Ulama Indonesia) in 2014. Prabowo also sponsored youth initiatives with an openly Islamist signature, such as the Indonesian Committee for Solidarity with the Muslim World (Komité Indonesia untuk Solidaritas dengan Dunia Islam, KISDI). Initially founded in 1987 as a satellite organization of the DDII with the personal support of Mohammad Natsir, KISDI aimed to mobilize Indonesia's Muslim youth for Islamic causes in Palestine, Kashmir, and Bosnia and to rally against US-led operations in the Muslim world. Prabowo and his coterie of military officers used KISDI for their own purposes, orchestrating a "divide-and-rule" campaign intent on sowing dissent within the Muslim camp, which they then could use to achieve their objectives. Not adverse to violence, by using thugs and street mobs recruited from the urban poor, Prabowo and his group sought to undermine the chances that the Muslim bloc would develop into a threat to the New Order regime (Feillard and Madinier 2011, 49–59).

From the government's perspective, there were other good reasons for such concerns. The DDII's active international networking led to the appearance on Indonesian soil of the Egyptian Muslim Brotherhood, Pakistan's Tablighi Jama'at, the Jordan-originated Hizbut Tahrir, and Malaysia's Darul Arqam, and Saudi Arabia had established a presence through its sponsorship of the Institute for Islamic and Arabic Sciences (Lembaga Ilmu Pengetahuan Islam dan Arab) and the opening of a branch of Muhammad ibn Saud University. The spread of these distinctly internationalist forms of *da'wa* came at the expense of the Indonesian variant propagated by the founders of the Tarbiyah Movement in the 1970s.

The presence of such foreign organizations also led to an increasing repoliticization of the Islamic discourse. By the mid-1990s, internationally sponsored campus *da'wa* institutes (*lembaga dakwah kampus*) were able to translate this repoliticization into real political capital as they managed to get their preferred candidates elected to the university senates (Feillard and Madinier 2011, 115–16). Proponents of a more cosmopolitan Islam in tune with Indonesia's cultural context objected to the distinctly Arab character of these new Islamization campaigns. This opposition was particularly strong among traditionalist Muslims, including NU chairman Abdurrahman Wahid and later also influential youth activists such as Ulil Abshar-Abdalla, who—ironically—was partly educated at the Institute for Islamic and Arabic Sciences.

Abdurrahman Wahid was also very suspicious of Suharto's overtures to Indonesia's practicing Muslims. This skepticism was informed by the NU's experiences under the New Order during the preceding fifteen years. Notwithstanding the involvement of the NU's youth wing in crushing Indonesia's political Left in the mid-1960s, the relationship between the Suharto regime and the NU had always been very problematic. Islamic modernism as represented by the Renewal and Tarbiyah Movements was tolerated and even accepted because its ideological underpinnings and the institutional transparency of organizations such as the Muhammadiyah and—to a degree—even the DDII had a greater affinity with the New Order economic-development agenda and regimented military outlook than with the more chaotic NU. As a consequence, no rapprochement had taken place with the traditionalist Islamic bloc.

The explanation for this apparent reversal in political fortunes of different groups within the Muslim segment of the Indonesian populace lies in the New Order's continuing desire to keep society under state control. The rural-based NU, with its deeply embedded scholarly networks across Java and its intimate teacher-student relations grounded in personal loyalty, formed an organic entity that was difficult to monitor. The government saw the NU, with its extensive network of Islamic schools and concomitant massive following among the Muslim peasant youth, as a formidable possible adversary and an obstacle to commanding popular support on the basic level of peasant society (Ricklefs 2012, 198–200).

Abdurrahman Wahid acknowledged the window of opportunity offered by the Reactualization Agenda for the dissemination of what he called
the "indigenization of Islam" (*pribumisasi Islam*)—that is, embedding the
religion in Indonesia's cultural settings. But he continued to harbor reser-
vations because in 1984 the agenda was accompanied by the reimposition
of Pancasila, or the Five Principles Doctrine of 1945, as the country's *asas
tunggal*, or "sole ideological foundation." Any actor in the public sphere—
encompassing not only civil and military government institutions, the
education system, and political parties but also Islamic mass organizations
such as the Muhammadiyah and the NU—had to formally subscribe to
Pancasila, thus curtailing the possibility of Islam becoming a competing
political ideology.

Confronted with this challenge, the NU's national congress of 1984
responded with a complete reorientation of the organization's activities.
Presented under the slogan "Return to the 1926 Founding Charter" (Kem-
bali ke Khittah 1926), the NU vowed to abandon party politics altogether
and to concentrate again on education and grassroots-level community
building. In the wake of this shift in focus, the NU established a number of
new NGOs geared toward training young cadres for the future coordina-
tion of these activities. Together with the NU student union, they became
seedbeds for intellectuals and activists, who began leaving their own mark
on Islamic activism from the turn of the century on, while some of the
student union's founding directors have since risen to senior offices in the
NU and to other prominent positions in Indonesian public life (Kersten
2015, 60–64).

Janus-Headed Muslim Youth Activism?

The ambiguity of the New Order vis-à-vis the public role of Islam in Indonesian society, exemplified by the simultaneous introduction of the Reactualization Agenda and imposition of Pancasila as the *asas tunggal*, can
be further illustrated with two developments, both of which were initiated by Muslim youth activists during what would turn out to be the final
decade of Suharto's rule. In 1990, five Muslim student leaders' impromptu
plan for a symposium at Brawijaya University in the East Javanese town

Malang was quickly turned into a grander scheme when they sought the mediation of more senior Muslim intellectuals, including Imaduddin Abdulrahim, a Tarbiyah Movement leader in the 1970s, and the economist M. Dawam Rahardjo, a leading Muhammadiyah intellectual and former member of Nurcholish Madjid's Renewal Movement. This request reflects not only the respect accorded to age and seniority in Indonesian culture but also a concomitant need for patronage if such youth initiatives are to be successful.

Abdulrahim and Rahardjo suggested turning the initiative into a more sustained effort to bring together various groups of Muslim intellectuals. To get the necessary official support (and permission), it was decided to approach Suharto's confidant, Minister of Technology B. J. Habibie. Suharto, seeing an opportunity to mobilize the Muslim intelligentsia for his own political purposes, gave his consent. He instructed Habibie to take charge of what was now turned into a government-led initiative for a formal discussion platform that became known as the Association of Indonesian Muslim Intellectuals (Ikatan Cendekiawan Muslim se-Indonesia, ICMI), designed to bring together Muslim government officials, technocrats, academics, activists, and—last but certainly not least—the leaders of Indonesia's Muslim mass organizations.

The ICMI was intended as a broad-spectrum organization, but its weakness was that the divergent social backgrounds of Indonesia's Muslim intelligentsia as well as concomitant differences in and clashes between ideological positions undermined its ability to operate effectively (Latif 2008, 430). However, the main vulnerability that plagued ICMI from the outset was the refusal of a key Muslim intellectual, NU leader Abdurrahman Wahid, to sign on to the project. He instead founded an alternative, more inclusivist, and critical body of intellectuals, which he called the Democracy Forum (Forum Demokrasi).

Thus, after the ICMI's initial success as a regime-friendly umbrella organization bringing together Muslim intellectuals of varying backgrounds, its ideological diversity and the inevitably resulting differences of opinion on how to relate and be loyal to the regime led to its fragmentation and its eventual demise when key intellectual figures became disenchanted and left the association either of their own volition or by unceremonious expulsion. Leading political scientist and Ciputat School member Bahtiar Effendy concludes that even though the ICMI has been perceived as a "watershed of the state's politics of accommodation towards Islam," its importance is outweighed by the continuing structural signif- icance of Muslim mass organizations such as the Muhammadiyah and the NU as well as of other state- and regime-related institutions, such as the New Order's government party, the Functional Group Party (Partai Golongan Karya, Golkar); the Indonesian Ulama Council; and the state bureaucracy in general (2003, 196). Such weaknesses aside, I suggest that the frustrations of Indonesia's Muslim youth over being sidelined after having such initiatives taken away from them also undermined the social support base for Suharto's attempts to ingratiate himself with the Muslim majority.

Eight years later, the formation of the Indonesian Muslim Students Action Union (Kesatuan Aksi Mahasiswa Muslim Indonesia, KAMMI) heralded a course of action of an entirely different nature that directly affected the regime change in 1999 and the transition toward democracy during what is called Indonesia's Reformation Period (Reformasi). Like the ICMI initiative, KAMMI's origins are rooted in a campus event, again held in Malang, but this time at the Muhammadiyah University in March 1998, during the economic meltdown that was seriously undermining Suharto's credibility. This gathering of the intercampus *da'wa* institute network dominated by the Tarbiyah Movement managed to bring together myriad Muslim student activists to form a pressure group and to mobi- lize Indonesia's Muslim student body to demand economic, political, and judicial reforms.

Although the new student union emerged on the puritan *da'wa* side of the Islamic spectrum, the use of "Action Union" in its name and KAMMI's founding "Malang Declaration" pointed to an ambition toward inclusiv- ity and a claim to represent "*all* Muslim students" (Kraince 2003, 166). Although KAMMI cooperated well with the Muhammadiyah's student union, it was dismissive of the NU's student union and irritated by the reluctance of the HMI's national leadership to criticize its former lead- ers for cozying up to the New Order regime. In spite of such ideological chasms, under the leadership of a twenty-six-year-old economics student named Fahri Hamzah, KAMMI demonstrated its organizational flair by mobilizing thousands of students across dozens of campuses within weeks of its establishment. Fahri Hamzah has since become a parliamentarian for the Islamist Justice and Prosperity Party (Partai Keadilan Sejahtera). While other student groups were calling for Suharto's resignation and democratization, KAMMI initially focused on "moral reform" without demanding that Suharto step down (Kraince 2003, 182). This stance changed when the military opened fire on student protesters in mid-May 1998, and Suharto's authority unraveled within days.

Regime Change, Reformation, and Polarization

The youth's role in bringing about regime change in Indonesia in 1999 prefigures or foreshadows the events unfolding elsewhere in the Muslim world since the beginning of Arab uprisings in 2010. Indonesia also offers some sobering lessons for aspiring but often impatient Muslim democrats. Although the replacement of the New Order by the Reformasi led to an unprecedented opening up of the public sphere in general and of the political arena in particular, as a result of the resilience of Indonesia's political—state and nonstate—elites it was not until 2014 that Joko Widodo (nicknamed Jokowi), a politician not tainted by associations with earlier regimes, established political parties, or Islamic mass organizations, finally rose to prominence and was elected as head of state.

An immediate indication of the continuing dominance of senior figures after 1998 was that although student organizations triggered the events leading to regime change, it took a figure such as Nurcholish Madjid, by then the eminence grise of the Muslim intelligentsia, to persuade President Suharto that it was time to go in order to avoid large-scale bloodshed. Suharto's departure, in turn, opened the way for the first fair and free general elections since 1955 and for the leaders of the traditionalist and modernist Muslim mass organizations to take up the top government positions: NU executive chairman Abdurrahman Wahid was elected president of the republic, and Muhammadiyah leader Amien Rais became Speaker of Parliament.

Although a wide array of Muslim parties and Islamist parties contested the elections, and in spite of the personal popularity of figures such as Wahid and Rais, these parties cornered only a modest part of the electoral market. The elections were instead won by more experienced party-political operators, including the New Order's "reinvented" governing Golkar Party, now led by former HMI chairman Akbar Tanjung, and the Indonesian Democratic Party of Struggle (Partai Demokrasi Indonesia–Perjuangan) under the daughter of the republic's founding president, Megawati Sukarnoputri. Political Muslims continued to make their influence felt primarily through alternative channels: the NU and the Muhammadiyah, Islamic higher education, and a wide array of Islamic NGOs and action groups, either affiliated with or operating independently from the mass organizations.

In the course of the first decade of the twenty-first century, a changing of the guard took place. Since the deaths of Nurcholish Madjid and Abdurrahman Wahid in 2005 and 2009, respectively, Muslim academics and activists of the second and third postcolonial generations are now the chief articulators of Islamic intellectual discourse in Indonesia and in some instances policy makers and executives, although perhaps not yet in the top echelons of political power.

These individuals include academics from the Ciputat School, such as Azyumardi Azra and Komaruddin Hidayat, both of whom have held office as rectors of the State Islamic University in Jakarta and have served the post-1999 governments in various advisory capacities.[1] After Nurcholish Madjid passed away in 2005, two younger members of the Ciputat School, Budhy Munawar-Rachman and Ihsan Ali-Fauzi, emerged as the chief custodians of Madjid's intellectual legacy. Although his ideas had already been widely disseminated during his lifetime through essay collections edited by his followers, they were now perpetuated through the publication of

---

1. Based on interviews and discussions with Azyumardi Azra in Banda Aceh on January 11, 2012, and in Jakarta on October 9, 2012, and with Komaruddin Hidayat on May 16, 2011.

an encyclopedia and the establishment of the Nurcholish Madjid Foundation, both under the direction of Budhy Munawar-Rachman. A longtime
Paramadina Foundation executive, Munawar-Rachman has also developed into a pedagogue and facilitator of interfaith dialogue and of the
intellectual development of young Muslims at a number of institutions of
advanced education. Focusing more on cultural activities, his colleague
Ihsan Ali-Fauzi has been the main force and instigator behind the Ahmad
Wahib Award for young essay writers. Established in 2003, the award was
named after another Renewal Movement activist who died prematurely, at
the age of thirty, in a traffic accident in 1973 (Kersten 2015, 56–57, 240–44).
Anies Baswedan—a US-trained political scientist and rector of Universitas Paramadina, the private university established by Nurcholish Madjid
in 1998—served as minister of education and culture in the Jokowi–Kalla
government (2014–16). A former HMI activist like Madjid, Baswedan has
also established his ideological-intellectual independence by not being
associated with either the NU or the Muhammadiyah. He won the run-off
for the Jakarta gubernatorial elections between Prabowo's Gerindra Party
and the Justice and Prosperity Party. In his final years, Nurcholish Madjid,
too, had displayed sympathies toward the latter party.

Aside from mentorship and custodial care, other young Muslim intellectuals have engaged more critically with Nurcholish Madjid's thinking.
These critiques are voiced in particular by young NU cadres who call
themselves "Islamic post-traditionalists," or "postra" for short (Kersten
2013, 2014a). They typically have received a combined religious-secular
education at NU and state-run schools before going on to working for
NU-affiliated NGOs. These young intellectuals draw on the writings of
Arab heritage thinkers, postmodern philosophers, and postcolonial theorists not only to criticize Madjid's reliance on the dominant discourses
of official Islamic historiography but also to challenge his association
with the New Order regime. By contrast, the "postra" intellectuals position themselves as representatives of a Muslim proletariat (Kersten 2015,
65–70, 109–17).

In terms of innovative and progressive Islamic thinking, the NU's
Islamic post-traditionalists appear to have overtaken the Muslim modernists. However, they do have a counterpart on that side of Indonesia's Islamic

spectrum in the Network of Young Muhammadiyah Intellectuals (Jaringan Intelektual Muhammadiyah Muda, usually referred to as JIMM). These intellectuals have been groomed by the social historian Kuntowijoyo and the anthropologist Moeslim Abdurrahman (both now deceased), while receiving political support from former Muhammadiyah chairman Ahmad Syafii Maarif as well as from Abdulmunir Mulkhan and M. Amin Abdullah—two professors from Yogyakarta's State Islamic University, who served with Maarif on the Muhammadiyah's central board between 2000 and 2005. Although this trio lost much of their influence following their purge from the central board as part of the Muhammadiyah's "conservative turn" under its new chairman, Sirajuddin Syamsuddin, it can be said that the network's intellectual proximity to the "postras" points to a meeting of the minds between progressive young Muhammadiyah and NU intellectuals that transcends the long-standing traditionalist/modernist divide of Indonesia's practicing Muslims (van Bruinessen 2013a).

After a decade of regressive polarization between progressive and reactionary Muslims, this convergence of progressive voices appears to have picked up new momentum, at least judging by the manifestos and declarations issued at the latest national congresses of the Muhammadiyah and the NU in August 2015. Both mass organizations position themselves as promotors of an Indonesian Islam geared toward contributing to the country's development and prosperity as well as toward the safeguarding of its religious plurality. This Indonesian variant of Islam was presented under different designations: Southeast Asian Islam (Islam Nusantara), Progressive Islam (Indonesia Berkemajuan), and Diversified Fiqh (Fikih Kebhinekaan) (Rais 2015; Rumadi 2015a, 2015b; Wahid et al. 2015). Young intellectuals such as Ahmad Rumadi of the NU and Fajar Riza ul-Haq and Ahmad Fuad Fanani of the Muhammadiyah are among the key articulators of these new Indonesian Islamic discourses.

This is by no means the full picture of Indonesia's Islamic discourses and activism at the beginning of the twenty-first century. The momentary breakdown of law and order after the regime change in 1999 and a redefinition of the role of the armed forces in Indonesia led to increased religiously inspired violence, with Muslim militias such as the Laskar Jihad and vigilantes of the Islamic Defenders Front (Front Pembela Islam, best known by the abbreviation FPI) turning on Christians, Shia Muslims, and Ahmadis. Also once the democratization process was more firmly on track from 2001 onward, Muslim proponents of liberal democracy and free-market economics united in the Liberal Islam Network (Jaringan Islam Liberal, best known by the abbreviation JIL) and continued to clash with *da'wa* activists and Islamist politicians on the other side of the Islamic spectrum; both groups employed the same confrontational rhetoric to challenge each other's viewpoints, exchanging accusations of either "intellectual invasion" or "Arabization," respectively (van Bruinessen 2013b).

If 1984 and 1998 were important watershed years for Indonesia's political system, the year 2005 functioned in a similar way for the issue of religious freedom in Indonesia. In the summer of that year, the Indonesia Ulama Council issued a fatwa in which the notions of secularism, pluralism, and liberalism were rejected as contrary to the teachings of Islam (Saputra and Andriansjah 2011, 87–95). While vigilantes of the Islamic Defenders Front considered this fatwa a license to intensify their persecution of Ahmadis and Shia Muslims, opponents of the fatwa argued that it undermined the republic's founding doctrine, the Pancasila, which, although no longer enforced as the country's sole ideological foundation, is still considered a guarantor of Indonesia's ethnoreligious plurality. In spite of the lip service paid to the doctrine's principles on grounds of what the erstwhile chairman of the governing Democratic (Demokrat) Party, former HMI student leader Anas Urbaningrum, referred to as "religious nationalism," the indecisiveness of then president Susilo Bambang Yudhoyono did little to alleviate tensions and in fact led to perpetuated intra-Muslim polarization (Kersten 2014b).

Conclusion

As an integral part of the Muslim world as well as part of a country with its own particular features, Indonesian Islam in the public sphere is embodied in a variety of institutions and manifested through a range of activities, including state-sponsored Islam, a religious education system, political parties, civil society organizations, and NGOs. But the religion is also claimed by unabashed Islamists, including vigilante movements, paramilitary groups, and terrorist organizations, which seek to challenge and undermine the existing political order.

Indonesia has also developed a distinctly Indonesian Islamic discursive tradition. Shaped by this tradition's dynamics of patronage and mentoring, custodial care and critique, Muslim youth activists have played and continue to play an important role in its articulation and dissemination. This tradition has resulted in vibrant intra-Muslim debates. In recent years, however, it has also led to a polarization of positions not just between Muslims and non-Muslims but also and perhaps even more sharply among Indonesian Muslims themselves.

References

Effendy, Bahtiar. 2003. *Islam and the State in Indonesia*. Singapore: Institute for Southeast Asian Studies.

Feillard, Andrée, and Rémy Madinier. 2011. *The End of Innocence? Indonesian Islam and the Temptations of Radicalism*. Honolulu: Univ. of Hawai'i Press.

Hamka [sic]. 1970. *Beberapa tantangan terhadap Islam dimasa kin*. Jakarta, Indonesia: Bulan Bintang.

Hassan, Mohammad Kamal. 1980. *Muslim Intellectual Responses to "New Order" in Indonesia*. Kuala Lumpur, Malaysia: Dewan Bahasa dan Pustaka.

Jabali, Fuad, and Jamhari. 2002. *IAIN & Modernisasi Islam di Indonesia*. Jakarta, Indonesia: Logos Wacana Ilmu.

Kersten, Carool. 2011a. "Cosmopolitan Muslim Intellectuals and the Mediation of Cultural Islam in Indonesia." *Comparative Islamic Studies* 7, no. 1: 105–36.

———. 2011b. *Cosmopolitans and Heretics: New Muslim Intellectuals and the Study of Islam*. New York: Columbia Univ. Press.

———. 2013. "Islamic Post-traditionalism in Indonesia: Revisiting Tradition and the Future of Islam." In *Alternative Islamic Discourses and Religious Authority*, edited by Carool Kersten and Susanne Olsson, 137–58. London: Routledge.

———. 2014a. "Islamic Post-traditionalism: Postcolonial and Postmodern Religious Discourse in Indonesia." *Sophia: International Journal for Philosophy and Traditions* 53, no. 3: 473–89.

———. 2014b. *Religious Intolerance versus Pluralism: Sectarian Violence in Indonesia*. Middle East–Asia Project paper. Washington, DC: Middle East Institute.

———. 2015. *Islam in Indonesia: The Contest for Society, Ideas and Values*. New York: Oxford Univ. Press.

Kraince, Richard Gordon. 2003. "The Role of Islamic Student Activists in Divergent Movements for Reform during Indonesia's Transition from Authoritarian Rule 1998–2001." PhD diss., Ohio University.

Kull, Ann. 2005. *Piety and Politics: Nurcholish Madjid and His Interpretation of Islam in Modern Indonesia*. Lund, Sweden: Department of History and Anthropology of Religions, Lund Univ.

Latif, Yudi. 2008. *Indonesian Muslim Intelligentsia and Power*. Singapore: Institute for Southeast Asian Studies.

Madjid, Nurcholish. 2002. *Manusia Modern mendambah Allah: Renungan Tasawuf Positif.* Jakarta, Indonesia: Iman.

———. 2003. "The Necessity of Renewing Islamic Thought and the Problem of the Integration of the Ummah." In *Nurcholish Madjid: The True Face of Islam—Essays on Islam and Modernity in Indonesia*, edited by Rudy Harisyah Alam and Ihsan Ali-Fauzi, 315–22. Ciputat: Voice Center Indonesia.

Marsden, Magnus. 2015. "From Trader to Taliban: Islam and Youth in Northern Afghanistan." Paper presented at the Department of Theology and Religious Studies, King's College London, Jan. 27.

Munhanif, Ali. 1996. "Islam and the Struggle for Religious Pluralism in Indonesia: A Political Reading of the Religious Thought of Mukti Ali." *Studia Islamika* 3, no. 1: 79–126.

Muzani, Saiful. 1994. "Mu'tazilah Theology and the Modernisation of the Indonesian Muslim Community: An Intellectual Portrait of Harun Nasution." *Studia Islamika* 1, no. 1: 91–131.

Rais, Ahmad Imam Mujadid. 2015. "Muhammadiyah's 'Progressive Islam': Guideline or Tagline?" *Jakarta Post*, Aug. 3.

Ricklefs, M. C. 2012. *Islamisation and Its Opponents in Java, c. 1930 to the Present*. Singapore: NUS Press.

Rumadi, Ahmad. 2015a. "NU, dari Nusantara untuk Dunia." *Kompas*, July 31.

———. 2015b. "NU Klarifikasi Istilah Islam Nusantara." *Kompas*, July 4.

Saeed, Abdullah. 1999. "Towards Religious Tolerance through Reform in Islamic Education: The Case of the State Institute of Islamic Studies in Indonesia." *Indonesia and the Malay World* 27, no. 7: 177–91.

Saputrah, Hijrah, and Adhika Rasetya Andriansjah, eds. 2011. *MUI, Himpunan Fatwa MUI sejak 1975*. Jakarta: Majelis Ulama Indonesia.

Van Bruinessen, Martin. 2013a. *Contemporary Developments in Indonesian Islam: Explaining the "Conservative Turn."* Singapore: Institute for Southeast Asian Studies.

———. 2013b. "'Ghazwul fikri' or Arabisation? Indonesian Muslim Responses to Globalisation." In *Dynamics of Southeast Asian Muslims in the Era of Globalisation,* edited by Ken Miichi and Omar Farouk, 43–70. Tokyo: Japan International Cooperation Agency.

Wahid, Abdul, Wawan Gunawan, Muhammad Abdullah Damaz, and Ahmad Fuad Fanani, eds. 2015. *Fikih Kebinekaan.* Bandung, Indonesia: Mizan.

Conclusion

Further Thoughts and the Challenges Ahead

TAHIR ABBAS and SADEK HAMID

The global aftermath of the events of September 11, 2001 (9/11), has profoundly altered the lives of millions of Muslims in both Muslim-majority and minority states, irrevocably shaping the future for generations to come (Rosen 2009). Many Muslim-majority states suffer from deteriorating social and economic conditions, blighted by poverty, violence, and discrimination caused by neoliberal structural reform policies, civil wars, and shifting social norms. This collection has explored some of the long-term repercussions of these deteriorating conditions upon a new generation of global youth who have grown up in the shadow of 9/11 and the tragic cycle of violence unleashed thereafter in a diverse range of geopolitical and cultural contexts. Yet despite the negative influences of coming of age at the beginning of the twenty-first century, many young Muslims have positively adapted to the challenges they face. Although this youth cohort is diverse in many ways, and its members experience different ways of being Muslim, they share numerous common features that transcend the specific conditions in which they live. This volume has demonstrated that even though Muslims are differentiated by their experiences and distinguished by gender, race, class, and local conditions, they share a parallel transnational consciousness of being young and Muslim in the age of the "global war on terror."

In Western nations, the hypervisibility of Muslims within the global context has produced fears about violent radicalization. In reality, young people tend to be concerned about more pressing issues, such as

economic disadvantage, racism and Islamophobia, and social marginalization (Mandeville 2009). There are more than thirty million Muslim
citizens in western Europe and approximately five million in the United
States. Most migrated in the post–World War II period and settled in and
adapted to their adopted countries while making valuable contributions
to these nations as active citizens, engaging with and participating in the
mainstream. However, as minorities they are often racialized, marginalized, and "Otherized" within these societies, routinely demonized by
media and political elites for issues that have nothing to do with them.
Muslims are considered a "problem"; however, much of this angst about
them is a projection of nations trying to define Muslims' role in a postcolonial, multipolar global era (Marranci 2004). Western Europe in the
early twenty-first century is in many ways experiencing an identity crisis
based on its struggle to reconcile the failures of the European Union (EU)
with the historical construction of a continental identity. Ironically, the
idea of Europe was in part a response to the encroaching power of the
Ottoman Empire, but there is still denial about a civilizational debt to
Islam. Much of "Old Europe" still resists the duty to accept its Muslim
minorities (Marquand 2012).

Young, Muslim, and Western European

The presence of Muslims in western Europe is indisputably redefining it
and reconfiguring notions of European-ness and thereby other national
identities across the region (Allievi 2012). Over the past decade, public
discussion about European Muslim young people is usually associated
with their alleged failure to integrate, their involvement in crime, and
their vulnerability to violent radicalization. The fixation on these three
dominant negative frames ignores the fact that the vast majority of these
youth are trying to live ordinary lives. Furthermore, the visibility of Muslims in Europe is contextualized within broader debates among the media
and political elites about immigration, secularism, and threats to national
identity. A continent with an ageing population but relatively higher birth
rates among Muslims and declining forms of traditional Christian religiosity appears to vindicate the rhetoric of anti-Muslim political parties that

warn of a potential "Islamization of Europe." This vindication has resulted in the imposition of various aggressive national social policies, ranging from mandatory language and integration courses and citizenship tests to restrictive measures such as the banning of burqas, head scarves, and mosque minarets. However, the fear of terrorism and the apparent rise of conservative forms of assertive religiosity among Muslim young people appear to be *the* most pressing concern among governments anxious about preserving social cohesion and security.

An important dynamic to consider is intergenerational change. Young western European Muslims are less likely to have spent significant amounts of time living in their countries of ancestral origin. They display clear generational differences in relation to the traditions and orientations of their parents and grandparents. They have more in common with their non-Muslim peers but also have different experiences. Various factors shape their identities, including ethnicity, nationality, religiosity, and education. These young people are unsurprisingly sensitive to Western norms and values through their socialization, including the state education requirement that they be able to speak the national language of the country in which they live. Most young Muslims, like their non-Muslim associates, want to be accepted and to "fit in." They will more often than not share similar tastes in food, dress, and leisure activities. They pass through the ambiguities of adolescence and are able to "code-switch" between the different cultural worlds in which they live. However, some find this process difficult owing to social prejudices that discriminate against them and to the inability to balance the pressure to conform to their parents' values and outlooks. This difficulty can lead to a sense of alienation from both their ethnic heritage and western European societies, an alienation that has been aggravated by increasing levels of racism and Islamophobia after the 9/11 attacks, the ongoing "war on terror," sporadic acts of terrorism, and the increasing popularity of Far Right political parties in Europe. Surveys conducted by polling agencies suggest that the majority of young Muslims in places such as Great Britain feel strongly attached to their nations. Only a small number claim to hate "the West" for its promiscuous liberal cultural norms and damaging foreign policies in the Muslim world (Pew Research Center 2015).

Apart from questions of identity and belonging, there is also the issue of economic participation and engagement in society. Too many western European Muslims are disproportionately represented in the most deprived urban areas, achieve relatively low levels of educational success, have higher levels of unemployment, or remain in lower-paid jobs. For instance, many French Muslims live in the segregated, marginalized *banlieues*, and a large number of British Muslims live in some of the poorest areas of the United Kingdom—a settlement pattern replicated right across the western European Muslim diasporas. Discrimination in employment practices is a common problem for young Muslims with Arabic-sounding names because they are less likely to be invited for job interviews. In addition to this "ethnic penalty" in the labor market, those who are employed can be subjected to discriminatory practices that deny them the right to pray at work and take time off for religious holidays and that cause them to be overlooked when attempting to seek promotion. Social discrimination also occurs in other areas of the public sphere. For instance, a recent report on British Muslims noted that the vast majority of Muslim young people are peaceful and reject the actions of violent extremist groups such as the Islamic State (ISIS), but this does not protect them from being singled out by government antiterrorism legislation (Shaffi 2015).

Regrettably, some young western European Muslims have entered into theaters of conflict in the Middle East, especially Syria and Iraq, and elsewhere. However, their doing so is more likely to be motivated by various drivers, such as a search for identity, anger, revenge, and even thrill seeking, rather than by religion (Abbas and Awan 2015). These dynamics have been identified among individuals who fought against the Soviet invasions of Afghanistan, Bosnia, and Chechnya as well as among individuals in the current period and during the emergence and subsequent demise of ISIS (Hegghammer 2010). The few thousand European-born Muslims fighting in the ranks of ISIS were drawn by "push–pull factors" that captivate Muslim young people to violent radicalism. In the case of young women, research suggests that the push factors include feeling socially and culturally isolated from their host cultures, adopting the view that Muslims as a global faith community are being persecuted, and feeling anger over a perceived lack of international action in response to this persecution.

The pull factors are said to be the pursuit of a utopic "caliphate state," the desire for belonging, sisterhood, and a romanticization of this experience (Saltman and Smith 2015).

The proto–Islamic State emerged in a power vacuum in Iraq and Syria, aided by a wider regional and global ambivalence toward the group in its early stages. Foreign interventions in Iraq, especially since 2003, further destabilized the region, leading to the possibility for such an organization as ISIS to emerge. Although there is the legacy of domestic political instability to consider, other significant concerns include a history of preexisting ethnic and sectarian differences and tensions, ongoing socioeconomic inequalities, and the lack of political participation among the populace. In addition, the demographic youth bulge and high unemployment among an educated and technologically aware group of people lead to multiple frustrations. ISIS was at its boldest in 2014 with the siege of Kobanî in Syria, but it suffered in the first half of 2016, losing ground as well as the value of its currency owing to the collapse of oil prices, until late 2017, when it was defeated by US air strikes supporting Kurdish forces on the ground. Syria's quagmire has led to Bashar al-Assad facing opposition from the United States and its allies, Turkey and Saudi Arabia, although Russia and Iran continue to support him. Meanwhile, Syrian refugees have fled north to Turkey and until recently into the EU through Greece. Over the past two years, the rise of ISIS has created considerable upheaval for Turkey, not least because of acts of terrorism that have threatened to destabilize the country through ISIS's attacks on tourist targets. Given the "Kurdish question" in Turkey, Turkey's foray into Afrin, Syria, is somewhat ambivalent, specifically given that it logistically and militarily supported rebel groups in the early stage of the conflict and since then has experienced a form of "blowback."

Reconstructing Identities

Many people remain perplexed by the overarching dynamics of existential questions about who we are, who we think we might be, and what we do not want ourselves to be seen as (Younge 2011). However, these questions around identity mask far deeper longings. We all are from somewhere, and we all are en route to somewhere else, but these journeys are not always as smooth or linear as we might imagine or conceive them to be. They are often full of struggles and pitfalls, chances taken and opportunities missed, especially for the young. Moreover, their details are not always fully recognized or appreciated. Indeed, when the question "Where are you from?" surfaces, in some cases the question limits the discussion by its framing as competition over imagined and misconceived identities. In these instances, we are witnessing a crisis of identity—not of the person being questioned but of the questioner.

When majority groups ask questions of the "other," they do so in societies that privilege certain constructed identities, which affects the idea of the nation, perceived and projected. The current "refugee crisis" that we are currently observing in the EU as Syrians flee war at home articulates everything about what is wrong with the EU (Lavenex 2001). The discussion of this "crisis" does not always reflect on the struggles and strife facing groups forsaking everything to make a new start in another home or on the tremendous barriers and restrictions they must cross along the way. When they do eventually get to their destinations, they are either welcomed half-heartedly or not at all. In Germany, the question of national identity highlights various contradictions that have also emerged in other western European societies (McGinnity 2016). In 2015, the German state hosted one million refugees from Syria and other parts of the world. At the same time, the rise of the group Patriotic Europeans against the Islamization of the West (Patriotische Europäer gegen die Islamisierung des Abendlandes, or PEGIDA) and other Far Right groups has created simmering tensions in certain towns and cities where local communities are anxious about the loss of their individual and collective identities—an anxiety based on their fear of the "other." These tensions oddly coexist with various EU laws in favor of immigration and with the fact that economic migration, an important element of the debate, is wholly necessary for western European nation-states, which are encountering virtually zero population growth (Bloom, Canning, and Fink 2010).

In reality, whether we are talking about people or nations, identities are always in a state of flux. However, identities are currently more fractured than ever because of globalization and its converse localization.

Ever-disappearing notions of collectivism, with individualism and consumerism reigning supreme, have further exacerbated the situation. Slow-to-modernize institutions of society, short-term policy making, and the forced projection of an imagined memory of the nation have led to manufactured but often unsustainable ethnonationalism by a dominant hegemon that looks to the past instead of to the future. In local-area contexts, less self-assured individuals and groups are compelled to subdue others by interrogating their identities and seeking to make them appear invisible, even unwanted. Migrants deciding to absorb the culture of a new society after they have made the choice to move to it are compelled to protect what they have because they confront politico-ideological opposition rather than because of an insistence not to integrate. The solution to this opposition is to take ownership of identity and propel it not as a function of wider interests but as a natural right. People on the move are a mixture of everything and nothing, of their pasts but also of their futures, of hopes and dreams but also of the fears and loathing expressed by dominant groups that seek either to welcome the weary travelers or to wholly reject them.

This search for identity and meaning can be seen as a lingering legacy of countercultural movements of the 1960s that exposed a deep chasm between generations, leading to progressive music, film, art, literature, and political activism, particularly in the Civil Rights and Black Power Movements in the United States. For a brief moment, it looked as if things were about to change. America has instead become increasingly paranoid and inward looking. It realized that economies such as Japan and Germany, battered by World War II, were now rising faster than it could have imagined. In response, it chose not to compete but to capitulate. Industrial sectors of the economy were downsized, and manufacturing shifted to parts of the world where labor and capital costs were reduced, leading to outcomes that were more profitable for firms. Emphasis was put on the financial sector of the economy, which up until then was only a small aspect of the gross domestic product of the United States and nations such as Britain. From the late 1970s on, the Middle East has been in a perpetual state of war and conflict owing to the legacies of colonialism, state mismanagement, and the proxy wars between the United States and Russia (Ali 2003). In the 1980s, Reaganomics and Thatcherism, combined with neoimperialistic foreign policy, became the order of the day. This new order eventually led to the collapse of the Soviet Empire in 1989. Since then, the banking and financial sectors of Western economies have been further boosted, industries decimated, and whole communities annihilated or forgotten. The combination of neoliberalism and globalization has pulled societies apart, while elites placate people with cheap credit, the allure of meritocracy, and the illusion of democracy (Picketty 2015).

The post-9/11 "war on terror" culture has perpetuated existing divisions and allowed neoconservatives to push forward their foreign-policy agendas. During the economic crisis of 2008, which was entirely owing to banks' greed and corrupt practices, governments handed out bailouts in the billions to the banks while cutting public spending. For at least another decade, everyday people will have to endure reduced incomes relative to inflation, along with cuts to welfare support and high-unemployment rates. In a deeply unequal economy, the opportunities for social mobility are virtually nil (Dorling 2015). There are huge inequalities throughout the world's economies as almost all nations have bought into the neoliberal paradigm, becoming consumer societies whose livelihoods depend on the service sector. In the West, ethnic and racial minorities often bear the brunt of these failed policies and are all too often criminalized and racialized. All that "we" hate about ourselves as a majority society "we" project onto the "other." Through media and political discourses, what "we" hate becomes a defining characteristic of the "other," normalizing the sense that these "others" are all the same. Inferior, threatening, and utterly undesirable, *they are not us. We are not they.* The result is that fascism has returned to the West. Hyperethnic nationalism is the new normal, combined with economic advantages for elite groups that have strong associations with big business. These groups have destabilized their countries and placed people in a permanent state of fear (Furedi 2005). Everywhere in the world, dissenting voices are silenced. The infiltration of our digital world by government security agencies has led to a culture of distrust (Greenwald 2015).

To achieve integration, western European political elites often lay the responsibility for change upon Muslim groups. This burden represents precisely what is wrong with western Europe's current approach to integration. Despite immense challenges facing Muslims in terms of racism and discrimination, research on alienation and marginalization persistently confirms that Muslims are making considerable efforts to integrate. They obey the laws of the land, take part in the politics of the nation, and behave as upright citizens (Norris and Inglehart 2012). However, a small number of Muslims intermittently fall out of the bottom of the system and follow a path to criminality, extremism, and radicalization. The prevailing discourse around radicalization habitually concentrates on the idea that it is a function of religion, yet a considerable body of literature recognizes it more as a function of politics and racism (Hussain and Bagguley 2012). Elite actors directly and indirectly encourage the majority to vent their frustrations on immigrant and minority groups. In the current climate, that usually means venting them on visible Muslim communities. In response, targeted communities may turn to more conservative forms of Islam that seem to offer communities a safe haven, protecting them from the deleterious consequences of anti-Muslim rhetoric. With this conservative Islamism, they also feel shielded from social problems affecting the wider non-Muslim community, such as alcoholism, teenage pregnancy, and domestic violence. As a result, conservative Muslim groups begin to embrace their religious identities in more observable ways. This turn has the unfortunate consequence of reaffirming the prevailing notions that Muslims are somehow refusing to adjust to the Western way of life and that they may even threaten the very existence of liberal society in secular Western nations.

Keeping the Faith in Youth

Young people who are invested in their faith or who experience "born again" religiosity tend to become committed to religion by means of their contact with conservative, activist organizations. Islamic youth organizations in various western European states are often youth branches of "adult organizations" such as the Milli Görüs Islamic Community (Gemeinschaft Milli Görüs) in Germany, the Union of Islamic Organizations of France (Union des organisations islamiques de France), the Islamic Religious Community (Comunità Religiosa Islamica) in Italy, and the Islamic Society of Britain and its Young Muslims group. Most of these organizations are affiliated with the Forum of European Muslim Youth and Student Organizations, which encourages networking and cooperation between them. Other transnational Islamist movements—such as the radical Hizb ut-Tahrir and the proselytizing Tablighi Jamaʿat and puritanical trends such as the Salafis—attempt to draw young people to their ideas without having formal youth structures. Those movements that have created youth organizations become environments where Muslim young people can learn about their faith, socialize, express their religious identities, and mobilize around religious, cultural, and political issues through attendance in weekly study classes, public lectures, annual conferences, camps, and online forums. Contrary to stereotypes, increased religiosity does not produce radicalization—though Salafis and Tablighi Jamaʿat are known for their highly conservative social attitudes and their generally isolationist approach to non-Muslim culture (Hamid 2016). Those young people who choose to join Islamic political movements do so in informed ways based on the ideological pragmatic strengths of each current of thought. Some have clearly decided to pursue the violent end of the spectrum of Islamism. As Olivier Roy (2017) has recently argued, the participation of French Muslim youth in violent extremism has more to do with an "Islamization of radicalism" rather than with the "radicalization of Islam." In Muslim-majority states, a number of potential dynamics explain patterns of global Islamic political radicalism, but few researchers have looked into the interconnected geopolitical dynamics underpinning global societies in an economic and sociological context. Indeed, uneven economic development, limited social freedoms, and striking inequality in much of the Middle East and North Africa region generate ongoing resentment against governments that have failed to deliver promises. Unending interventions by Western political, economic, and military actors with short-term interests further exacerbate these grievances.

Muslim populations are growing throughout the world, and they are in the West to stay. In the next few decades, a number of major European cities such as Amsterdam, Bradford, Birmingham (Abbas 2006), Malmø, and Marseille may become Muslim-majority cities in their demographic makeup. This change presents both challenges and opportunities for these cities. Tackling these complex problems requires holistic, long-term solutions that consider the histories and contemporary realities of Western Muslim communities. Rather than enforcing heavy-handed policies, governments would be wiser to address socioeconomic inequalities. Social deprivation and discrimination alienate young people, impair their productivity, and in worst cases contribute to violent radicalization. This radicalized minority is largely underground but is manifested in the rhetoric of groups such as Shariah4 UK and through social media platforms such as Twitter, which encourage young Muslims to migrate to Syria. These factors, in addition to acts of terrorism, have energized xenophobic groups in a vicious cycle that results in increased Islamophobia and anti-Muslim hate crime.

The mainstreaming of Islamophobia within media and political discourses also needs to be challenged as religious extremists exploit feelings of social marginalization to recruit young people looking for acceptance, hope, and sometimes revenge. Anti-Muslim sentiment actually helps vindicate the binary narratives of groups such as ISIS and al-Qaeda to turn alienated Muslim youth in western Europe against it (Ahmed 2015). An encouraging sign, however, is that positive work is being carried out within Muslim communities across Europe in the form of various grassroots projects and institutions that offer social services and capacity-building programs. This work is being done by youth-led, faith-based agencies such as Muslim Action for Development and Environment in Europe, an initiative of the Forum of European Muslim Youth and Student Organizations that helps young Muslims to apply Islamic teachings to help to solve environmental problems, and the Al-Mizan Trust, which is a British charity that supports homeless young people. These and other agencies work with various faiths and secular organizations to respond to wider social problems in their countries. The future will be determined by how many Western nations can practice inclusivity and respond to the needs of all of their citizens.

The contributions in this collection highlight a variety of peaceful forms of youthful resistance that are contributing to positive social transformation in many Muslim-majority states as well as in Muslim-minority contexts. They constitute a richly textured set of accounts that demonstrate the diversity of outlooks, experiences, and strategies illustrating how youth shape politics and social movements around the world. This online generation has taken advantage of new communication technologies and the benefits of globalization. Academic studies and popular media, however, have paid scant attention to the positive social change initiated by young people, overlooking the most dynamic demographic of all societies. This volume has demonstrated how the expression of Islam is vastly different among young Muslims and how these different expressions may contrast sharply with scriptural prescriptions. The understanding of Muslim young people can no longer be discerned merely through their relationship with their religion (Dessing et al. 2016). Even studies that examine young people's involvement in Islamist movements rarely account for the generational shifts taking place within these groups or for the need to pay attention to the newer forms of religiously inspired and secular trends challenging state hegemonies, such as those described by Yusuf Safarti and Chloe Gill-Khan in this volume. Similarly, static representations of Muslim young people are inadequate when trying to understand the multiple ways in which youth identities are developed and evolving in a continuous state of "becoming" rather than "being," as Aminul Hoque and others in this volume have shown in their chapters. Hence, Muslim youth activism is not necessarily an overtly religious commitment but rather can be driven by the pursuit of social justice, challenging discrimination and protesting against oppressive state policies that define the modus operandi, as demonstrated by Shehnaz Haqqani and Idrisa Pandit in their chapters.

This volume has attempted to contextualize the global and local issues that affect the lives of today's Muslim young people and to disrupt the monochromatic representations of them by foregrounding their agency and ability to effect positive change. Encouragingly, many Muslims are working with other faith groups in Europe and elsewhere to constructively challenge the counterproductive policies of state institutions (Back et al. 2009). Young Muslims in particular are increasingly at the forefront of these initiatives, demonstrating their capacity to affect positive social change, as discussed in this volume. Many more areas remain unexplored, such as the consumer lifestyle choices made and remade in the context of wider national and global dynamics. Future studies could explore the intersections of Muslim youth and the global problems of drug misuse and gang membership. An equally worthy topic is the emergence of Muslim youth subcultures and patterns of disengagement from religion among young people who identify as agnostic or atheist (Cottee 2016). These trends are an outcome both of the huge shifts taking place in the world and of changes within Muslim communities. They are both personal and political and are likely to shape the present and the future.

References

Abbas, Tahir. 2006. *Muslims in Birmingham, UK*. Oxford: Centre on Migration Policy and Society, Oxford Univ.

Abbas, Tahir, and Imran Awan. 2015. "Limits of UK Counterterrorism Policy and Its Implications for Islamophobia and Far Right Extremism." *International Journal for Crime, Justice, and Social Democracy* 4, no. 3: 16–29.

Ahmed, Nafeez Mosaddeq. 2015. "ISIS Wants to Destroy the 'Grey Zone.' Here's How We Defend It." *Open Democracy*, Nov. 16. At https://www.open democracy.net/nafeez-ahmed/isis-wants-destroy-greyzone-how-we-defend.

Ali, Tariq. 2003. *A Clash of Fundamentalisms*. London: Verso.

Allievi, Stefano. 2012. "Reactive Identities and Islamophobia: Muslim Minorities and the Challenge of Religious Pluralism in Europe." *Philosophy and Social Criticism* 38, nos. 4–5: 379–87.

Back, Les, Michael Keith, Azra Khan, Kalbir Shukira, and John Solomos. 2009. "Islam and the New Political Landscape: Faith Communities, Political Participation, and Social Change." *Theory, Culture & Society* 26, no. 4: 1–23.

Bloom, David E., David Canning, and Günther Fink. 2010. "Implications of Population Ageing for Economic Growth." *Oxford Review of Economic Policy* 26, no. 4: 583–612.

Cottee, Simon. 2016. *The Apostates: When Muslims Leave Islam*. London: Hurst.

Dessing, Nathal M., Nadia Jeldtoft, Jørgen S. Nielsen, and Linda Woodhead, eds. 2016. *Everyday Lived Islam in Europe*. London: Routledge.

Dorling, Danny. 2015. *Inequality and the 1%*. London: Verso.

Furedi, Frank. 2005. *Politics of Fear: Beyond Left and Right*. London: Continuum.

Greenwald, Glenn. 2015. *No Place to Hide: Edward Snowden, the NSA, and the Surveillance State*. New York: Penguin.

Hamid, Sadek. 2016. *Sufis, Salafis, and Islamists: The Contested Ground of British Islamic Activism*. London: I. B. Tauris.

Hegghammer, Thomas. 2010. *Jihad in Saudi Arabia: Violence and Pan-Islamism since 1979*. Cambridge: Cambridge Univ. Press.

Hussain, Yasmin, and Paul Bagguley. 2012. "Securitized Citizens: Islamophobia, Racism, and the 7/7 London Bombings." *Sociological Review* 60, no. 4: 715–34.

Lavenex, Sandra. 2001. "Migration and the EU's New Eastern Border: Between Realism and Liberalism." *Journal of European Public Policy* 8, no. 1: 24–42.

Mandeville, Peter. 2009. "Muslim Transnational Identity and State Responses in Europe and the UK after 9/11: Political Community, Ideology, and Authority." *Journal of Ethnic and Migration Studies* 35, no. 3: 491–506.

Marquand, David. 2012. *The End of the West: The Once and Future Europe*. Princeton, NJ: Princeton Univ. Press.

Marranci, Gabrielle. 2004. "Multiculturalism, Islam, and the Clash of Civilisations Theory: Rethinking Islamophobia." *Culture and Religion* 5, no. 1: 105–17.

McGinnity, Frances. 2016. "A Threat in the Air? Perceptions of Group Discrimination in the First Years after Migration: Comparing Polish Migrants in Germany, the Netherlands, the UK, and Ireland." *Ethnicities* 16, no. 2: 290–315.

Norris, Pippa, and Ronald F. Inglehart. 2012. "Muslim Integration into Western Cultures: Between Origins and Destinations." *Political Studies* 60, no. 2: 228–51.

Pew Research Center. 2015. *Facts about the Muslim Population in Europe*. Washington, DC: Pew Research Center, Nov. 17. At http://www.pewresearch.org /fact-tank/2015/11/17/5-facts-about-the-muslim-population-in-europe/.

Picketty, Thomas. 2015. *Capital in the Twenty-First Century*. Cambridge, MA: Harvard Univ. Press.

Rosen, Nir. 2009. *Aftermath: Following the Bloodshed of America's Wars in the Muslim World: The Death of Iraq and the Birth of the New Middle East*. New York: Nation Books.

Roy, Olivier. 2017. *Jihad and Death: The Global Appeal of Islamic State*. London: Hurst.

Saltman, Marie Erin, and Melania Smith. 2015. *Till Martyrdom Do Us Part: Gender and the ISIS Phenomenon*. London: Institute for Strategic Dialogue.

Shaffi, Wahida. 2015. *Muslim Youth Speak Ten Years On*. Leeds, UK: Leeds Muslim Youth Forum.

Younge, Gary. 2011. *Who Are We—and Should It Matter in the 21st Century?* London: Penguin.

Contributors · Index

Contributors

Tahir Abbas is currently assistant professor at the Leiden University Institute of Security and Global Affairs. He was previously a senior research fellow at the Royal United Services Institute in London (2016–17), Remarque Visiting Fellow at New York University (2015–16), and professor of sociology at Fatih University in Istanbul (2010–16). Abbas is author of *The Education of British South Asians* (2004), *Islamic Radicalism and Multicultural Politics* (2011), and *Contemporary Turkey in Conflict* (2016) as well as the editor of *Muslim Britain* (2005), *Islamic Political Radicalism* (2007), *Islam and Education* (2011), and *Muslim Diasporas in the West* (2016).

Sameera Ahmed has been the director of the Family and Youth Institute since 2006. She holds a PhD in clinical psychology, an MS in biology, and a certificate in family life education, and she currently serves as an assistant clinical professor in the Department of Psychiatry and Behavioral Science at Wayne State University. Ahmed is associate editor for the *Journal of Muslim Mental Health* and is currently a fellow at the Institute for Social Policy and Understanding. In addition, she is a licensed psychologist in the states of Michigan and Ohio.

Asma Bala is a doctoral student in the Department of Religious Studies at the University of Waterloo. She is currently researching the intersection of religion and human rights in the context of Islam and Canadian civil society organizations. Her research examines the overall contribution of these institutions to civil society as both "Canadian" and "Islamic" organizations that operate in a secular state system. Her research aims to shed light on these institutions' universality and inclusiveness.

Martijn de Koning graduated from Vrije Universiteit Amsterdam as an anthropologist. In 1999, he began his work on the project Schoolcareersupport of the

Nour Mosque in Gouda and the Social Work Organization Woonhuis. In 2002, he joined the research group Between Secularization and Religionization at the Vrije Universiteit. In 2008 he defended his PhD dissertation, "Looking for a 'Pure' Islam: Identity Formation and Religious Experience among Moroccan-Dutch Youth." He worked at the International Institute for the Study of Islam in the Modern World until January 2009. Since 2007 he has worked at Radboud University Nijmegen and since 2013 at the University of Amsterdam. In 2014 he coauthored *Salafisme: Utopische idealen in een weerbarstige praktijk* (Salafism: Utopian Ideals and Unruly Practices), with Joas Wagemakers and Carmen Becker.

Jürgen Endres is a researcher at the Center for Research on Religions at the University of Lucerne and a member of the Group of Researchers on Islam in Switzerland. He holds a doctoral degree in Islamic studies from Leipzig University. His current research interests are Islam in Europe, Muslim authorities in Switzerland, and Islamic fundamentalism.

Chloe Gill-Khan has a PhD from the School of Oriental and African Studies at the University of London (2012). She is working on a monograph based on her doctoral research, examining comparative British and French methods of colonial statecraft and their post-1960s models of integration. Gill-Khan is author of "French Republican Secularism and Islam in North African Diasporic Cultural Production" (2013) and "Asian Britain: A Visual Chronicle of South Asian–British Histories" (2015).

Sadek Hamid has written widely about British Muslims, young people and religious identity formation, and public policy. He has held teaching and research positions at the University of Chester, Liverpool Hope University, and most recently at the Oxford Centre for Islamic Studies at Oxford University. He is author of *Sufis, Salafis and Islamists: The Contested Ground of British Islamic Activism* (2016), coauthor of *British Muslims: New Directions in Islamic Thought, Creativity, and Activism* (2018, with Philip Lewis), editor of *Young British Muslims: Between Rhetoric and Realities* (2017), and coeditor of *Youth Work and Islam: A Leap of Faith for Young People* (2011, with Brian Belton).

Shehnaz Haqqani is currently a PhD student at the University of Texas at Austin. She received her bachelor's degree from Emory University (2011) and her master's from the University of Texas at Austin (2013). Her academic research interests include the construction of religious interpretive authority in Islam, Islamic feminism, Muslim televangelism, and Pashtun/Afghan immigrants in the West. She is also interested in the gendered nature of (religious) knowledge and authority, and her dissertation, which explores this issue in addition to other related concerns, highlights the tensions between Muslim feminist scholars of Islam and traditionalist Muslims.

Aminul Hoque is a lecturer in the Educational Studies Department of Goldsmiths University of London and a visiting lecturer at London Metropolitan University. He gained his doctorate from Goldsmiths in 2011, and the in-depth ethnographic research for his dissertation forms the basis of his book *British-Islamic Identity: Third-Generation Bangladeshis from East London* (2015). He is also a journalist, and his inaugural radio documentary *Islamic Pride* was shortlisted for the prestigious Sony Awards in 2004. His writing focuses on issues of educational policy, identity, and social justice. In 2008, he was made a Member of the Order of the British Empire for services to youth justice in East London.

Carool Kersten is associate professor in the study of Islam and the Muslim world at King's College London. His interests are the intellectual history of the contemporary Muslim world and Islam in Southeast Asia. He is a founding member of the British Association for Islamic Studies. His key publications include *Cosmopolitans and Heretics: New Muslim Intellectuals and the Study of Islam* (2011), *Alternative Islamic Discourses and Religious Authority* (2013), *Demystifying the Caliphate* (2013), *Islam in Indonesia: The Contest for Society, Ideas, and Values* (2015), and *The Caliphate and Islamic Statehood* (2015).

Hadiyah Muhammad is a health behavior and health education student at the University of Michigan. She has a master's degree in public health from the School of Public Health at the University of Michigan. Her research focuses on mental health issues in US Muslim communities and on identifying the intervention efforts and instructional programs best suited for mosques and Islamic centers of learning.

Idrisa Pandit is associate professor and director of the Studies in Islam project in the Humanities Department at Renison University College, Ontario. Her PhD is from the University of Illinois at Urbana-Champaign, where she was also a Mortenson Postdoctoral Fellow. In 2007, Pandit was named one of the "top-twenty Muslim women who inspire" by the Canadian Council of Muslim Women. In 2010, she was the finalist in the Volunteer Centre's Volunteer Impact Awards for Innovative Involvement. She is coeditor of *Interfaith Grand River: Our Story* (2014, with Darrol Bryant and Bob Chodos).

Yusuf Sarfati is associate professor of politics and government at Illinois State University, where he teaches comparative politics of the Middle East. He received his PhD from Ohio State University in 2009. He serves as the director of the Middle Eastern and South Asian minor program at Illinois State. Sarfati's research interests revolve around social movements, democratization, and politics and religion. His research has appeared in various journals and edited volumes. Sarfati is also the author of *Mobilizing Religion in Middle East Politics: A Comparative Study of Israel and Turkey* (2013).

Andreas Tunger-Zanetti is a researcher at the Center for Research on Religions at the University of Lucerne and a member of the Group of Researchers on Islam in Switzerland. He earned his doctoral degree in Islamic studies in 1994 from the University of Freiburg. His research interests are Islam in Europe and religion in the public space and the media. He is coeditor of *Debating Islam: Negotiating Religion, Europe, and the Self* (2013, with Samuel M. Behloul and Susanne Leuenberger). Since 2011, he has been a coauthor of the country report on Switzerland in the *Yearbook of Muslims in Europe*.

Munazza Yaqoob is the former chair of the Department of English on the women's campus and founder and director of the Critical Thinking Forum at the International Islamic University, Islamabad. She was Study of US Institutes Fellow for the Multinational Institute for American Culture and Society at New York University. She is the author of two books and numerous research papers published in national and international journals. Her areas of interest include comparative literature, critical and cultural theory, and Pakistani and South Asian literature in English. She is a member of executive board of the Pakistan-US Alumni Network Islamabad, the board of the International Comparative Literature Association, and the International Islamic University Board of Studies and Research Committee. She is currently working as director of the two-year grant project Consciousness Raising of Pakistani Women on Academic and Social Issues.

Jasmin Zine is professor of sociology at Wilfrid Laurier University, Ontario. Her PhD is from the Institute for Studies in Education at the University of Toronto–Ontario in 2012. Zine's areas of interest include critical race and ethnic studies, postcolonial theory and research methodologies, education and social justice, representation, Canadian Muslim studies, and Muslim women's studies. She is author of *Canadian Islamic Schools: Unraveling the Politics of Faith, Gender, Knowledge, and Identity* (2009) and "Safe Havens or Religious 'Ghettos?' Narratives of Islamic Schooling in Canada" (2007).

Index